Vhat is this n

the rural t

THE URBAN
SOUTH

Published for

THE INSTITUTE FOR RESEARCH
IN SOCIAL SCIENCE

by

THE UNIVERSITY OF NORTH CAROLINA PRESS

THE URBAN SOUTH

RUPERT B. VANCE

and

NICHOLAS J. DEMERATH

EDITORS

With the Assistance of

SARA SMITH

and

ELIZABETH M. FINK

CHAPEL HILL

THE UNIVERSITY OF NORTH CAROLINA PRESS

1954

To

DONALD R. YOUNG

in appreciation of his aid and encouragement to
social scientists of the South
while he was director of the
Social Science Research Council

PREFACE

THE contributors to this symposium write as students of urbanism; they also write as students of regionalism. This then is a book on cities; but unlike writers of certain other books, its authors are able to live at peace with the idea that cities are valuable adjuncts to living and are here to stay. On the other hand, it seems clear that they have not been able to live at peace with the idea that the region they study is permanently assigned to a status which, to say the least, has been called backward and undeveloped. Moreover, they are willing to admit that one attitude may bear some relation to the other: that is to say, advancing urbanization may indicate an advancing region.

Not so many years ago one of our distinguished university presses published a book with the rather strange title, *Cities Are Abnormal*. The next census, that of 1950, reported large gains in our cities and the smallest proportion of United States population on farms in history. This account of the urbanward movement suggests if anything a contradictory thesis. Cities are growing more numerous and bigger; evidently *they are here to stay*. This can be taken as the leitmotif of the present volume. If modern man is to destroy his cities by A-bombs, H-bombs, or by any other means, he has calculated to destroy civilized and social life as it exists. Urban functions, we sincerely believe, are necessary—and if they cease, life as we now know it will also cease.

This volume represents integration of a series of studies on the process of urbanization in the most rural region of our nation—the South. As such it should serve to redress an agrarian bias, for even some of the best southern studies have proceeded as though cities were unimportant, if not nonexistent, in the South. Urbanism is growing, as the volume makes clear; it is creating new problems as others are being superseded.

Urbanization, then, we take as an index of social change in the South in its most dynamic period. Throughout the treatment the attempt is made to clarify the relation of urbanism to population change, to industrialization, to commerce and finance, and to our major political and social processes. In fact there is a feeling that a "breakthrough" has occurred in the region's position; this "breakthrough" is well represented in the present urban development and it may well have occurred in the decade 1940-1950.

This, as we have indicated, is also a book on the South—a subject which for several decades has attracted much of the research effort of the group centering at the University of North Carolina. In this context, our book follows a course set by several preceding volumes. It accepts the American South as something of a cultural and an economic entity and then proceeds to trace its recent social changes. But there may be a difference. Regionalism (and one can hardly write of the South today without being called a regionalist) has been said by its critics to make its point by delineating differences. Our contributors, however, concentrate on ways in which the South is becoming more like the nation and the differentiation is diminishing. These characteristics are well summed up in the way men now live and work together in the collective life of larger communities—urbanism. If the outlying areas of our nation are to partake more of the characteristics of the central core of power, wealth, administration, and finance in this country, they will of necessity become more urban. This urbanization process will go somewhat beyond the simple demographic characteristics of increased size and density of population; it will go over into important metropolitan processes and functions.

If regionalism is dependent on differentiation—and there is no known reason why differentials are not important—such analysis as follows may lead to further refinements. To be explicit, we are finding in many fields, economic and demographic, trends toward the convergence of differentials as in fertility, health, and income. Less and less will we be able to think of our regional differences as those of kind—rural vs. urban, for example; rather they will become differences of degree—in this case, degree of urbanization and concentration. To some students this may mean the need is passing for regional analysis; it can hardly mean the attainment of identity. In any case, the possible demise of regionalism does not concern us here. In the present volume we are more concerned with change, process, and function. To treat of function it is evident that we must allow our area an identity. Granted this obvious assumption, we can proceed.

Regionalism, it may be noted, is one illustration of the many ways in which science has been conscripted in the service of society. Contrary to certain canons of objectivity, regionalism is seen as social therapy—an attempt to do something as well as to study something. This is no doubt why regional study has been so highly developed in the South—reputedly one of the nation's more backward areas. It represents the section's conscious effort to use science to escape from its undeveloped status. Certainly the attempt to amputate regionalism from considerations of regional planning is likely to be fatal to both disciplines.

Regionalism also represents a convergence of many scientific disciplines on a phenomenon, simply because the phenomenon itself tends to converge within the confines of an area. In both instances—analysis and action—urbanism is most pertinent to the questions under discussion. Thus it can be presumed that this particular region has been at a disadvantage because it was understaffed with cities. This situation is changing and as the economy matures this change may be so managed as to improve the region's status. Finally, nearly as many threads of social science converge in the study of urbanism as in that of regionalism itself. Cooperative scholarship is thus calculated to shed light on a dynamic process. This is our hope and on this base we stand.

The book itself has a history dating back to the Southern Regional Committee of the S.S.R.C. Over two decades the Social Science Research Council under the direction of Robert T. Crane and Donald R. Young sought to give aid and comfort to research efforts of social scientists in southern universities. The last topic considered by the Committee under the chairmanship of Raymond D. Thomas was urbanism, and several research conferences were held on the Urbanization of the South. Contributors were secured and a volume was planned with O. D. Duncan of Oklahoma A and

M College as editor. With the disbanding of the Committee, the project lapsed for a time.

Subsequently, new support was secured, the undertaking was accepted as a project of the Institute for Research in Social Science, University of North Carolina, and the volume was pushed through to completion. The present editors wish to compliment the contributors on their patience and perseverance throughout all our delays and tribulations. Editors are a trial even to themselves; what they must be to the writers of these chapters we shudder to contemplate. We were already convinced of the ability of our editorial aides, Sara Smith and Elizabeth Fink; we hereby embarrass them with a public commendation of their good nature under arduous circumstances. The editors especially acknowledge their indebtedness to Donald Young, to the Committee on Urban Studies of the Southern Regional Committee and to its first chairman, O. D. Duncan. We are especially grateful to Gordon W. Blackwell and Katharine Jocher of our own Institute. They have aided the undertaking in every way possible.

Rupert B. Vance
Nicholas J. Demerath

Chapel Hill, 1954

CONTENTS

xi

Part One

URBANIZATION OF THE SOUTH

Introduction

THE contributions to *The Urban South* have been organized around three topics: (1) the urbanization process, (2) organizational aspects of southern cities, and (3) social change and the impact of urbanism on tradition.

Not urban society, but urbanization as the process occurs in a rural region, sets the problem for Part One. The reader will note that a significant definition of the components of urbanization emerges as these chapters unfold. (1) *Urbanization involves an increase in the number of points at which population concentrates and a growth in the size of these concentrations.* Chapter 2 traces the emergence and development of this spatial pattern in the South. (2) *Urbanization means an increasing shift from agrarian to industrial, service, and distributive occupations,* and this is traced in Chapter 3. Finally (3) *urbanization means a redistribution of the population and the peopling of the cities;* this is discussed in Chapters 4 and 5 both from the point of view of migration and the effect of urbanization on the reproductive behavior of the population.

An overview is needed, however, to place southern urbanization in its widest possible context. To do this requires one who is acquainted with European urbanism firsthand, practiced in arts of "American" sociology, and cognizant of the southern scene. This characterization is "tailor-made" for Rudolf Heberle and his chapter on the mainsprings of southern urbanization. What delayed urbanization in the South? What causes can be assigned for the growth of different type cities? Rudolf Heberle concludes that while the South is not one of the heartlands of modern capitalism, the growth

3

of urban places is due to the same general "factors" to be found in urbanization the world over.

At the mid-century, census records showed that the South was almost exactly one-half urban and one-half rural with the rural population almost equally divided between those living on farms and those living in villages and suburbs (rural-nonfarm). What time schedule did the South follow in its process of urbanization? When did nuclei of urban concentrations emerge and how did they grow? In a careful review of census data from 1790, T. Lynn Smith is able to shed light on these problems and to suggest the extent of the South's lag in urbanization. Since the editors have not felt they were required to edit out all duplication, readers may compare two sets of causes assigned to account for the growth of the urban South.

Did the South's breakthrough to urbanization and a mature economy occur around 1950? A study recently completed under the highest auspices found the current rate of metropolitan development in the South proceeding at a faster pace than the rate at which the North developed its larger metropolitan centers (Donald Bogue, *Growth of Metropolitan Areas*). Certainly the decade showed the "South moving rapidly toward an industrial and commercial economy which is organized around cities and metropolitan areas. This change in economic and social organization is requiring the South to redistribute its population in new patterns and to acquire new skills and take on new characteristics." This consideration documented by Donald Bogue in a thoughtful paper sets the stage for Lorin Thompson's analysis of employment and occupational change, and advancement from the primary to the tertiary economy is shown to be very real. Women have advanced in employment faster than men while the Negro's retirement from agriculture has not been balanced by sufficient occupational mobility in southern cities. Chapter 3 documents the rapid trend toward urban occupations.

In its impact on the people, urbanization means a redistribution of the population. Thus for every three city dwellers in 1940, the South had four in 1950; for each five farm residents in 1940, only four remained in 1950. The cities, we are told, grow by migration, the rural areas by virtue of their high birth rates. Two chapters accordingly deal with peopling the southern city (1) by migration, and (2) by reproduction. Homer Hitt shows us how much migration goes outside the South, an estimated 2 million net, a loss of 5 percent from 1940 to 1950. The stream to southern cities from its rural areas was much greater and in addition there is now an important stream of migration between cities. Not least significant in Professor Hitt's paper are his findings as to the kinds of people who migrate.

Robert M. Dinkel's chapter on differential fertility adds one more component to our definition, namely: (4) *urbanization involves the spread of urban ways of living to the surrounding rural areas*. Thus, over time, urbanization tends to lower birth rates both for those who move and those who stay at home. The facts of Chapter 5 serve to indicate that southerners are still having enough children to maintain their growing cities with some left over for export to other regions. There is a trend toward convergence in family size, regional-national and rural-urban. The question is raised as to whether occupation does not reflect the effect urbanization has on the replacement of the population.

CHAPTER ONE

The Mainsprings of Southern Urbanization

RUDOLF HEBERLE

STUDY OF THE "mainsprings" of urbanization in the South may well proceed from the assumption that urban places in this region, generally speaking, have developed in response to the same "factors" as they have elsewhere in the Western world. Just as the growth of cities in the United States is explainable in terms of the same general "factors" as urbanization in Europe or in Australia, the increase in the number and size of urban places in the South is due to the same general "factors" as urbanization in the rest of the United States. The increased productivity of agriculture, the development of commerce and transportation, the growth and concentration of manufacturing industries in certain localities, settlement and natural increase of population—all these are general "factors" of urbanization in the Western world. Stated in these terms, the growth of urban places in the South presents no particular problem.

The real problem is this: What is the relative importance of each of these general "factors" in the South, and how is the particular geographic pattern of urban places in the South to be explained?

Before going into these questions it should be understood that cities do not merely grow, as if they were natural organisms under the influence of external, non-human forces. In fact the cases where urban places came into existence or grew without the concerted effort of organized groups of men are probably quite rare. Quite apart from the act of incorporation, many cities came into existence by a definite act of "founding." In many cases growth of a place into a city was stimulated by the deliberate placement of industrial, commercial, or transportation establishments in a given locality. Also, the choice of a town for a garrison or other military installations has often been the impetus to rapid growth. On the other hand, many "founded" urban places have failed to grow into larger cities because "external" conditions were unfavorable to the development of a city in a particular locality. In some cases growth of a city has been strangled by deliberate measures of competitors in other cities. It is well known that this factor has been important in the case of certain southern cities.

Urbanization in the South is a recent phenomenon in comparison with other regions of the New World. In Mexico, Peru, and other parts of Latin America many urban places can be traced back to pre-European times and many have grown up from Indian villages; in Europe many contemporary urban places have been locations of Roman, Celtic, and even prehistoric settlements. In the South, however, very few cities are located at the site of an aboriginal settlement; even in these cases there is usually no actual continuity between the ancient and the modern town. Practically all cities in the southern United States owe their existence to European colonization.

More precisely, urbanization in the South occurred during those centuries of western history which saw the rise and highest bloom of modern capitalism. This is important because it simplifies our task of analyzing the conditions and factors of urbanization in the region; we are, in the South, not confronted with a heterogeneous system of urban places dating in part from pre-capitalistic days, as we are in Europe or Asia or Latin America. When southern cities developed, the technology, the economic and political systems, as well as other civilizational aspects of southern society were essentially the same as in North America in general and in Europe. The South, however, has not been a heartland of modern capitalism; rather it was one of the frontier provinces of the Euro-American economic system. In this hemisphere, the South had an economic (not political!) function resembling that of the Balkan and eastern European region in the other hemisphere. The similarities are striking: agricultural surplus production concentrated on large estates or plantations; crop specialization for export in vast areas (as in Roumania or Hungary); late development of secondary industries and these very largely limited to the extraction and first processing of products of such primary industries as lumber, steel milling, canning, paper, basic chemical and oil refining. Furthermore, in the

South as in eastern Europe, until recently, one observes a predominance of low wage industries producing low grade consumer goods (the textile industry in the Piedmont and in Poland). In both regions the result has been a sparsity of large cities, a predominance of small market towns, a high rate of fertility, and a strong tendency of migration to distant industrial areas and to better agricultural labor markets. The comparison could be carried much further into the sphere of capital investment and trade relations, but that would lead us beyond the scope of this chapter. It is enough for the present to realize that the so-called "colonial" character of the South's economy has retarded the urbanization of the region, although we find here some of the oldest cities in the United States.

I. THE DEVELOPMENT OF SOUTHERN CITIES,
ORIGIN AND GROWTH

Let us consider the various factors which have both facilitated and retarded the origin and growth of cities in the South.[1] For obvious reasons, urbanization began along the seacoast. Here the oldest cities were "founded" places: military, naval, and administrative outposts of the Spanish, French, and British Empires, intended at the same time to be ports of export and import. It is important to realize that these cities like New Orleans, Mobile, Charleston, and Savannah were all founded during the age of mercantilism, when the empire governments took a very active hand in the economic exploitation of the New World colonies. Hence it seems quite futile

---

1. For empirical data pertaining to the following, see Chapters 2, 3, 4 and 5 in this volume. In this chapter, a discussion of vital processes and migration as factors of urbanization has been intentionally omitted in view of the fact that these problems are treated in the more specialized contributions to the symposium.

It may be pointed out that, while in the New England and the Middle Atlantic states one-third of the population was classified as urban in 1860, and while the East North Central states reached this stage in 1890 and the West North Central states in 1910, the South Atlantic and West South Central divisions reached it only in 1930, and the East South Central states had not reached it in 1940. From Bureau of the Census, "Urban Population of the United States, 1790-1930," Release of October 31, 1939, Table 4; and *Statistical Abstract of the United States, 1942* (Washington: Government Printing Office, 1943), Table 8. Cf. also Rupert B. Vance, *All These People* (Chapel Hill: The University of North Carolina Press, 1945), p. 19.

to try to disentangle the political and economic functions of these cities during the first phases of their existence. The important point is that their locations were deliberately chosen; and, as the later fate of some of these cities—like St. Augustine (1565)—shows, the choice was not always the wisest from an economic point of view. Following the establishment of United States hegemony in the South, the political and military factors in urban development became less important. Urbanization then became very largely the concomitant of the economic development of the region. The major exceptions to this rule are some of the state capitals and some of the minor cities where naval or military establishments, and more recently, air force bases or training fields have furnished the "mainspring" for growth.

Towns whose major function is that of a center of higher learning, like Chapel Hill, North Carolina, are far fewer in the South than in New England. A society consisting of a relatively thin social class of planters, most of whom were not men of great wealth, and a broader layer of family farmers over a basis of Negro slaves (and later, sharecroppers), is not in the position to maintain a large number of small and exclusive colleges. Nor does the intellectual climate of the South seem to have been as favorable to the growth of college towns as that of New England and the Middle Atlantic states.

On the other hand, life in the subtropical climate created at an early date a demand for resort places and spas where planters and businessmen could escape the heat or cure their malaria, gout, and other ailments. Thus, we find quite a number of old seacoast towns and some cities in the hill country which owe their origin in this indirect way to the advantages of a local climate or to mineral springs. Hot Springs, Arkansas, Warm Springs, Virginia, Asheville, North Carolina, Biloxi, Mississippi, and Bay St. Louis, Mississippi, are examples of these older resort cities. The recent spectacular development of resort cities in Florida (Miami and others) has its origin in a national rather than regional demand for resort places.

Turning to the economic factors,[2] we find that with few exceptions (like Birmingham) southern cities did not originate as industrial communities. This is particularly true of the larger cities. The South, remaining for a long time a rural region with a colonial type

2. The following section of this chapter is largely adapted from Rudolf Heberle, "Social Consequences of Industrialization of Southern Cities," *Social Forces*, 27 (October 1948), pp. 30-34.

of agriculture, developed most of its older and now outstanding cities as ports, railway, and commercial centers, as local trading and marketing towns, or as temporary residences of wealthy planters' families.[3]

The oldest industries in the South, those engaged in processing the products of the farm and the forest, were largely located in rural communities and small towns. The cities, therefore, for a long time had to depend almost entirely on commerce and trade.[4] Purely commercial cities, however, seldom attain large size. Those old cities of the South whose commercial importance diminished as the transportation system changed were doomed to stagnation unless they attracted manufacturing industries. For example, one notes the string of minor shipping and trading centers which, as early as 1840, had grown up behind the coastal port cities. All of these "second line" centers were located at the head of navigation on rivers flowing from the Appalachian region to the Atlantic or Gulf. In 1840, this group consisted of: Richmond and Petersburg, Virginia, Columbia, South Carolina, Augusta, Macon, and Columbus, Georgia; later Montgomery, Alabama, was added to this group. On the Mississippi such places as Donaldsonville, Baton Rouge, Port Hudson, Port Gibson, Natchez, Vicksburg, and Mayersville may be named. Some of these places were reduced to insignificance when river traffic and local cotton production declined; others stagnated and some were saved from oblivion through industrialization or because they became administrative and political or educational centers.[5] In contrast to the most important European com-

3. Walter J. Matherly, "The Emergence of the Metropolitan Community in the South," *Social Forces*, 14 (March 1936), pp. 311-325. See also F. B. Simkins, *The South, Old and New* (New York: Alfred A. Knopf, 1949), pp. 68-69.

4. See W. F. Ogburn, *Social Characteristics of Cities* (Chicago: The International City Managers' Association, 1937), p. 29.

5. See the instructive demographic map diagrams in T. Lynn Smith, "The Emergence of Urban Centers in the South," in T. Lynn Smith and C. A. McMahan, *The Sociology of Urban Life* (New York: The Dryden Press, 1951). R. W. Shugg, *Origins of Class Struggle in Louisiana* (Baton Rouge: Louisiana State University Press, 1939), p. 42, enumerates the following major towns in ante-bellum Louisiana (besides New Orleans): Baton Rouge, Alexandria, Natchitoches, Shreveport, Donaldsonville, and Opelousas. Today, only Baton Rouge and Shreveport, both industrialized, are major cities; the others have been surpassed by Lake Charles and Monroe, both industrial cities.

mercial cities which were also old centers of handicraft, producing
many commodities for long-distance trade, the older southern cities
lacked such a broad basis of secondary production. Until late in
the nineteenth century they were places of export and import trade,
mainly exporting products of primary industries and importing the
products of European handicraft and manufactures. Apparently,
the wealth of planters and merchants did not support a broad layer
of local artisans and craftsmen. This fact has been a great hindrance
for the rise of manufacturing industries in the region and possibly
also accounts for the minor role of industrialization in the later development and growth of "secondary" industries: the extraction of
coal, oil, natural gas, and other minerals, the construction industry,
and most important of all, the manufacturing and mechanical industries.

The role of an industy as a city-building agent depends in the
first place on the factors which determine that industry's location.
Some of these industries are consumer-oriented,[6] like bakeries, printing shops, gas and power plants and, by and large, the construction
industries. Their location tends to correspond to the distribution
of population;[7] they are to be found in all larger communities and
in fairly fixed ratios to the population of an urban place and its
trade area. In city development such industries are of less importance as compared with others presently noted. They develop as
urban society develops and they are part and parcel of it. A great
deal of the earlier industrial growth in the South has been of this

6. The terminology with regard to location of industries is that of Alfred
Weber's, on whose theory this section is based. See Alfred Weber, "Indus-
trielle Standortslehre," in *Grundriss der Sozialökonomik*, VI (Tübingen,
1923); and Alfred Weber, *The Theory of the Location of Industry*, trans.
by Carl Joachim Friedrich (Chicago: University of Chicago Press, 1929).

The ecologists and regionalists are also referred to A. Lösch, *Die räumliche
Ordnung der Wirtschaft*, 2nd ed. (Jena: G. Fisher, 1944). This truly remarkable work, which is based largely upon Thünen's, Weber's, and
Christaller's theories, contains a wealth of ideas and empirical demonstra-
tions and ought to become a basis for future research, theoretical or empirical, on the spatial distribution of economic activities. Since it also deals
with the location and internal ecology of cities, it should be taken seriously
by urban ecologists. The writer regrets that he did not have the time to
utilize Lösch's work for the present chapter.

See also Edgar M. Hoover, *The Location of Economic Activity* (New
York: McGraw-Hill, 1948).

7. Edgar M. Hoover, *op. cit.*, p. 35 f.

sort and, for that matter, so also has much of the more recent industrialization.[8] Other industries are either raw-material oriented, like steel mills and sugar refineries, or labor-oriented, like most of the southern textile industries. Among these two groups are the truly city-building industries, the "dominant" industries in city development. These industries draw people into cities, and their growth tends to accelerate urban growth. Consequently, our analysis should be primarily concerned with them.

In the South it so happens that a large proportion of the industries which are raw-material oriented are also "secondary" in respect to city development. This is due not merely to the presence of resources, but is a consequence of the well-known freight rate structure, which according to some authorities has prevented the development of production of finer grades of finished goods in the South.[9] Whether these raw-material oriented industries will be located in cities or in rural areas, whether they tend to develop large industrially diverse urban communities or to create only small or medium-sized industrially specialized towns, depends on the nature of their main raw materials and the location of resources, and also on the industry's dependence upon cheap transportation facilities and other factors.[10]

8. It should be noted, however, that with the increasing dependence of the rural population upon urban industry and commercial services, the development of these consumer-oriented industries tends to be increasingly influenced by the demands of rural customers in the metropolitan region of the city. Bakeries, for instance, sell increasing proportions of their production in rural territory. But a large-scale bakery is not likely to be established except in a city of considerable size.

9. See, however, the contrary opinion in Calvin B. Hoover and B. U. Ratchford, *Economic Resources and Policies of the South* (New York: Macmillan, 1951), p. 78 f.

10. Vance, *op. cit.*, p. 276, reproduces a table from Harriet L. Herring, *Southern Industry and Regional Development* (Chapel Hill: The University of North Carolina Press, 1940), which shows the share of the South in 55 industries in 1939. Among the 20 industry groups of whose total wage earners the Southeast had 25 percent or more, only about ten may be considered as definitely city-building industries. Of the entire list the same proportion is probably in this class.

In Louisiana the writer found that of all workers in manufacturing industries in 1940, 57.6 percent were living in urban communities, 33.7 percent were rural-nonfarm, and 8.7 percent rural-farm.

In the lumber industry, however, only 29 percent of the workers were living in urban communities, whereas in the paper industry 51.5 percent

One of the oldest industries in the South and one of the most important industries in regard to employment is the lumber industry. It is definitely raw-material oriented. The rapid exhaustion of timber resources made it a temporary industry in many localities. The sawmills were rarely located in large cities but rather were spread over the countryside. Consequently, this industry created a large number of small mono-industrial communities but contributed little directly to the growth of larger cities. However, in many cases it laid the foundation for a larger community, as some of the sawmill towns developed beyond the mono-industrial stage and became cities of more diversified industrial structure. In some cases this was due to the establishment of additional wood-using industries. The furniture industry, the production of paper and cardboard containers, and the rayon industry belong in this group. The wood-using industries are, as a rule, more concentrated locally than the lumber industry. Consequently, the workers in these industries tend to be living in cities, while the sawmill workers tend to be living largely in rural areas and small towns. A striking example of city development due to the sequence of sawmills and paper mills is the town of Bogalousa, Louisiana, a small urban community of very recent origin. Another example is Monroe in northern Louisiana.

In other cases the continued growth of lumber towns was due to the agglomeration of new industries oriented towards *different* raw materials at the location of the lumber industry. This happened in several cities of the deep South and coastal Southwest with the coming of the petroleum industry. Oil refineries and chemical plants using the products and by-products of oil refineries, as well as natural gas, were in several cases established in old lumber industry towns.

Reasons for this "agglomeration" of two different industries were

---

were classified as urban residents. In the crude petroleum and gas production, only 41.0 percent were living in urban communities, 49.6 percent were classified as rural-nonfarm residents, and 9.4 percent lived on rural farms, while in the group petroleum products and chemical industries, 51.0 percent were urban, 42.8 percent were rural-nonfarm, and 6.2 percent rural-farm. Although these data need considerable refinement, they do give an idea of the differences in urbanizing effect between various industry groups. See Rudolf Heberle, *The Labor Force in Louisiana* (Baton Rouge: Louisiana State University Press, 1948).

probably the dependence of both upon water transportation,[11] the location of their respective raw materials in the same general areas, and the advantage, for the more recent industries, of finding already a local supply of industrially experienced yet not too highly specialized labor. Baton Rouge [12] or Lake Charles and the area of Beaumont-Port Arthur in the southeastern corner of Texas are good examples of this sequence.

However, the job-creating capacity of the petroleum and basic chemical industries is low and the direct effect of these industries upon urban growth not very strong. On the other hand, they are both high wage industries which exert a considerable stimulus upon the development of trade and services; they also attract a variety of auxiliary industries.

Among the raw-material oriented branches of the food industry, which are very important with regard to employment in the Deep South, none can be considered as city-building industries if taken by themselves. The canning and drying of seafood and of fruits and vegetables are typically rural industries, scattered over many small towns and villages. Cane sugar refineries, too, tend to be located in rural communities. As city-fillers, they have been important in many southern towns; rice mills have contributed to the growth of several cities in the southwestern part of the region.

The greatest city-building industry, the iron and steel industry, is largely concentrated, except for Chattanooga, in the Birmingham metropolitan area. Here, of course, was an ideal location for this industry because iron, coal, and limestone—the three basic materials in steel production—occur in this same locality. Birmingham, which was *founded* in 1871, is a conspicuous example of the urbanizing force of the iron and steel industry. It is probably the one outstanding example in the South of purely industrial origin of a large city.

11. Oil refineries are not necessarily located near the origin of petroleum, which can be transported economically over long distances by pipeline or water transportation. The Baton Rouge refinery receives petroleum in both ways, from oil fields in the region and from Venezuela. Coastal lumber mills also receive part of their raw material (valuable tropical timber) from overseas. The shipment of bulky products like sawn timber and gasoline by waterway is of course also advantageous.

12. According to Stanley F. Horn, *This Fascinating Lumber Business* (New York: Bobbs-Merrill Co., 1943), p. 120, one of the "earliest and finest" cypress sawmills with a capacity of 40,000 feet a day was built in Baton Rouge in 1884.

However, Birmingham has for a long time been lagging behind the chief northern centers of iron and steel production as far as diversification is concerned. This has been explained by the relatively restricted size of the southern market for steel products.[13]

An even more striking example of purely industrial origin of a city is Oak Ridge, Tennessee, child of World War II and of the most recent industry in the region. While its population in 1950 was approximately 30,000, it may grow into a considerably larger center, provided that other industries locate at the same place.

If we now turn to the labor-oriented industries in the South, we have to consider in the first place the South's notorious problem child: the cotton textile industry. This industry had its main period of growth in the South at a time when electrification together with a relatively ample labor supply in rural areas made concentration in large cities unnecessary and decentralization in small urban communities possible. Thus, the growth of the textile industry in the Piedmont, while certainly contributing to urbanization, did not result in the development of an American Manchester or Chemnitz. With few exceptions, the southern textile towns are small.[14] However, in some cases textile mills have been located in larger cities where an already established industry employing men left a sufficient supply of female labor unutilized. The agglomeration of the hosiery industry at a furniture manufacturing center like High Point, North Carolina, illustrates this case. The fuller utilization of the labor force will, of course, result in larger aggregate payrolls which in stimulating the growth of trades and services contribute to further urbanization.

13. Andreas Predoehl, "Die örtliche Verteilung der amerikanischen Eisen- und Stahlindustrie," *Weltwirtschaftliches Archiv*, 27 (Jena, 1928), pp. 240, 246, 270, 276, 289.
For a discussion of the South's potential role as location for iron and steel production see Hoover and Ratchford, *op. cit.*, pp. 12-13.

14. According to Vance, *op. cit.*, p. 307, Table 84 (Percent and Number of Manufacturing Establishments by Size of City and Type of Manufacture, North Carolina Catawba Valley, 1938), the furniture and chemical industries were more concentrated in larger cities than the textile industry. Among the latter, plants making wearing apparel, silk and rayon, and dyeing and finishing plants were more concentrated in cities of 10,000 or over than plants making cotton yarns and cotton fabrics. Only 35 percent of all establishments in the area were in cities of 25,000 and over; 61.5 percent were in cities 10,000 or over.

The concentration of the cigarette and tobacco industry in two urban areas, Winston-Salem and Durham, appears to be the result of a combination of labor and raw-material orientation. Without the additional factor of an extraordinary concentration of capital, this industry as such would scarcely have created any important urban centers.

The growth of labor-oriented manufacturing industries is dependent not only on an ample supply of adequately qualified or trainable labor but also on the institutional arrangements under which manual workers can be secured. The Negro population, which constitutes about one-fifth of the labor force in the South today, was until emancipation not free to leave the open country and to migrate to towns and cities. Even after the freeing of the slaves the institution of share-cropping operated as a restriction of migratory mobility of workers. It is reasonable to assume that this has been one factor among others in delaying urbanization in the region. Furthermore, when the great exodus of rural Negroes began during World War I, much of it by-passed southern cities, going directly to the big manufacturing centers in the North. A similar situation developed during World War II, when large masses of southern Negroes migrated to war production centers in the Great Lakes region and on the Pacific Coast where high wages and non-discriminating employment policies offered a strong attraction.

Needless to say, migration in general from the South toward industrial centers in other parts of the country very likely contributed to a retardation of city growth in the region. The relatively late development of manufacturing industries in the South had also the effect of permitting the substitution of commuting instead of permanent cityward migration of workers. Had the main phase of industrialization occurred before the age of the automobile, much larger masses of workers who now are journeying back and forth between their rural homes and urban places of work might have congregated in urban centers. Without this "urbanization" of the countryside many towns and cities would have grown somewhat faster than they actually did.

A more precise appraisal of the urbanizing effect of various types of industries would have to be based upon thorough studies of comparative production costs, including shipping costs for raw materials and products for industrial plants in various locations. It would also take into consideration such additional factors of location of industry as water and overland transportation facilities and the availability of sources of fuel or power, the water supply [15] (very important in the chemical industries), and finally the climate. In certain parts of the South we find strings of small industrial cities lined up along main railroads. Some of these places were founded by railroad companies; others had their origin in older towns which expanded when the railroads came. Among the old river towns previously mentioned, those which became stations on main railroads were saved from stagnation or decline. The importance of water power and later of electric power (generated by water power) for the location of industries in the Piedmont and its influence upon the development of a chain of small manufacturing towns and cities in that region is well known. More recently the immense supply of natural gas in the southwestern part of the region has become an important attraction for chemical industry plants and is beginning to exert an influence upon the growth of cities in that part of the South. However, since natural gas can be easily distributed, it does not lead to large concentrations of industry and therefore has no strong urbanizing effect. Similarly, the warm climate, by reducing fuel consumption for heating of factories, offices, and residences of workers, facilitates decentralization of plants and of industrial settlements, since distance from fuel distribution points will not significantly increase the fuel costs. Furthermore, the fact that highways are open practically the year round makes the decentralized location of factories and residences less hazardous than in a northern climate. The factor of water supply for industrial plants may work for decentralization of industry or it may lead to concentration along waterways; no generalization as to city-formation seems possible.

In appraising the effect of industrialization upon the growth of cities, it is necessary to consider not only the immediate but also the indirect effects. The latter were dramatically demonstrated during World War II when increases in manufacturing employment in cities like New Orleans were accompanied by very strong increases

15. See the interesting discussion in Hoover and Ratchford, *op. cit.*, pp. 232 f. and 372.

of tertiary employment in trade, transportation, and services,[16] in spite of the fact that all expansions in nonessential branches of business were discouraged during the war.

II. GEOGRAPHICAL DEVELOPMENT OF SOUTHERN CITIES

We can now attempt to explain the pattern of the geographical distribution of urban places in the region as it results from the various factors of urbanization discussed in the preceding sections of this paper. This approach to a classification of cities seems to us more appropriate in the context of this paper than the conventional classification of cities by functions. The larger cities in particular are bound to be multi-functional, or else they would not be large cities; which of the functions is the most important cannot be determined, let us say, simply on the basis of employment in major industrial divisions. Take, for example, Baton Rouge, Louisiana, which has been classified (by Chauncy D. Harris) as a "university" city. On the one hand one could argue that it is the seat of the state university merely because it is the state capital and that the "political" function is primary; on the other hand one could point out that the city's significance in the national community is that of a center of highly integrated basic chemical production of eminent significance for the economy of the nation, and that this industrial function overshadows all others. In this writer's opinion, Baton Rouge is no more a university city than Durham, North Carolina.

Be that as it may, we are here concerned with the process of urbanization, and we shall therefore attempt to group the cities with regard to the "mainsprings" of their origin and growth. We may consider the demographic map of southern urban places as a composite of different "systems" of towns and cities, which owe their existence and present size to various predominant factors and combinations of factors. In this composite we can discern four major systems:

(a) The oldest layer of cities in the South consists of a small

16. Rudolf Heberle, "Survey of the War-Time Labor Force of Louisiana," U. S. Employment Service, Louisiana (1945), p. 22 f. and *passim*. In New Orleans these increases were concentrated in the central business district rather than in the "neighborhood" shopping centers; in other words, they occurred in establishments serving the war industry workers and soldiers.

number of military and political outposts which at the same time served as centers of colonial trade—New Orleans, Mobile, Savannah, and Charleston. Since these functions could in colonial days be concentrated only at a few strategic points in this vast and wild region, the system of these cities is far-flung and widely scattered. This oldest layer of cities was limited to the coastal region, never penetrating farther inland than ocean-going sailing vessels could conveniently go in the pre-steamer age.

(b) A second and more numerous system of relatively old but smaller urban places consists of local trading and service centers which grew up or were founded by enterprising businessmen as the population increased, moved westward, and gained in wealth. Here we find the cotton and oil presses, rice mills and other plants processing farm products; but the main reason for the existence of these places is the presence of hardware and dry-goods stores and other services which have to be located at short distances from the rural consumer. The size and density of these trading centers is essentially a function of the spatial extent of their trading area, of the density of population in this area, and of economic factors such as the value of farm products produced in the area and the aggregate purchasing power of the rural population and other factors such as the location of highways, railroads, and waterways. The geographical distribution of these places at any given time corresponds roughly to the distribution of the population.

As a sub-group in this system may be regarded the county seat towns (in Louisiana, parish seat towns); their density depends on the size of the counties, which varies considerably thoughout the region, and their size depends on the density of population in the county as well as on the wealth of the people. Many of these towns have become the locations of activities other than the administrative and commercial ones and thus have experienced exceptional population growth. Some smaller state capitals may also be classed in this group either because they were founded in locations of optimum accessibility to the state's population of the time or because they developed at minor inland trade centers.

(c) Interspersed through these two systems we find a limited number of larger, subregional commercial centers in the hinterland: Atlanta, Dallas, Memphis, Lexington, Fort Worth, San Antonio, Kansas City (Mo.), and also some smaller cities with similar functions such as Shreveport. Today most of these cities are also seats of manufacturing plants; but their origin, their life-giving functions have been commerce and transportation, and the geographical location of these cities is at "breaks" in transportation or at locations that for other reasons had strategic significance for commerce rather than for the establishment of manufacturing industries.

A group in an intermediate position between (b) and (c) consists of the old river ports in the southeastern states which have been mentioned previously. Only a few of them—for example, Richmond and Vicksburg—rose to nearly the importance of group (c) cities.

Characteristic of cities in this third system is a concentration of wholesale business enterprises (or their regional branch offices), headquarters of certain industrial enterprises (e. g., oil producing companies), department stores, mail-order house regional offices, banks, law firms, and many other enterprises and services which operate over a large subregion. Of necessity these cities are also railroad centers.

(d) Finally, we can distinguish a system of urban places which owe either their origin or their present size or both to the fact that they are locations of secondary industry. They range in size from Birmingham, with a population of half a million in the metropolitan area, to small mono-industrial lumber mill and textile towns of less than 10,000 inhabitants.

The mining towns of the coal mining areas of the Appalachian Mountains present a particular problem since many communities which have the size of urban places according to the census definition are not incorporated and therefore do not appear in the census tabulations as urban communities.

We pointed out before the reason for the South having only very few large cities which owe their existence or development to the agglomeration of raw-material oriented industries like many of the big manufacturing cities of the North. Characteristic for the South is rather the large number of small industrial towns and cities based upon the processing of lumber, oil, and agricultural products. In the labor-oriented industries, two contradictory tendencies can be observed in a society where labor is free to move: the workers tend to concentrate at the large labor markets, where employment opportunities are most numerous and diverse, while employers, unless the nature of their enterprise ties them also definitely to the large labor markets, tend to move away from the big cities in order to evade high land prices, taxes, and high wage levels. This latter tendency has been strong in the South where industries with high skill demands are rare and where docility of labor has been a major attraction for manufacturers. This is evidenced by the sugar-coated advertising of entrepreneurs who want to establish a plant in a small community with an ample supply of labor and without competing enterprises, in order to attain a virtual monopoly over the local labor market.

On the workers' part this tendency has been abetted by lack of knowledge of employment opportunities in distant large cities and probably in many cases by the desire to be able to fall back on farming in old age or depression, both contributory factors in holding labor in small cities and in the surrounding country. The result has been a wide dispersion of manufacturing industries in many relatively small cities with a corresponding sparsity of large cities.

Distances between large cities are much greater than in the older manufacturing regions of the North, and there are in the South no very large clusters of smaller cities. While in some highly industrialized subregions, like the Piedmont, we find strings of cities lined up along the railroads and highways, there are no large compactly urbanized areas. Even in the more densely industrialized parts of North Carolina, which have been studied by Howard W. Odum, Rupert B. Vance, and Harriet L. Herring and their associates, there appears to be evolving a new constellation pattern of urban communities, consisting of small central cities with still smaller satellite communities and considerable dispersion of workers in the open country.[17] Similar patterns are to be observed along the Gulf Coast from Pensacola to Galveston.

However, it is hardly justifiable to infer from these local observations that a general tendency toward industrial decentralization exists in the region. The boom of World War II did not result in a significant measure of decentralization of industry; on the contrary, most of the gains in population and in manufacturing employment

17. Vance, *op. cit.*, chaps. 19 and 20 (especially pp. 306 and 317).

occurred in already established industrial centers.[18] It seems that the new manufacturing cities tend to assume a very loose, widespread pattern like the triangle of Beaumont, Orange, and Port Arthur or the Houston, Texas City, Galveston areas. Houston, now the largest center in the whole region, has developed largely as a port city.

There arises in this connection the question of whether important new cities will now come into being in the region. This could happen in two ways: by growth of villages to the size of urban places and by founding of new cities in connection with new industrial plants. The possibility of the latter is of course unpredictable. It is however safe to assume that those new industrial towns that do appear are not likely to grow to large size. The other form of urbanization is not likely to become important; with the improvement of transportation facilities, more and more of the retail businesses and service establishments are likely to be concentrated at a smaller number of central places, each of which will serve a larger area. It may therefore be assumed that those hamlets, villages, and small towns which have the advantage of a central location to a large rural trade-and-service area will eventually grow to urban size, while the majority of these places is likely to stagnate or to decline, except those which become suburbs or satellites in an expanding metropolitan area.[19] This prognosis is in keeping with observed trends in the development of small places and the tendency of commercial, educational, and other non-agricultural activities in rural areas to become concentrated in the larger villages, which has been demonstrated for the pre-war decade.[20]

The future growth of cities in the South will depend on three major trends: the increase of population in the region, the increase in secondary industry, and the changes in agriculture. These three basic movements are obviously closely interrelated. The rate of

18. Rudolf Heberle, "The Impact of the War on Population Redistribution in the South," *Papers of the Institute of Research and Training in the Social Sciences, Vanderbilt University*, Number Seven (Nashville, Tennessee: Vanderbilt University Press, 1945), pp. 24-30.

19. These assumptions seem to be in agreement with the findings in Donald J. Bogue, "Changes in Population Distribution Since 1940," *American Journal of Sociology*, LVI (July 1950), 47, 52, 54, concerning the decline of population in rural areas of the South, 1940-1947.

20. T. Lynn Smith, "The Role of the Village in American Rural Society," *Rural Sociology*, 7 (March 1942), pp. 10-21, emphasizes the ascendancy of the villages over the smaller places as trade and service centers.

population increase will depend very largely on the variations in
the level of migration from and to the region, if it can be assumed
that no very great changes in the rate of natural increase of population are to be expected in the next decades. Secondary industries,
especially of the city-building and city-filling varieties, will receive
a stimulus if the labor force in the region continues to increase;
extension of existing or establishment of new industries will be discouraged if a large-scale exodus of workers should take place.

The changes in agriculture, i. e., diversification and mechanization,[21] are already "setting free" in some areas considerable numbers
of farm workers who, if they stay in the region at all, tend to con-
gregate in the nearby smaller urban places, where unknown proportions of them are absorbed into secondary and tertiary industries.
Smaller numbers will eventually migrate over longer distances and
reach the larger cities. This movement out of agricultural areas is
counterbalanced in some parts of the South, however, by the trend
to industries scattered in towns and villages. The depopulation of
the agricultural areas is not likely to be balanced by the movement
of urban people into the country, the latter being confined by and
large to the immediate vicinity of the cities.

21. A. L. Bertrand, *Agricultural Mechanization and Social Change in
Rural Louisiana*, Louisiana State University, Agricultural Experiment Station, Louisiana Bulletin No. 458 (June 1951).

CHAPTER TWO

The Emergence of Cities *

T. LYNN SMITH

The FIRST SECTION of our symposium is devoted to an exposition of urbanization as a process. The complex of economic and social changes accompanying urbanization has proved difficult to present in the scientific depth desired. In its primary aspects, however, urbanization is best viewed as a redistributon of population, involving both (1) an increase in the number of points at which population concentrates, and (2) a growth in the size of these concentrations.

While urbanization in our Western civilization has impressed some students as a continuous and irreversible process, it is not safe to assume that the growth of urban populations is necessarily eternal. For nations and regions there may well exist a ceiling above which the trend of urbanization will not ascend. Presumably in a given economy it would prove neither profitable nor rewarding to exceed this limit. Thus cities in the most urban regions will slacken in growth as they approach an assumed upper limit; in rural regions, however, urbanization may continue at an increasing rate. To the extent they take over functions previously carried on elsewhere, such regional centers might lower the ceiling on urban growth in other regions.

The emergence and growth of southern cities viewed against the backdrop of an urban nation may well illustrate some of the above assumptions without actually subjecting them to a scientific test. Certainly we know that the South—among the first of the nation's

* This paper appeared in an earlier form as "The Emergence of Urban Centers in the South" in T. Lynn Smith and C. A. McMahan (eds.), *The Sociology of Urban Life* (New York: The Dryden Press, 1951), pp. 159-171.

areas to be settled—long lagged in urban development. It is the purpose of this chapter to supply the historical perspective and time schedule for this phenomenon. When and where did the South's urban centers emerge and how fast have they grown? How fast is urbanization proceeding in the South as compared to the nation? Interesting in themselves, the answers to these questions also shed light on the discussions to follow.

THE RISE OF URBAN CENTERS

The Census of 1790 showed that Charleston with 16,359 inhabitants was the fourth city in the nation; only Philadelphia, New York, and Boston contained larger populations. At this date, the other six places classed as urban were Baltimore, Salem, Providence, Portsmouth, Richmond, and Albany. A decade later Charleston was in fifth position, having yielded fourth to Baltimore. Six new urban centers were added in 1800 but if the new national capital is excepted, only one of them—Petersburg, Virginia—was in the southern region. At the beginning of the nineteenth century, Louisville contained only 359 inhabitants, and Cincinnati had the grand total of 750. By 1810 the Louisiana Purchase had added New Orleans to the southern cities, giving the region another large center which ranked just below Charleston, sixth in size in the nation. By this time the South's leading centers of population were Charleston, with 24,711 people; New Orleans, 17,242; Richmond, 9,735; Petersburg, 5,668; Savannah, 5,215; and Louisville, 1,357.[1]

Thirty years later, important urban centers were still conspicuously absent in the South. New Orleans with 102,193 inhabitants in 1840 stood in a class by itself and ranked fourth in the nation. Only seven other southern cities (Charleston, Louisville, Mobile, Norfolk, Petersburg, Richmond, and Savannah) contained as many as 10,000 inhabitants each. In 1840 there were no population centers whatsoever deserving to be classed as urban in the states of Arkansas, Mississippi, North Carolina, and Tennessee, or in Florida Territory. At that time, before the "iron horse" had made any great headway in rearranging the pattern of transportation routes, nearly all of the

1. J. D. B. DeBow, *Statistical View of the United States . . . Being a Compendium of the Seventh Census* (Washington: Beverley Tucker, 1854), p. 192.

sizeable population centers were ports, most of them on the ocean. Louisville was the only one of the region's "river towns," besides New Orleans, to emerge as an important urban center. Memphis, Vicksburg, and Baton Rouge were still in the small town category. Although more than 6,000,000 persons were living in the South, Richmond (20,153) was the region's only state capital with as many as 10,000 inhabitants. Its closest rival, Nashville, with a population of 6,929, was still just an overgrown town. The astounding development of governmental services that eventually was to cause southern capitals to expand so fast as to burst at the seams was not to come for many decades.

On the eve of the Civil War (1860), New Orleans with 168,675 inhabitants was still the only metropolis in the South, although Louisville had begun to come to the fore. No other southern city had passed the 25,000 mark, but to the ranks of those with more than 10,000 inhabitants had been added Alexandria, Virginia; Augusta, Georgia; Covington and Newport, Kentucky; Memphis and Nashville, Tennessee; and Donaldsonville and Lafayette (a suburb later incorporated into New Orleans), Louisiana. By this time 32 additional towns had emerged from the village category and gave promise of further development. Of these, six were in Georgia, five in Mississippi, four in Kentucky, four in Alabama, three in Virginia, two in North Carolina, two in Louisiana, one in Florida, one in Arkansas, and four in Texas, which had entered the Union. As late as 1860 no towns of 10,000 inhabitants were to be found in North Carolina, Florida, Mississippi, Arkansas, and Texas.

It is doubtful that the twenty years of war and reconstruction greatly retarded the development of urban centers in the South. Certainly by 1880 the region was much more thickly dotted with cities and towns. New Orleans and Louisville had grown considerably, while Richmond and Charleston had outdistanced other cities in their class. Centers boasting more than 10,000 inhabitants now totaled 25: five in Virginia, five in Georgia, four in Texas, three in Kentucky, three in Tennessee, two in Alabama, and one each in South Carolina, Mississippi, and Arkansas. The important future centers—Birmingham, Knoxville, Durham, Raleigh, Charlotte, Jackson, Fort Worth, and Shreveport—had not yet left the small town category, while Atlanta, Memphis, Nashville, Chattanooga, Dallas, Houston, and San Antonio remained in their swaddling clothes.

As the twentieth century opened, the South contained only six of the nation's 50 large cities. At that time New Orleans held eleventh position; Louisville was eighteenth; Memphis, thirty-seventh; Atlanta had advanced to forty-third; Richmond was forty-sixth; and Nashville, a newcomer, was forty-seventh. Trade and transportation were still the chief bases of urban existence in the South, but new urban centers were appearing at many places throughout the South. Manufacturing centers such as Birmingham, Charlotte, and Fort Worth were only commencing their growth, while Tulsa was still a small village of 1,390 inhabitants. In 1900 Houston, Dallas, San Antonio, Oklahoma City, and the Florida cities were just beginning the expansion that would soon bring them to positions of prominence in the nation.

In the first two decades of the twentieth century many western cities made bids for national prominence. Because of this competition the South's representation among the nation's 50 leading cities in 1920 was held to seven only. Had it not been for the phenomenal growth of the Texas cities with three newcomers—San Antonio, Dallas, and Houston—occupying forty-sixth, forty-seventh, and fiftieth positions, respectively, the South's showing would have been poorer. New Orleans, finding it difficult to maintain the pace, had dropped to twenty-second place by the close of World War I; Louisville had fallen to thirty-fourth; but Atlanta's continued gains put her in thirty-eighth position, and Memphis was forty-fifth. Houston had not yet shown signs of its great future growth.

Between the two World Wars, growth of urban centers in the South got underway in earnest. In 1920 only seven of the nation's largest cities were found in the region; by 1940, the South could boast 14 of the nation's 50 largest cities. Cities along the Gulf Coast mushroomed at an astounding speed, and places like Oklahoma City, Birmingham, and Nashville came forward rapidly. By 1950 the South's 14 representatives ranked as follows: Houston, fourteenth; New Orleans, sixteenth; Dallas, twenty-second; San Antonio, twenty-fifth; Memphis, twenty-sixth; Louisville, thirtieth; Atlanta, thirty-third; Birmingham, thirty-fourth; Fort Worth, thirty-eighth; Miami, forty-second; Oklahoma City, forty-fifth; Richmond, forty-sixth; Norfolk, forty-eighth and Jacksonville, forty-ninth. In all, however, they had 4,852,000 people—less than half of the population of New York and Philadelphia taken together.

The emergence of small centers is also important since many of them are destined to become centers of commerce, trade, industry, and of cultural life in the decades that lie ahead. It is impossible to give the full details concerning these small places, but some essential facts have been compiled in tabular form. Table 1 gives the total number of urban places (those having 2,500 or more inhabitants) in the southern region at each census from 1790 to 1950. Comparable data for the United States serve to show the South's proportion of urban centers at each decade. These tabulations show urban

TABLE 1. Number of Urban Centers in the United States and the 13 Southern States, 1790 to 1950

Year	Number of Urban Places			Number with More Than 10,000 Inhabitants			Number with 10,000 or Less Inhabitants		
	United States	South	Percent in South	United States	South	Percent in South	United States	South	Percent in South
1790	24	5	20.8	5	1	20.0	19	4	21.1
1800	33	5	15.2	6	1	16.7	27	4	14.8
1810	46	7	15.2	11	2	18.2	35	5	14.3
1820	61	12	19.7	13	3	23.1	48	9	18.8
1830	90	18	20.0	23	4	17.4	67	14	20.9
1840	131	25	19.1	37	8	21.6	94	17	18.1
1850	236	41	17.4	62	10	16.1	174	31	17.8
1860	392	62	15.8	93	14	15.1	299	48	16.1
1870	663	80	12.1	168	24	14.3	495	56	11.3
1880	939	119	12.7	223	31	13.9	716	88	12.3
1890	1,348	222	16.5	354	53	15.0	994	169	17.0
1900	1,737	320	18.4	440	67	15.2	1,297	253	19.5
1910	2,262	480	21.2	597	100	16.8	1,665	380	22.8
1920	2,722	643	23.6	752	136	18.1	1,970	507	25.7
1930	3,165	790	25.0	982	188	19.1	2,183	602	27.6
1940	3,464	922	26.6	1,077	223	20.7	2,387	699	29.3
1950	4,284	1,217	28.4	1,262	330	26.1	3,022	932	30.8

Source: U. S. Censuses of Population, 1790 to 1950.

places with populations of less than 10,000, and those having larger numbers of inhabitants. A second compilation, Table 2, shows the number of urban places in each of the 13 southern states for the years 1860, 1900, 1920, 1940, and 1950.

It is interesting to note that the total number of urban centers in the South increased from five in 1790 to 62 at the outbreak of the Civil War and to more than 1,200 at the mid-century. In 1870 the 13 southern states contained only 12.1 percent of the nation's urban centers, but in the following years the emergence of towns and

TABLE 2. Number of Urban Places in the South, 1860-1950, By States

State	1860	1900	1920	1940	1950
13 Southern States	62	320	643	922	1,217
Alabama	5	27	39	59	85
Arkansas	1	15[a]	41[a]	53[a]	64[a]
Florida	2	12	30	70	95
Georgia	9	31	59	78	106
Kentucky	8	34	51	56	74
Louisiana	4	15	38	54	72
Mississippi	5	22	32	48	54
North Carolina	4	28	55	76	87
Oklahoma	—	13	63	74	86
South Carolina	2	20	32	50	83
Tennessee	4	22[b]	47[b]	57[b]	71[b]
Texas	5	56[a]	119[a]	196[a]	272[a]
Virginia	13	27[b]	39[b]	53[b]	78[b]

[a] Texarkana counted in both states, but only once in total.

[b] Bristol counted in both states, but only once in the total.

Source: U. S. Censuses of Population, 1860 to 1950.

cities in the southern region was even more rapid than the corresponding developments in other sections of the country, with the result that by 1950 these states contained 28.4 percent of all such urban places. It is significant that the South contains a disproportionately large share of the smaller urban centers. In 1950 only one-fourth of all places of more than 10,000 inhabitants were located in the southern region, whereas almost one-third of the smaller urban centers were found in the 13 southern states. Since 1880 each passing decade has found the South with a greater percentage of the nation's urban centers, large and small, but until 1940 the gain in places of less than 10,000 inhabitants was more rapid. The last decade reversed this trend. Figure 1, which shows the distribution of population by size of place for 1950, highlights the emergence of these large centers against the region's backdrop of smaller towns and cities.

Were it not for the fact that urbanism in the South has always been overshadowed by the national trend, increases in urban centers in southern states would have received more attention. In 90 years the number of urban places in Arkansas increased from 1 to 64, in Texas from 5 to 272, in Florida from 2 to 95; and none of the other 13 states was very far behind. Oklahoma, legally opened to

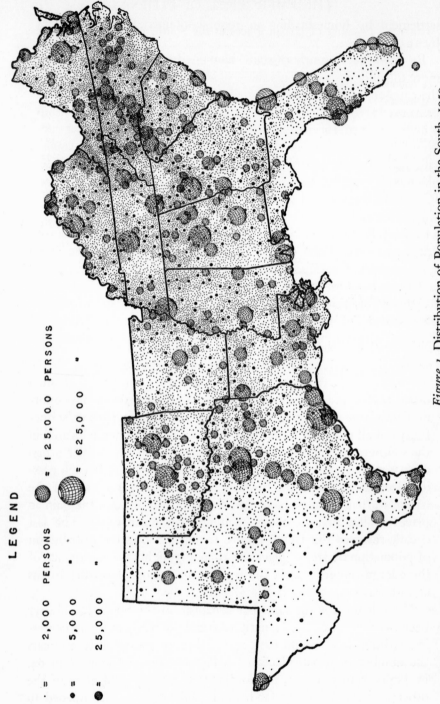

LEGEND

= 2,000 PERSONS
" = 5,000   "
" = 25,000   "

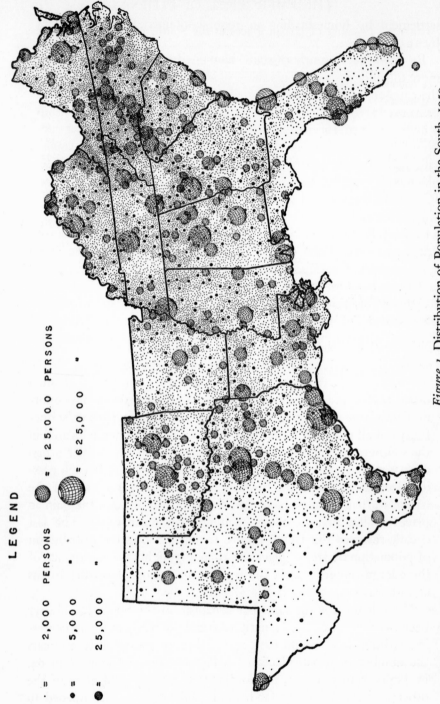 = 125,000 PERSONS

 = 625,000   "

Figure 1. Distribution of Population in the South, 1950

settlement by homesteading in 1909, contained 86 urban places by 1950.

By 1950 the 13 southern states contained 29 cities of 100,000 or more inhabitants. The lion's share of these had mushroomed out of the category of large town or small city only during the twentieth century. In 1900 there were only three cities in the entire region which qualified for inclusion in the 100,000 or more category: New Orleans, which passed the 100,000 mark prior to 1840, Louisville before 1870, and Memphis during the closing decade of the nineteenth century. In 1910 Birmingham, Atlanta, Nashville, and Richmond were added to the group. Ten years later the number was increased by five: Dallas, Forth Worth, Houston, San Antonio, and Norfolk. Between 1920 and 1930 Jacksonville, Miami, Tampa, Oklahoma City, Tulsa, Chattanooga, and Knoxville all passed the 100,000 mark. Charlotte alone was added to the list between 1930 and 1940; but Mobile, Montgomery, Little Rock, Savannah, Baton Rouge, Shreveport, Austin, Corpus Christi, and El Paso all passed the 100,000 line between 1940 and 1950. In addition, Arlington County, Virginia, one of Washington's suburbs which is classed as

TABLE 3. Metropolitan Areas in the South of over 400,000
Population, 1950

Rank	Areas	Population	Percent in Central City	Percent Increase, 1940-1950
18	Houston	806,701	73.9	52.5
22	New Orleans	685,405	83.2	24.1
23	Atlanta	671,797	49.3	29.7
24	Dallas	614,799	70.7	54.3
25	Louisville	576,900	64.0	27.8
27	Birmingham	558,928	53.3	21.5
33	San Antonio	500,460	81.6	48.0
34	Miami	495,084	50.4	84.9
36	Memphis	482,393	82.1	34.7
38	Norfolk-Portsmouth	446,200	65.8	72.3
41	Tampa-St. Petersburg	409,143	54.1	50.4

Source: U. S. Bureau of the Census, *U. S. Census of Population: 1950*. Vol. I, *Number of Inhabitants*, Chapter I: U. S. Summary, Tables 26 and 28.

urban under a special rule, more than doubled in population during the last decade and had almost 135,000 inhabitants by 1950.

Only Houston, 596,163, and New Orleans, 570,445, reached the half-million club by 1950, giving the South 2 out of 18 such cities in the nation. The rise of the census metropolitan areas is also considered since the entire population centering around the large city is integrated in one urban social and economic system. Of the 33 metropolitan areas of 500,000 and over in population, the South has seven: Houston, 806,701; New Orleans, 685,405; Atlanta, 671,797; Dallas, 614,799; Louisville, 576,900; Birmingham, 558,928; and San Antonio, 500,460 (Table 3). If Dallas-Fort Worth were counted together as are Minneapolis-St. Paul, the Texas concentration would be the South's largest, reaching 976,052 population. The high rate of growth shown from 1940 to 1950 suggests the South will in the near future develop some four other areas in the half-million category—possibly Miami, now 495,084 population; Memphis, 482,939; Norfolk-Portsmouth, 446,200; and Tampa-St. Petersburg, 409,143.

THE POPULATION OF URBAN CENTERS

Urbanization in the South seems to be progressing in much the same manner as in the United States as a whole except that it has lagged by about fifty years. At the opening of the nineteenth century the entire nation was almost exclusively rural, only 6.1 percent of the population then living in what would have been classed as urban centers on the basis of present census criteria. Even then, however, there were great regional differences, and in the southern states the corresponding percentage was only 1.8 (Table 4). After the Louisiana Purchase gave the South New Orleans—one of the nation's most populous centers—the Census of 1810 showed only 2 percent of the region's population living in towns and cities of 2,500 or more. In the United States as a whole the corresponding percentage was 7.3 percent. Not until the decade 1840-1850 did the South reach a degree of urbanization comparable with that of the United States at the time of the first census in 1790. At the outbreak of the Civil War the stage of urbanization in the South resembled that of the nation in 1820. In 1900 the South apparently was urbanized to the extent reached by the whole country in 1850.

Not until 1940 did the percentage of urban dwellers in the region equal that of the nation in 1890. Thus, in historical perspective urbanization in the South seems to parallel rather closely the process in the nation, with a lag of some fifty years. The rate of urbanization stepped up, however, so that by mid-century the South appeared to resemble the nation of forty years before (Table 4).

TABLE 4. Growth of Urban Population in the United States and the 13 Southern States, 1790 to 1950

Year	Urban Population United States	South	Percentage of Population in Urban Centers United States	South
1790	201,655	28,655	5.1	1.8
1800	322,371	40,154	6.1	1.8
1810	525,459	70,090	7.3	2.6
1820	693,255	108,507	7.2	2.8
1830	1,127,247	174,199	8.8	3.4
1840	1,845,055	301,524	10.8	4.7
1850	3,543,716	493,662	15.3	6.0
1860	6,216,518	742,381	19.8	7.2
1870	9,902,361	1,013,687	25.7	9.4
1880	14,129,735	1,377,982	28.2	9.4
1890	22,106,265	2,382,800	35.1	13.4
1900	30,159,921	3,339,779	39.7	15.2
1910	41,988,932	5,308,070	45.7	20.1
1920	54,157,973	7,503,288	51.2	25.4
1930	68,954,823	10,827,860	56.2	32.1
1940	74,423,702	12,873,317	56.5	34.8
1950 (old def.)	88,927,464	17,912,854	59.0	42.9
1950 (new def.)	96,467,686	19,653,073	64.0	47.1

Source: U. S. Censuses of Population, 1790 to 1950. See Chapter 3, Table 6, for the new definition of urban population.

From 1790 to 1950 the density of settlement in the United States increased from 4.5 persons per square mile to 50.7. In 1790 only 28,655 persons or 1.8 percent of the South's population lived in places of 2,500 or more as compared to 5.1 percent for the nation. By 1950 almost 18 million southerners were classified as urban (Table 4). This was 42.9 percent of the regional population as contrasted with 59.0 percent for the nation (Table 4, Old Definition). If the farm population be taken as the obverse of the urban population, it can be noted that the nation's farm population in 1950 stands at its low point, 16.6 percent of the total, compared with 34.9 percent in 1910. In 1920 over half of the South's population—51.3 percent—was on farms; by 1950 this proportion was cut almost in half, 27.1 percent. Farm tenancy had fallen to 26.0 percent of the nation's farm operators, approximately the level returned in the 1880 Census.

This indication of basic change in the urban "stance" of the population is reinforced by a glance at the several states. States that were less than 20 percent urban at the turn of the century were 40 to 60 percent urban in 1950 by any definition (Table 5). Okla-

TABLE 5. Rank of Southern States by Percent of Urban Population, 1900-1950

1950 New Urban Definition			1950 Old Urban Definition			1900		
Rank	State	Percent Urban	Rank	State	Percent Urban	Rank	State	Percent Urban
13	Florida	65.6	13	Texas	59.8	26	Louisiana	26.5
16	Texas	62.7	16	Florida	56.5	31	Kentucky	21.8
25	Louisiana	54.8	24	Louisiana	50.8	32	Florida	20.3
30	Oklahoma	51.0	26	Oklahoma	49.6	33	Virginia	18.3
34	Virginia	47.0	35	Virginia	40.3	34	Texas	17.1
36	Georgia	45.3	36	Georgia	40.1	36	Tennessee	16.2
37	Tennessee	44.1	37	Alabama	40.1	38	Georgia	15.6
38	Alabama	43.8	39	Tennessee	38.4	41	South Carolina	12.8
41	Kentucky	36.8	42	Kentucky	33.5	42	Alabama	11.9
42	South Carolina	36.7	44	Arkansas	32.3	44	North Carolina	9.9
45	North Carolina	33.7	46	North Carolina	30.5	45	Arkansas	8.5
47	Arkansas	33.0	47	South Carolina	28.8	46	Mississippi	7.7
48	Mississippi	27.9	48	Mississippi	27.6	47	Alabama	7.4

Source: U. S. Bureau of the Census, *U. S. Census of Population: 1950*. Vol. I, *Number of Inhabitants*, Chapter I: U. S. Summary, Table D.

homa made the greatest gain, 7.4 to 49.6 percent urban. Dramatically enough, the least urban state in 1950—Mississippi—exceeded 1900's most urban state—Louisiana—by 27.9 percent to 26.5 percent urban. This gain is relative as well as absolute, for the composite rank of southern states in urbanization went from 37.3 in 1900 to 34.7 in 1950. The rate of urbanization in the South exceeded that for the nation without perceptibly decreasing the half-century gap.

FACTORS IN URBAN GROWTH

The factors responsible for the emergence and growth of urban centers in the South probably do not greatly differ from those in the urbanization of other sections of the country. They merely got underway later; and by the same token it may be that they have not yet spent their force as fully in the South. The forces contributing to urbanization include the following factors: (1) the growth of population; (2) the improvement of agricultural methods which made it possible for smaller proportions of the population to produce enough food and fiber to feed and clothe the whole; (3) the progress of invention and discovery, the division of labor by areas and tasks, specialization, and other developments included in what is known as the industrial revolution, all of which resulted in the wholesale transfer of farm and home processing establishments to the towns and cities; (4) the abrupt decline in the degree of self-sufficiency on the part of the individual family, and the corresponding skyrocketing of trade and commerce; (5) revolutionary improvements in the systems of communication and transportation; (6) the discovery and perfecting of a large number of new industrial processes and the building of hundreds of new factories in which thousands of products are now manufactured; (7) the tremendous expansion of governmental agencies and services, including the welfare agencies and the great state universities, which has aided in the mass transfer of populations from rural to urban areas; and (8) the development of the territory adjoining the Gulf Coast as one of the nation's principal winter playgrounds, and as a residential area to which thousands of persons go to spend the declining years of their lives. Before the Civil War none of these factors except the commercial one had played any important part in the rise of southern towns and cities.

It may be impossible to indicate specific periods in which each of the factors enumerated has exerted its preponderant influence in the growth of southern towns and cities. Only a hundred years ago nearly all of the cities in the South owed their existence to favorable locations as seaports. A little later, trade and commerce had become great enough for a few river ports to grow into cities of some importance. Prior to the Civil War, however, few other factors had gained sufficient importance to affect urbanization in the South.

But when railroads came to be the backbone of the American transportation system—during the last quarter of the nineteenth century —a host of inland towns and cities came to the front. As a matter of fact, this rearrangement of routes resulting from the perfecting of rail transportation was probably the most important factor in determining the precise locations for concentrations of population in the South. By 1900 important towns were aligned along the principal railways like beads on a string. Roanoke, Charlotte, Knoxville, Chattanooga, Dallas, Fort Worth, Montgomery, and especially Atlanta were among the chief beneficiaries of this development.

Late in the nineteenth century, manufacturing in the modern sense took its place among the factors contributing to the growth of new towns and the expansion of some already in existence. The phenomenal rise of Birmingham is the most spectacular case; but by 1900 industry had already heavily contributed to population increase in such cities as New Orleans, Louisville, and Memphis, and to the continued rise of a host of smaller places. The twentieth century, however, is crucial, for industrialization is now coming into its own as a basis for the urbanization of the South. The remarkable development of the textile industry in the Piedmont section of North Carolina and the continued expansion of heavy industry around Birmingham did not stand alone. The development of the oil industry and the building of meat-packing facilities played an important part in the rise of the Texas and Oklahoma cities. Although these changes overshadow developments in other parts of the South, they should not obscure the rapid process of industrial expansion underway in the Louisville, Memphis, Nashville, New Orleans, and Atlanta areas.

Finally came the rise of the whole Gulf Coast area, beginning roughly at the end of World War I. This can be seen as a part of the tendency of population to concentrate at water's edge, noted by R. D. McKenzie. In an area stretching from Florida to Brownsville, this movement toward urbanization is seen to be compounded of three parts: recreation, retirement, and a very real industrial development.

What are we to conclude from our review of the emergence of southern cities? It can hardly be said that the South "lost the jump" in urban development, for the region never held the lead. The familiar contrast of an agrarian area in an industrial nation explains the facts, but the trends we have observed now point to a future urbanization of respectable dimensions in the South. If cities are needed for the functions of a developed economy, the South is growing them as it matures its economy. The "breakthrough" was related to the demands of two World Wars, but the decade of the mid-century, 1940-1950, appears to have contributed the greatest push. Southern cities will grow as auxiliaries of our great centers, not duplicate them. To a people reared in the agrarian tradition, this should be a benefit—not a disaster.

CHAPTER THREE

Urbanization, Occupational Shift and Economic Progress

LORIN A. THOMPSON

THE CONCOMITANTS OF URBANIZATION

No account of the urbanization of a nation or of a region is complete without an analysis of the available labor force, its trend and utilization. Urbanization as redistribution of the population involves more than movement from country to city. It involves mass shifts in the occupations of a people, since a function of migration itself is to place a working force in position to climb the occupational ladder. Specifically urbanization means the transfer of workers from (1) agriculture to (2) manufacturing and (3) the service and distributive occupations. Occupational mobility carries with it the rewards of increased income, and since these payments are made by the economy as a going concern it is not surprising to find that the conditions of individual advancement are also those of economic progress.[1]

In his world-wide study, *Conditions of Economic Progress*, Colin Clark[2] found that both economic efficiency and per capita incomes increased as the proportion of a nation's working population engaged in the (1) primary industry (agriculture) decreased while the proportions in (3) tertiary industry (commerce, services, administration, distribution, etc.) increased. Proportions engaged in

1. See discussion in W. S. and E. S. Woytinsky, *World Populations and Production* (New York: Twentieth Century Fund, 1953), pp. 349-377. Erich W. Zimmermann, *World Resources and Industries* (rev. ed.; New York: Harper and Brothers, 1951), chaps. 7, 8, and 9 are excellent in this connection.
2. Colin Clark, *Conditions of Economic Progress* (rev. ed.; New York: Macmillan, 1952).

(2) secondary industry (manufacturing) appear in the more advanced countries to rise to a maximum and then to recede. This maximum was reached, Clark contends, for Britain in the Census of 1901; France in 1901; Switzerland in 1910; the United States in 1920; Japan in 1920; Germany in 1925; while in Australia, Italy and Denmark the maximum had not been reached by 1940.

In the United States the major shift from primary industry went hand in hand with economic advance. From 1820 to 1900 the proportions of workers in agriculture declined from 72.3 percent to 35.9 percent of the total, while manufacturing increased from 12.4 percent to 29.6 percent, and commerce and services increased from 15.3 percent to 34.5 percent. In terms of percentage change, commerce, trade and administration absorbed half the workers displaced in agriculture from 1820 to 1900 while the other half went into manufacturing. Since 1900 the proportion in manufacturing has remained constant (around 30 percent), while reductions in the proportion in agriculture to 18.9 percent in 1940 were accompanied by increases in transportation, trade and administration or in the professions and other services.[3] These changes continued through the 1940's when agriculture declined from 18.9 to 12.5 percent of all employed workers while tertiary industry increased to 53.8 percent of the total. In Table 1, which shows the components of the three sectors, only personal service among the two upper levels lost in percentage of workers.

Obviously economic development, diversification of occupational structure, and rising per capita incomes have accompanied the urbanization of nations. The South too is undergoing the process of urbanization. In 1900 it was 15 percent urban; in 1920, 25 percent; by 1950 it had grown to 42.9 percent urban (or 47.1 percent under the new definition). In the same periods the rest of the nation, already far ahead, grew from 50 percent urban to 61.3 to 65 percent (70 under new definition). To what extent has the economic and occupational structure of the South moved ahead with the region's urbanization?

Within the space of a single chapter only major phases of this development can be reviewed. The changes for the region as a whole were not necessarily duplicated within each of the 13 south-

3. Rupert B. Vance, *All These People* (Chapel Hill: University of North Carolina Press, 1945), chap. 11, especially pp. 148-153.

TABLE 1. Percentage Distribution by Industry Groups of Employed Persons, United States, 1940-1950

Industry Group	1940	1950
All Groups	100.0	100.0
Primary (Agriculture, etc.)	18.9	12.5
Secondary	30.2	33.7
Manufacturing and Mining	25.6	27.6
Construction	4.6	6.1
Tertiary	50.9	53.8
Trade	16.8	18.7
Transportation and Communication	6.9	7.8
Professionals and Related	7.3	8.3
Public Administration	3.2	4.4
Personal Services	8.9	6.2
Finance, Business Services, etc.	5.3	5.9
Other	2.5	2.5

Source: U. S. Census of Population, 1950.

ern states. Each state has had its own pattern of development, and its rate of urban growth comes near to reflecting its economic development.

THE SHIFT FROM AGRICULTURE

The changing pattern of employment in the main sectors from 1890 to 1950 is given in Table 2 for the southern states and the rest of the nation. The table gives the usual three-fold division: (1) agriculture, forestry and fishing; (2) manufacturing; and (3) trade, service and all other industries.

Colin Clark's prime requisite of economic advance—the shift from primary industry—has come to the South in much the fashion it came to the nation in an earlier period. Until 1930 the South's economy was primarily agricultural and its pattern of employment was greatly influenced by tobacco and cotton farming, both requiring large amounts of hand labor. From the 1930's, mechanical energy has increasingly been substituted for human and animal energy; as a result, the pattern of farming has changed, and the amount of labor required in southern agriculture has dropped sharply. In number of workers in agriculture, forestry and fishing, the South reached its peak in 1930, both in absolute numbers and in relation to the nation. In 1890 the South had 4.2 million agricul-

TABLE 2. Percent of Total Workers Engaged in Agriculture, Forestry and Fishing; Manufacturing; and Trade, Service and Other Industries, the Southern States and the Rest of the United States, 1890-1950

	Agriculture, Forestry and Fishing		Manufacturing		Trade, Service and Other Industries	
	Southern States	Rest of U. S.	Southern States	Rest of U. S.	Southern States	Rest of U. S.
1950	21.3	9.0	17.6	28.3	61.1	62.7
1940	34.9	12.9	15.3	26.4	49.8	60.7
1930	42.8	14.6	19.0	32.4	38.2	53.0
1920	50.7	17.6	17.5	35.6	31.8	46.8
1910	60.9	21.8	13.7	33.7	25.4	44.5
1900	61.6	25.5	10.5	29.8	27.9	44.7
1890	65.3	29.4	9.8	29.8	24.9	40.8

Source: U. S. Census of Population, 1950.

tural workers; the rest of the nation, 5 million. By 1930 the South had 5.5 million such workers to 5.3 million for the non-South. Since then the pattern has changed markedly, declining in 1950 to 3.2 million in the South, 3.8 million outside.

The agricultural revolution which the South underwent during the decades 1930-1950 was totally without precedent in the region. Mechanized agriculture and improved farming practices, first developed in the North and West, are now taking effect in the South. They include such improvements as hybrid corn and new and improved grasses suited for southern pastures. A contemporary southern saying puts it: "Yankees coming South; Negroes going North; cotton going West; livestock coming East; money coming in!" In spite of the great exodus from agriculture, efficiency of physical production has held up so that farmers and government are still hard put to it to hold down surpluses.

The changes in the proportion of workers engaged in agriculture, forestry and fishing, 1890 to 1950, stand out as most striking (Table 2). In 1890 more than 65 percent of all workers in the southern states were engaged in primary industry compared to only 29.4 percent outside. By 1930 this had dropped to less than 15 percent in the rest of the nation; in the South it remained around 43 percent (Table 2). Depression, New Deal and World War II shocked and revitalized southern agriculture so that it no longer follows traditional paths. Agricultural workers in the South declined from 5.5 million in 1930 to 3.2 million in 1950. Their proportion was cut in half; by 1950 they comprised little more than one-fifth of all workers. In the rest of the nation they dropped to 9 percent.

Nevertheless the pressure toward urbanization continues strong in the South as an analysis of farm incomes will show. In 1939 the gross value of farm products was 2.08 billion dollars in the South and 6.26 billion dollars in the rest of the nation. In this year agriculture in the two areas employed 4.3 million and 4.7 million respectively. Net income in agriculture was estimated at 1.9 billion dollars in the South and 3.3 billion outside. The value of marketings per worker in agriculture was $485 in the South compared to $1,318 in the non-South, while net incomes per worker were $460 and $701 respectively. The figures accurately state the different economic potential in agriculture for the South and the rest of the nation. These differences have long been associated with the high migration rates of workers from southern agricultural areas into other areas and occupations. As 1950 figures show, differences in the value of farm products per worker in agriculture are being reduced; there will be less pressure on agricultural workers to move from the South into other regions. Increased mechanization and improved methods of farming in southern agriculture, however, will continue to exert pressure on agricultural workers engaged in marginal production and on those who are underemployed.

THE SHIFT TO SECONDARY INDUSTRY

Shifts to higher levels of employment are now apparent in every phase of the southern economy. While agricultural employment was declining, employment in manufacturing, construction, trade, and the service industries expanded. Development of these industries has resulted in a redistribution of the South's population: urban and urban fringe areas have grown, and rural-farm areas have declined. The southward movement of industry has been well publicized and, no doubt, deserves the notice it has received.

Around 1890-1900 only about 10 percent of all southern workers were engaged in manufacturing compared to 30 percent in the rest of the nation. In the year 1920 the rest of the nation attained its highest proportion in manufacturing industry—35.6 percent; for the South the percentage was half as much, 17.5 percent. The South attained its highest employment in manufacturing, 19.0 percent, in 1930. Since then proportions in manufacturing have declined in both areas, reaching 17.6 percent in the South and 28.3 percent in the non-South in 1950 (Table 2). Physical volume of output was increased due to increasing production per worker.

Analysis of the trend in employment of the working force reinforces these conclusions. From 1930 to 1940, total employment in the South declined from 12.7 million to 12.2 million, a loss of 569,000 or 4.5 percent. During the decade 1940-1950, however, employment increased by 2.8 million or 22.7 percent (Table 3). The percentage increase in total civilians employed in the South was 20.1 percent, 1940 to 1950, compared to 27.2 percent in the rest of the nation.

Generally speaking, the increases in employment paralleled population increases, which were 12.7 percent for the southern states compared to 15.1 percent in the rest of the nation. That the South should have a lower proportionate increase in employment during its greatest period of development has its logical explanation. Analysis by occupational groups shows losses in farm owners and managers, farm laborers, unpaid family workers and farm and domestic servants at much higher rates than in the rest of the nation (Table 3). When these losses are accounted for, the South gained in all categories of industrial and service workers at much higher rates. The increase in the percentages of craftsmen, foremen, and kindred workers, from 7.9 to 11.6 percent, is a real index of the improved manufacturing position of the South. The proportion of semi-skilled operators also increased, in this instance from 13.9 percent in 1940 to 17.5 percent of total employment in the South in 1950. For the rest of the nation the corresponding figures were 19.4 and 20.6 percent (Table 3). Increases in these classifications indicate the degree of technological improvement and advancement in manufacturing industries. Auxiliary forces in the third level of commerce and administration are discussed below but attention is called to the higher rate of increase among owners and executives, 47.3 percent in the South compared to 36.2 percent outside.

The fact that the construction of industrial plants came later in the South has given the area its share of adequate plants, high capitalization and improved layouts. Because of industry's high output

TABLE 3. Percentage Distribution of Employed Workers by Occupational Group, Southern States and the Rest of the United States, 1940-1950

	Southern States			Rest of U. S.		
	1940	1950	Percent Change 1940-50	1940	1950	Percent Change 1940-50
Employed	100.0	100.0	20.1	100.0	100.0	27.2
1. Professional, Technical & Kindred Workers	5.9	7.2	46.8	8.7	9.3	35.4
2. Farmers & Farm Managers	20.7	13.4	−22.1	8.1	5.7	−10.7
3. Mgrs., Officials, Proprietors (except farm)	6.6	8.0	47.3	8.6	9.2	36.2
4. Clerical & Kindred Workers	5.7	8.8	84.8	11.2	13.4	52.7
5. Sales Workers	5.2	6.4	47.7	7.5	7.2	22.8
6. Craftsmen, Foremen & Kindred Workers	7.9	11.6	76.2	12.8	14.6	45.4
7. Operators & Kindred Workers	13.9	17.5	51.6	19.4	20.6	34.9
8. Private Household Workers	6.8	4.1	−27.5	3.8	1.9	−35.6
9. Service Workers (except private household)	5.4	6.8	50.5	7.7	7.9	30.4
10. Farm Laborers & Unpaid Family Workers	6.0	3.2	−35.4	1.3	1.1	.5
11. Farm Laborers (except unpaid foremen)	7.6	4.5	−29.2	3.1	2.0	−17.4
12. Laborers (except farm and mine)	7.5	7.0	11.8	6.8	5.8	9.1
13. Occupation Not Reported	.8	1.5	119.7	1.0	1.3	62.0
Number Employed 1940	12,050,926			32,837,157		
1950	14,475,591			41,763,858		

Source: U. S. Censuses of Population, 1940 and 1950.

per worker, increases in capitalization, physical production and auxiliary workers in the South may have proportionately exceeded the increase in number of workers in manufacturing. In spite of the region's rapid advances, however, manufacturing indices in the South, such as proportions of workers, volume of production, value added, etc., rarely exceed two-thirds of the nation's averages.

THE SHIFT TO TERTIARY INDUSTRY

If the battle of increased physical output in agriculture and manufacturing is being waged in the field of management, administration, finance and distribution, we should turn to tertiary industry for the test of economic advance in the South. How has the region fared in the area of the services? Measured in terms of working force, the South made its "economic breakthrough" in 1950. In that year the proportion of the region's working force in commerce, service and all related fields practically equalled that of the rest of the nation, 61.1 percent to 62.7 (Table 2). The impact of this transition on the South's economy and on urbanization is not yet fully realized. It can be better appreciated when we realize that before 1910 this group had never climbed above 25 percent. From 1930 to 1950 the proportion increased from 38.2 to 61.1 percent. Along with this shift has gone a comparatively rapid increase in incomes in southern states, although the region's level of per capita income is still about 72 percent of the national average.

That this shift involved a real increase in occupational skills is shown by detailed analysis. Thus the proportion of all workers engaged in professional and technical occupations in the South increased from 4.5 percent in 1930 to 5.9 in 1940 and to 7.2 in 1950. These figures, however, are not strictly comparable (Table 3). Managers, officials, and owners, except on farms, increased from 6.6 to 8.0 percent of all employed, 1940-1950. There were likewise substantial increases in the employment of clerical and kindred workers, 5.7 to 8.8 percent. Expansion among sales workers was also large in the South—from 5.2 to 6.4 percent of total employed. When other service workers are added, the South's proportions employed in tertiary industry increased from 28.8 to 37.2 percent compared to an increase in the rest of the country from 43.7 to 47.0 percent.

We included skilled craftsmen, foremen and kindred workers in the discussion of manufacturing but it is difficult to draw the line between such technical skills and the broad realm of overhead services. If added, proportions of third level workers then increased from 36.7 to 48.8 percent in the South, 56.5 to 61.6 percent elsewhere. When household service is added, the South's proportion employed in this third broad level increased from 43.5 percent to 52.9 percent compared to an increase in the rest of the country from 60.3 to 63.5 percent, 1940 to 1950. In each category the South started at lower levels and changed at faster rates so that its differences from the national pattern of occupations is growing smaller

(Table 3). Private household workers offer an exception to be discussed below.

WOMAN'S PLACE IN THE NEW SOUTH

Economic advance has usually meant increased gainful employment for women. From 1920 to 1950 the percentage of females aged 14 and over in the nation's labor force increased from 23.3 to 28.9 percent. With the growth in urbanization and service employment, women during the past two decades have left their homes and entered the labor force in increasing numbers.

Thus, in the southern states between 1940 and 1950 employment of males increased 14.9 percent and of females 37.2 percent. (See Table 4.) In the rest of the nation the increase in the civilian employment of males was 22 percent and of females 42.5 percent. Of the total increase in the civilian employed of more than 2.4 million in the South, 43.5 percent was among female workers; they constituted 23.5 percent of the total labor force in 1940 and 26.9 percent in 1950. In the non-South, 25.3 percent of the total civilian labor force was female in 1940, 28.3 percent in 1950. Thus of the total increase of 9 million workers, about 3.5 million or 40 percent were women.

The South's smaller rate of increase in the employment of women—as of men—was due to greater percentage losses in agriculture and domestic service. In all other services and in industrial groups the South showed constantly higher percentage gains in the employment of women (Table 4).

The generalization that employment of women increased at a higher rate than that of men finds one surprising exception. Among professional and technical workers, males increased at higher rates than females both in the South, 54.3 to 37.9 percent, and outside, 40.6 to 27.9 percent.

THE NEGRO'S PLACE IN THE NEW SOUTH

In economic advance there is a significant contrast in the South's ability and willingness to make use of women and Negroes in its occupational hierarchy. That is not to say that Negroes have lost where women have gained, for the situation is much more com-

TABLE 4. Percentage Change of Employed Workers, by
Occupational Groups by Sex, Southern States and
the Rest of the United States, 1940-1950

	Percent Change			
	Southern States		Rest of U. S.	
	Male 1940-50	Female 1940-50	Male 1940-50	Female 1940-50
Employed	14.9	37.2	22.0	42.5
1. Professional, Technical & Kindred Workers	54.3	37.9	40.6	27.9
2. Farmers & Farm Managers	—21.6	—36.1	—10.9	—3.4
3. Mgrs., Officials, Proprietors (except farm)	41.6	92.9	32.3	68.8
4. Clerical & Kindred Workers	44.1	123.4	26.3	74.7
5. Sales Workers	30.5	96.9	10.8	55.7
6. Craftsmen, Foremen & Kindred Workers	75.3	126.9	44.3	87.4
7. Operators & Kindred Workers	50.3	55.2	30.5	47.9
8. Private Household Workers	—55.2	—25.6	—17.5	—36.5
9. Service Workers (except private household)	27.6	84.5	19.3	48.4
10. Farm Laborers and Unpaid Family Workers	—39.9	—22.9	—33.3	411.0
11. Farm Laborers (except unpaid foremen)	—32.4	3.0	—20.8	210.6
12. Laborers (except farm and mine)	11.5	22.3	8.7	19.8
13. Occupation Not Reported	135.4	98.0	68.3	53.0
Number Employed 1940	9,214,984	2,835,942	24,534,921	8,302,236
1950	10,584,928	3,890,663	29,934,534	11,829,324

Source: U. S. Censuses of Population, 1940 and 1950.

plicated than that. Against the background of changing employment in the South, it appears that women are gaining not where Negroes have lost—that is, in agriculture—but where it would seem logical that more Negroes should go—that is, in the services. This situation deserves analysis in some detail.

In the whole area of tertiary industry, only one occupation—personal service—has lost workers. The decline in household workers, 1940-1950, from 6.8 to 4.1 percent in the South and from 3.8 to 1.9 percent outside, is no contradiction of our thesis. Apparently both economic progress and individual advancement took women from underpaid domestic service into more alluring fields. The demand for domestic help for working wives had to be met by more household appliances—not by more servants. This has had especial repercussions in the pattern of racial employment in the South. Between 1940 and 1950 the decline in personal service was 8.0 percent. During both decades (1930-1950), however, increases were noted in personal service employment among whites: 10.3 percent between 1930 and 1940 and 5.1 percent between 1940 and 1950. Among Negroes the decline from 1930 to 1940 was 5.1 percent; from 1940 to 1950, 14.5 percent. In 1930 Negroes comprised about 70 percent of persons employed in personal service; in 1950 they comprised only about 62 percent. Thus while Negroes lost in both agriculture and household service, white women were entering all the service fields.

In the 20-year shift from agrarian to urban pursuits, from physical production to clerical management, from unskilled to more skilled occupations, one important fact about races stands out. The number of employed white workers in the South increased by 2.7 million, 1930-1950, while the Negroes lost 940,000—almost a million civilian employment (Table 5). During this time total non-white population in the South increased from a little less than 9 million in 1930 to 9.5 million in 1950. In 1930, southern Negroes made up 33.1 percent of the employed labor force; by 1950 they were only 22.6 percent.

TABLE 5. Distribution of Civilian Employment in the Southern States, by Color, 1930-1950

	1930		1940		1950		Percent Change	
	Number	Percent	Number	Percent	Number	Percent	1940-50	1930-40
All Occupations	12,725,634	100.0	12,050,926	100.0	14,475,591	100.0	−5.3	20.1
White	8,510,523	66.9	8,708,623	72.3	11,201,236	77.4	2.3	28.6
Negro	4,215,111	33.1	3,342,343	27.7	3,274,355	22.6	−20.7	−2.0

Source: Census of Population, 1950, Series B.

Obviously Negroes displaced in agriculture were not assimilated into manufacturing, trade, and other service industries as fully as were the whites in the South during the past two decades. Many of the rural workers moved to southern cities. In many cases, however, the Negroes' adjustment to the changing economic pattern was migration from the area.

The detailed patterns of occupational change between whites and Negroes are rather mixed and varied. Increases in transportation, construction, and all other employment were somewhat less for Negroes than for whites. In professional service, wholesale and retail trade, and manufacturing, the percentage increases among Negroes were slightly higher than among whites. Considering the low bases from which Negroes started, this does not mean substantial increases in numbers. For the Negro, the mainstream of occupational mobility has been to cities outside the South.

SHIFTS BY INDUSTRY AND BY RESIDENCE

What has been the impact of this economic reorganization on the urbanization of the South? First, we should hope to compare two types of movement: (1) the movement out of agricultural industry with (2) the movement out of rural areas. We can show that in 60 years the South has transferred its labor force from 65.3 percent located in agricultural pursuits to 78.7 percent following non-agricultural callings. Not all who work in urban industries live in urban areas. Is it possible to relate the facts of occupational mobility more closely to urbanization? We know that from 1930 to 1940 employed persons in agriculture declined by 1.2 million or 22.2 percent, while total non-agricultural employment showed a small increase of 538,000 or 7.4 percent. In this period there was a loss of employment in rural areas of some 776,000 persons and a gain in the urban employed of 206,000, leaving a net loss in total employed of 569,000 for 1930-1940. From 1940 to 1950 agricultural employment declined 1.1 million or 25 percent, while total non-agricultural employment increased by 3.5 million or 44.7 percent. In terms of residence this meant a decline of 150,000 employed persons living in rural areas, while the employed in urban areas increased from 4.9 to 7.8 million—a gain of 2.9 million or nearly 60 percent. A part of the increase of those employed in urban areas resulted from the change in census definition (Table 6). The relation between the two sets of figures appears reasonably close when it is realized that large numbers of rural people work in urban centers.

We have discussed the shift between the races. The decline in those agriculturally employed, 1930-1940, represented a loss of some 611,000 Negro and 602,000 white workers; from 1940 to 1950, agriculture lost 597,000 whites and 468,000 Negroes.

TABLE 6. Employment in the Southern States by Rural and
Urban Areas, 1940-1950

	1950 (New definition)	1940 (Old definition)	Change 1940-1950	Per-cent Change
Total	14,911,923	12,156,326	2,755,597	22.7
Urban	7,782,626	4,876,461	2,906,165	59.6
Rural-nonfarm	3,488,436	2,571,032	917,404	35.7
Rural-farm	3,640,861	4,708,833	—1,067,972	—22.7
	Old definition estimated	Adjusted		
Total	14,911,923	12,156,326	2,755,597	22.7
Urban	7,166,626	4,876,461	2,290,165	47.0
Rural-nonfarm	4,104,436	2,571,032	1,533,404	59.6
Rural-farm	3,640,861	4,708,833	—1,067,972	—22.7

Source: U. S. Census of Population, 1950. Prior to 1950 the urban population, with certain adjustments, was that residing within the corporate limits of places of 2,500 and over. In 1950 the census classified as urban all population residing in urban-fringe areas around cities of 50,000 or more and in unincorporated places of 2,500 or more. The new definition upped the nation's 1950 urban population from 88.9 million to 96.5 million, or from 59 percent to 64 percent of the total. All this increase came out of the rural-nonfarm population, which was reduced from 25.7 to 20.7 percent of the U. S. total. The rural-farm population remained 13.3 percent of the total under each definition.

The South's urban nonwhite residents, however, increased from 2.6 million in 1930 to 4.3 million in 1950 (by new urban definition) or to slightly more than 4 million (by the old urban definition). The percentage of nonwhites living in urban places shows approximately the same pattern of development as the proportion of whites living in urban places. For example, in 1930, 32.1 percent of the total population of the southern states lived in urban areas; in 1940, 34.8 percent; in 1950, 47.1 percent (new urban definition) or 42.9 percent (old urban definition). The corresponding percentages for the nonwhites were 29.7, 34.2, and 45.1 or 42.5. While increases in the white urban population in the South were much larger both in absolute numbers and in percentage change than for the non-whites, the distribution of the two races between urban and rural follows the same pattern.

Total employment in the South, including military personnel, is given in Table 6 for 1940 and 1950 for urban, rural-nonfarm and rural-farm population groups. The first part of the table shows each population sector according to the 1950 definition of urban, and the 1940 data according to the old definition. The second part of the table incorporates an estimated adjustment of 1950 data to conform to the 1940 definition. On the first basis, urban employment in the South increased by more than 2.9 million or 59.6 percent. On the basis of the adjusted definition, the urban increase was 2.3 million or 47.0 percent. This difference is the result of including in the urban classification 1.7 million persons who would have been classified as rural-nonfarm under the old definition.

The increase in rural-nonfarm employment during the past decade was 917,404 or 35.7 percent according to the prevailing definitions of 1940 and 1950 respectively. Under the old definition for both years, the rural-nonfarm increase becomes 1,533,404 or 59.6 percent. The 1950 adjusted employment figures for rural-nonfarm and urban were estimated from the 1.7 million involved in the differences in definition. It was assumed that 36 percent (or 616,000) of this rural-nonfarm or urban population was employed. On this basis the total rural population of the South would have increased during the decade by 465,000 or 6.4 percent instead of declining by 150,000 (Table 6). Now that the population of densely settled areas outside corporate limits is classified as urban rather than rural-nonfarm, difficulties of definition will be less.

THE IMPACT OF ECONOMIC REORGANIZATION
ON URBANIZATION

What relation can we find between where workers live, rural-urbanwise, and where they work by type of industry? Stated in terms of change, have southern people moved into urban-centered industries faster than they have moved into urban places? We have no figures on those who commute from rural residences to work in urban-centered enterprises, nor can we estimate the amount of employment in establishments located in rural areas. Table 7, however, serves to estimate the combined effect of rural commuting and industrial decentralization on the employment of workers residing in rural-farm, rural-nonfarm, and urban territory by type of industry—primary, secondary, and tertiary. Thus we can see at a glance that of the South's 3.6 million employed labor force living on farms in 1950, only 72.0 percent worked in agriculture and related fields. Some 15.8 percent were in manufacturing, professional services or trade. Rural-nonfarm residence with 3.3 million employed is definitely associated with secondary and tertiary in-

TABLE 7. Percentage Distribution of Civilian Employment of Urban, Rural-Nonfarm, and Rural-Farm Populations, by Selected Industry Groups, Southern States and the Rest of the United States, 1950

	Urban		Rural-nonfarm		Rural-farm	
	Southern States	Rest of U. S.	Southern States	Rest of U. S.	Southern States	Rest of U. S.
Total Employment	100.0	100.0	100.0	100.0	100.0	100.0
Agriculture, Forestry and Fishing	1.9	1.0	12.7	7.4	72.0	70.2
Construction	7.7	5.6	9.1	8.8	3.2	3.0
Manufacturing	19.9	31.8	24.1	26.3	9.1	9.6
Transportation, Communication & Other Pub. Utls.	9.2	9.0	6.4	8.0	1.7	2.4
Wholesale and Retail Trade	24.0	21.4	17.3	18.4	4.3	4.4
Personal Service	11.5	6.2	7.4	5.1	1.9	1.5
Professional & Related Services	9.7	9.4	7.5	8.9	2.4	2.9
All Other	16.1	15.6	15.5	17.1	5.4	6.0
Number	7,557,905	30,847,642	3,280,426	6,579,430	3,637,260	4,336,786

Source: U. S. Census of Population, 1950.

dustry. Almost a fourth, 24.1 percent, of this category worked in manufacturing compared to 19.9 percent of employed urban residents. The proportion in trade, 17.3 percent, also exceeded those employed in primary economy, 12.7 percent. We conclude from this analysis that the work pattern is more urban than the residence pattern—a fact which is due to the location of plants and other enterprises in rural territory, plus a great deal of commuting of rural dwellers to work in urban centers. Thus figures on urbanization in the South do not adequately represent the region's shift to industrial and service employment.

Comparison with the rest of the nation, however, serves to show a less urbanized pattern of employment. In the South's greatest discrepancy, fewer in all residence categories work in manufacturing and more in agriculture. But construction was more important in the South, indicating new capitalization in plant facilities. In the services and trade the South's future seems definitely urban.

CONCLUSION

In the drastic readjustment of its economy from 1930 to 1950 the South made more economic progress than in any four previous decades. This is evident in the sizeable shifts from extractive to manufacturing and service economies as shown by the occupational shift of the working force.

A recent study found that at the current rate metropolitan development in the South was proceeding faster than the rate at which the industrial North developed its metropolitan centers.[4] Donald Bogue writes, "The South is moving rapidly toward an industrial and commercial economy which is organized around cities and metropolitan areas. This change in economic and social organization is requiring the South's population to redistribute itself in new patterns and to acquire new skills and take on new characteristics."

In this development a striking contrast can be observed in the employment of two population components: southern women and southern Negroes. Opening up of the service and distributive fields was conducive to the employment of women, who entered the new labor force in large numbers. In sharp contrast, the Negro in his exodus from southern agriculture found little welcome in the South's expanding sectors and large numbers exercised their privilege of occupational mobility by migrating outside the region. They also continued their migration to southern cities so that in their rural-urban distribution the two races still follow much the same pattern.

In this developing economy, many rural residents commute to work in urban places, and many enterprises including industrial plants are located in rural areas. When the population enumerated by rural-urban residence was checked against the industries in which they work, the proportions employed in urban-centered industries were found to exceed those living in urban areas. Thus figures on southern urbanization actually understate the trend toward "urban" industry and services. In the rural-nonfarm areas of the South, for example, higher proportions of the working population are employed in manufacturing than in the cities themselves. The maturation of the South's economy is definitely leading the march to urban centers.

4. Donald J. Bogue, *The Growth of Metropolitan Areas, 1900 to 1950* (Washington: Government Printing Office, 1953).

CHAPTER FOUR

Peopling the City: Migration*

HOMER L. HITT

Modern cities typically are not peopled through their own reproductive efforts. Most of the large cities of the United States would wane in population within a few decades were it not for the continuous flow of migrants they receive. The rapid growth of our cities before World War I depended on the influx of immigrants from Europe. After the drastic reduction of foreign immigration, the nation's cities grew primarily by large movements of migrants from rural areas. Estimates of the annual movements to and from farms indicate that the net gain to towns and cities of the nation from the rural-urban exchange of population during the 26 years from 1920 through 1945 amounted to 16,578,000.[1]

Migrants to cities, however, do not come solely from rural districts. Significant numbers originate in urban areas. The importance of these urban migrants in the cityward stream is suggested by the report of the 1940 Census that of the 8,230,003 urban residents in 1940 who migrated to cities between 1935 and 1940, 5,663,353 had lived in other urban centers in 1935.[2] While not contributing to

* Parts of this chapter appeared in "Migration and Southern Cities" in T. Lynn Smith and C. A. McMahan (eds.), *The Sociology of Urban Life* (New York: The Dryden Press, 1951), pp. 319-334.
1. See Bureau of Agricultural Economics, *Farm Population Estimates, United States and Major Geographical Divisions, 1910-1946* (United States Department of Agriculture, June 1946), mimeographed.
2. U. S. Bureau of the Census, *Sixteenth Census of the United States: 1940. Population, Internal Migration, 1935 to 1940, Color and Sex of Migrants* (Washington: Government Printing Office, 1943), Table 2. These figures undoubtedly overstate urban residence in 1935. Criticisms of migration data, well-known to students in the field, are not repeated here.

the total growth of the urban population, this movement is an important factor in the redistribution of the urban population.

Many aspects of urban life are influenced by migration.[3] The size and composition of the labor force of each city are in part determined by the number and characteristics of the entering and departing migrants. Within the realm of urban government, the make-up and stability of the electorate are closely related to the prevailing pattern of migration. Educational needs are also related to the number and the social and economic characteristics of migrants. A city's problems in the fields of health, housing, and recreation bear a distinct relation to its migration experience. Indeed, virtually every important phase of urban life is affected by the entry and departure of residents and, for that matter, by their redistribution within the city.

We have every reason to think that the role of migration in peopling southern cities has been generally similar to that in urban development elsewhere in the nation. Rural areas, by sending surplus population to urban centers of the South, have served as the source of the bulk of the net migration gains of the cities. These migrants, including more males than females, have moved to cities in search of economic opportunity at a youthful age when they could make the maximum contribution to the urban labor force. An attempt is made in this paper to fill in some of the details on this migration to the urban South and at the same time to compare it with cityward migration in other regions of the nation. The analysis revolves around two topics: (1) the sources and magnitude of the migration to southern cities and (2) the selectivity of this migration.

THE MOVEMENT TO SOUTHERN CITIES

Southern cities are ideally situated to gain population from rural-urban migration. They are surrounded by the most prolific large group of people in the nation—the southern farm population, often referred to as the "seedbed" of the nation. In an area of high reproduction, the highest peaks of fertility are found in the more remote sections, such as isolated parts of Texas, Louisiana, and

3. See Ronald Freedman, *Recent Migration to Chicago* (Chicago: The University of Chicago Press, 1950).

Arkansas, and in the Appalachian Mountains of eastern Kentucky and Tennessee, western Virginia, and Alabama. The region's natural increase of rural people regularly outdistances the "carrying capacity" of agriculture. For the past few decades, agriculture has been capable of absorbing less than half of the youth reaching maturity on southern farms. Large-scale migration from the agricultural districts has been inevitable. A substantial portion of these migrants go to towns and cities of the South, although large numbers of them have moved to urban areas outside the region.

Of the nation's native-born population in 1930, an estimated 28,700,000 were born in the Southeast. Of these, a total of 24,100,000 were born in rural areas, and the balance—4,600,000—in urban centers. Only about 17,500,000 of the rural-born remained in their area of birth. Thus, over 6,500,000 had migrated elsewhere. Among these migrants, 3,800,000 had moved from the region, while 2,900,000 had gone to southern cities. However, 400,000 had moved into the region, leaving a net loss of 3,400,000. These data mean that prior to 1930 the rural districts of the Southeast had exported 2,900,000 of their natural increase to the region's cities, had sent 3,800,000 to other regions, and had continued to grow.[4]

Additional information regarding the interregional shift of population involving southern migrants may be gained from state-of-birth data for 1950.[5] Of the native-born residents of the United States in 1950, 49,934,010 were born in the census South.[6] Of the southern-born persons, 7,411,900 (14.8 percent) were living (and thus had migrated since birth) outside the South. On the other hand, those born elsewhere but residing in the South in 1950 numbered only 3,415,470. As a result of these interregional movements, the South sustained a net loss of nearly 4 million persons. These 1950 data do not provide information as to urban or rural residence of birth. However, information on rural or urban resi-

4. Howard W. Odum, *Southern Regions of the United States* (Chapel Hill: University of North Carolina Press, 1936), p. 463.

5. U. S. Bureau of the Census. *U. S. Census of Population: 1950*. Vol. IV, *Special Reports*, Part 4, Chapter A, State of Birth (Washington: U. S. Government Printing Office, 1953).

6. It is to be noted that the Census South does not correspond to the Southern Region as defined for the purpose of this study. It includes, in addition to the 13 states of the region as delineated by this study, West Virginia, Delaware, and Maryland.

dence in 1940 indicates that the migrants both entering and departing from the South were predominantly destined for urban areas. Only 11.5 percent of those born in the South and living elsewhere resided on farms in 1940 whereas the corresponding percentage for those born elsewhere but living in the South was 15.6.

Recent population changes in urban and farm areas of the South, viewed in the perspective of knowledge of natural increase in these two areas, show the importance of migration for the growth of southern cities. The farm population of the 13 southern states, despite its high rate of natural increase, failed by approximately one-half million to hold its own between 1920 and 1940 and sustained a loss of over 4 million between 1940 and 1950. In sharp contrast, the urban population of these states registered a net increase of more than 10 million persons in the 30 years prior to 1950, and this in spite of a low urban rate of natural increase.[7] The rapid and continuous urban growth in the South, coupled with a declining farm population, can be accounted for only by a large flow of people from the region's farms to its cities.

Estimates of the annual flow of migrants to and from the farms of the South between 1920 and 1948 inclusive are shown in Figure 1.[8] It is evident that the farms of the South paid a heavy and almost continuous tribute to urban areas.[9] The net gain registered during this 28-year period by nonfarm territory was 9,518,000. This re-

7. In this connection, the net reproduction rates for urban whites and nonwhites of the census divisions comprising the South as compiled by the Bureau of the Census from 1940 data, and thus applying to the 5-year period 1935-1939, were well below the replacement level. These rates for the urban whites of the South Atlantic, East South Central, and West South Central divisions were 71, 79, and 81, respectively. The corresponding figures for the urban nonwhites were 73, 70, and 68. See *Sixteenth Census of the United States: 1940*, Series P-5, No. 13. See also discussion in Chapter 5 in this book.

8. The official annual estimates of the movement of persons to and from farm areas are made by the Bureau of Agricultural Economics of the United States Department of Agriculture. Begun in 1920, this service has now compiled and made available data through 1948 for the nation and the nine census divisions. By combining the reported figures for the South Atlantic, East South Central, and West South Central divisions, estimates have been obtained for the Census South, upon which the following analysis of the movement to and from farms in the region is based.

9. In this analysis, the migrants leaving southern farms are construed to have moved to urban territory. Although this was not the case for all of them, the overwhelming majority undoubtedly had cities as their destination.

sulted from the departure from farms of 24,479,000 and the arrival on them of 14,961,000 persons.

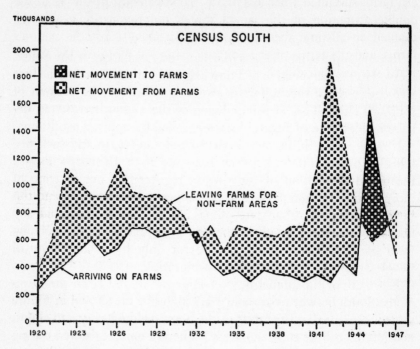

Figure 1. Migration to and from Farms in the Census South, 1920-1948

Except for two brief periods in 1932 and 1945-46, net migration gains were consistently registered by urban areas at the expense of the farms. The reversal of the usual pattern in 1932 was due for the most part to the depression-caused backing up on southern farms of many youth who normally would have migrated. The migration balance in favor of farm areas in 1945-1946 seems to have resulted primarily from reconversion of industry and demobilization of the armed forces, both of which sent thousands back to the land.

The migration gains, although substantial, varied over a wide range, and fluctuations in their magnitudes even in successive years were often considerable. The lowest urban gain, 108,000, was registered in 1931, when the depression began to slow down the movement away from farms in the South. Farms outside the South actually showed a slight gain rather than a loss that year. The greatest annual gain for urban areas occurred in 1942, when southern farms sustained a net loss of 1,622,000 persons. In this year, the double attraction of the armed forces and the nation's industry drained an all-time record number of persons from the nation's farms, and the farms of the South contributed more to this urbanward stream than did those of all other parts of the nation combined. These data indicate that the net annual migration gain in urban areas at the expense of southern farms varied for most of the period between 200,000 and 500,000 persons.

Comparable data for other regions indicate that the net contribution of southern farms to towns and cities during the past quarter of a century substantially exceeded that of the farms of the rest of the nation combined. Although these estimates shed no light on the region of destination, it may be confidently assumed that the bulk of this net migration was to urban areas of the South. Other data, some of which have been reviewed, show that substantial numbers were drawn to the cities of the North and West, and especially to the former.

Notwithstanding the South's net loss in recent decades, southern cities have attracted considerable numbers of migrants from outside the region. State-of-birth data, for example, indicate that 9.1 percent (1,350,960) of urban residents of the census South in 1940 had been born outside the region. Three-fifths of these migrants (805,393) were born in the North Central region, approximately one-third of them (462,192) in the Northeast, and the balance (83,375) in the West. The states outside the region sending the largest contingents of their natives to the urban South included, in order of magnitude, the adjacent states of Pennsylvania, Missouri, and Ohio; following these were New York, Illinois, Kansas, and Indiana.

Southern cities, however, have depended upon outside migrants much less than northern and western cities have depended upon recruits from outside their regions. This is convincingly demonstrated by the comparison of state-of-birth data for selected southern and non-southern cities, such as New Orleans, Atlanta, Chicago, and Los Angeles. In 1940 the native populations of both New Orleans and Atlanta were highly homogeneous in origin, the "lion's share" of each having been recruited from the respective state of location and nearby states. In contrast, Los Angeles and Chicago were extremely heterogeneous. Indeed, the southern states themselves had made generous contributions to their populations. Los Angeles, which stands alone among the large cities of the nation with respect to the widespread origins of its native American residents, numbered among its 1940 inhabitants about 60,000 native Texans, 27,000 native Oklahomans, 17,000 native Arkansans, 14,000 native Louisianians, 12,000 native Tennesseans, 7,500 native Georgians, 7,000 native Alabamans, and 6,500 native Mississippians. Chicago had drained even more substantial numbers from the South, including 50,000 from Mississippi, 23,500 from Tennessee, 27,000 from Alabama, 24,000 from Georgia, 23,500 from Louisiana, 21,000 from Arkansas, and 14,000 from Texas. These data demonstrate that the South has both peopled its own cities and sent large contingents of migrants to the urban areas of other regions. Stated somewhat differently, persons born in the rural South have migrated from their native region to a much greater extent than those born in other sections of the country.

Negroes, as is generally known, have played a large part in the migration from farms to cities within the South as well as to urban centers of other regions. Many interesting features of the Negro's cityward trek are revealed by the analysis of the state-of-birth data for the Negroes residing in selected cities in 1940. For one thing, they demonstrate that Negro migration to northern cities followed the main lines of transportation. New York and Philadelphia drew large contingents from the South Atlantic states, but few from other states. Chicago, on the other hand, drew most of its Negro migrants from states adjacent to the Mississippi River, especially Mississippi.

The significant fact from the standpoint of this particular treatment, however, is the striking contrast posed by the areas of origin of Negroes residing in southern cities. They, for the most part, were born in the same states in which they were residents in 1940. The great bulk of Atlanta Negroes (over 90 percent) were native Georgians, and the great bulk of New Orleans Negroes (over 90 percent) were native Louisianians. Even Mississippi, despite its proximity to New Orleans, sent only a fraction of the number of Negroes to this city that it sent to Chicago, several hundred miles to the north.

Internal migration figures assembled by the 1940 Census, which cross-tabulated residence in 1935 and residence in 1940, provide additional information on the flow of population to southern cities, in spite of the fact that these data have the serious limitation of considerable overstatement of urban residence in 1935 and consequent understatement of rural residence.

The 1940 Census defined migrants as "those persons who lived in 1935 in a county (or quasi county) different from the one in which they were living in 1940." Since cities of 100,000 or more population were considered quasi counties, much of the migration to and from cities in this size-class represented merely an exchange between them and their surrounding suburban areas. According to this definition, 15.1 percent of the urban population of the census South in 1940 was classified as migrants and 83.9 percent as nonmigrants. Corresponding figures for the urban population of the United States, 11.1 and 87.8, show that migrants were relatively more numerous in the cities of the South than in those of the nation as a whole. Migrants were proportionately less numerous in the region's cities of 100,000 and over than in other urban areas, the percentages being 13.2 and 16.4 respectively. In farm areas of the South, only 8.8 percent of the population was classified as migrants in 1940. Thus, according to the 1940 Census, proportionately almost twice as many of the urban as the farm people of the South were classified as migrants.

Slightly more than one-half (51.6 percent) of the migrants to the urban centers of the census South resided in the same state in 1935 as in 1940. In comparison, 23.9 percent had migrated between contiguous states and 24.5 percent moved between non-contiguous states. It is interesting to note that the large cities of the region (100,000 or more population) recruited proportionately more of their migrants from outside the state than did the other urban territory. The contrast was particularly great for those migrants moving between non-contiguous states. Specifically, 36.1 percent of the migrants to the large cities and only 18.4 percent of those to other urban centers were so classified. Of those migrants counted in the region's rural-farm areas, only 5.5 percent were from non-contiguous states, indicating the predominantly local character of the movement to southern farms.

Movement to the urban South between 1935 and 1940 to a considerable extent involved exchange of persons among urban centers. Because of the problem of overstatement of urban residence in 1935 in these data, the number of the migrants actually moving from other cities cannot be known. According to these data, three out of five (60.5 percent) of the migrants in the urban South had lived in an urban center in 1935. Approximately one out of five (21.4 percent) reported 1935 residence on a farm, 18.9 percent in rural-nonfarm territory, and 3.2 percent reported rural residence without specifying farm or nonfarm. Allowing for a substantial overstatement of urban residence in 1935, it is clear that large numbers of migrants to the southern cities originate in urban territory.

Among the residents of the urban areas of the census South in 1940 there were 1,119,718 persons, or 48.4 percent of all migrants, who reported residence five years earlier in another state. The other state for the majority of these persons (652,068) was located in the southern region. For them, migration from the 1935 residence to their urban residence of 1940 had been across one or more state lines but, except in unusual instances, within the South. The balance of these migrants (467,650) reported residence in a state outside the South in 1935. Their migration to the urban South constituted both an interstate and interregional transfer. Among the non-southern states, New York had been the state of residence of the largest number in 1935, followed by the border states of Missouri, Illinois, and Ohio. From the standpoint of broad areas of origin, 220,072 reported 1935 residence in the North Central region, 183,583 in the Northeast, and only 63,995 in the West.

The 1950 Census reports for standard metropolitan areas throw some light on migration to the large population centers of the South in the 1949-50 period.[10] According to these preliminary data, approximately 5 percent of the population in the 57 metropolitan areas of the nation reported having moved from another county in the preceding year.[11] The proportion of migrants varied widely among the individual cities. In general, the same ones experiencing heavy migration between 1935 and 1940 were char-

10. *Seventeenth Census of the United States: 1950*, Series PC-5.
11. For a brief penetrating analysis of these migration data, see Metropolitan Life Insurance Company, "Recent Movement to Large Population Centers," *Statistical Bulletin*, 33 (February 1952), pp. 7-10.

acterized by high rates of migration in this recent period. This uniformity suggests the continued operation of long-term forces favorable to the movement to large population centers. From a regional standpoint, migrants were relatively most numerous in the metropolitan areas of the South and West, reflecting the industrialization of those regions. The metropolitan areas of the North contained, by and large, the fewest persons reporting residence one year earlier in another county.

The migration rate (the number of migrants per 1,000 population) among the 17 metropolitan areas of the census South ranged from 155 in Washington, D.C., the highest in the nation, down to 37 in Wheeling, West Virginia-Steubenville, Ohio.[12] Other than Washington, large cities of the South in which 10 percent or more of their population were migrants included Miami (rate of 113), Norfolk-Portsmouth (106), and Tampa-St. Petersburg (102). Memphis, Atlanta, and Dallas followed with rates of 89, 88, and 85, respectively. Somewhat surprisingly, Houston, with a rate of 68, ranks fairly low in this regard, followed by Birmingham (51) and New Orleans (47). Since members of the armed forces are included in these migration figures, the presence of training stations tends to swell the migration rate.

Suburban areas both in the South and in the nation generally had more migrants than the cities which they surround. Considering the rapid growth of suburban areas in recent years, their higher migration rates are not surprising. Composite migration rates for the 32 metropolitan areas for which data are available were 65 in the suburbs and 41 in the central cities. The contrast was particularly marked in Washington in which the rate for the central city was 70 and for the suburbs 259. Corresponding rates for Atlanta were 60 and 115; for Louisville, 46 and 107; for Memphis, 67 and 189; and for New Orleans, 32 and 119. These differential migration rates reflect the continued shift of population from central cities to their suburbs. Modern transportation makes it possible for workers to live at some distances from the crowded cities in which they work. Extensive housing and shopping developments in outlying locations are accompanying and, in some instances, encouraging the growth of suburban living. In the South the higher migration

12. *Ibid.*, p. 8.

rate in the suburbs was fairly general with the Texas metropolitan areas of Dallas, Houston, and San Antonio the only exception.

Racial comparisons are made possible by the separate tabulation of these 1949-50 migration data for whites and nonwhites in eight metropolitan areas of the South. Migration rates were considerably greater for whites than for nonwhites in each of these areas. Taken in the aggregate, the rate for the former group was 121 and for the latter, 36. The following are rates for whites and nonwhites respectively in selected areas: Atlanta, 109 and 29; Nashville, 83 and 35; Memphis, 113 and 42; Birmingham, 66 and 25; and New Orleans, 55 and 31. The diverting of Negro cityward migrants to urban areas outside the South undoubtedly contributes to this racial differential.

THE PEOPLE WHO MOVE TO SOUTHERN CITIES

In studying the impact of migration upon the urban community, the researcher has frequently concentrated upon the selectivity of the cityward population movement. The formidable array of selectivity studies, however, has yielded few definite and clear-cut results. Despite their acknowledged limitations, the 1935-40 migration data make possible consideration of two highly meaningful aspects of the selectivity of cityward migration in the South. One aspect centers upon the differentials between migrants and nonmigrants in the region's cities. The other concerns the differentials among migrants from the various residential backgrounds, i.e., from urban, rural-farm, and rural-nonfarm territory.

The procedure followed in treating these two aspects of selectivity is simple and direct. In order to reduce the computations necessary, the census South is used as the area of study. Its urban population in 1940 is divided into migrants and nonmigrants, and the nonmigrants are further subdivided into three groups—urban, rural-nonfarm, and rural-farm—according to their 1935 type of residence. It is thus possible to make direct comparisons between migrants and nonmigrants and among migrants from different types of residence (1935-40) with respect to a variety of social and economic characteristics. In this analysis attention is successively devoted to differentials in (1) race, (2) age, (3) sex, (4) education, and (5) occupation.

Race.—A comparison of the various migrant groups in the urban South in 1940 discloses wide differences among them in the relative importance of the two races. The 1935-40 data show that nonwhites were relatively less numerous among migrants than among the settled population of southern cities. (Table 1.) Indeed they were proportionately only one-half as numerous, comprising one-eighth (12.7 percent) of the migrants but one-fourth (25.8 percent) of the nonmigrants. Essentially this same differential prevailed among both males and females. Nonwhites constituted one-fourth of the migrants who resided on farms in 1935, approximately their proportion of nonmigrants. In comparison, only about one-tenth of those who lived in either urban or rural-nonfarm territory were nonwhite. In these latter two categories, nonwhites were slightly more numerous among those migrants from rural-nonfarm than from urban areas. Closely similar racial differentials among the three migrant classes prevailed among both males and females.

Nonwhites were thus substantially less numerous, relatively speaking, among the total migrants to southern cities than among the nonmigrants residing in these centers. Data already cited from

TABLE 1. Racial Composition of the Urban Residents of the Census South, by Migration Status * and Sex: 1940

Race and Sex	Non-migrants	Migrants			
		Total	Urban	Rural-nonfarm	Rural-farm
Total	100.0	100.0	100.0	100.0	100.0
White	74.2	87.3	89.9	88.4	75.6
Nonwhite	25.8	12.7	10.1	11.6	24.4
Males	100.0	100.0	100.0	100.0	100.0
White	74.9	88.1	90.6	88.9	76.6
Nonwhite	25.1	11.9	9.4	11.1	23.4
Females	100.0	100.0	100.0	100.0	100.0
White	73.5	86.6	89.3	87.9	74.7
Nonwhite	26.5	13.4	10.7	12.1	25.3

* Migration status as used in this and subsequent tables refers to the two-fold division of residents into nonmigrant and migrant classes and to the further differentiation of migrants into three categories (urban, rural-nonfarm, and rural-farm) according to type of residence in 1935.

Source: U. S. Bureau of the Census, *Sixteenth Census of the United States: 1940. Population, Internal Migration, 1935 to 1940, Age of Migrants* (Washington: Government Printing Office, 1946), Tables 11, 12, 12a, and 12b.

the 1950 Census showed a considerably lower migration rate for nonwhites for the 1949-50 period. Comparable figures for the three migrant groups, however, disclose that the nonwhite is proportionately more than twice as important among the farm-urban migrants as among the other two migrant groups. The relatively great importance of the nonwhite in the movement to southern cities from farms would be expected, for all studies have shown the rapid rate of urbanization among Negroes of the region. Apparently they do not participate as frequently as whites in the movements from one urban center to another.

Age.—The crucial bearing which age has on a wide range of demographic and social phenomena makes age differences between migrants and nonmigrants of major interest to demographers. Indirect procedures utilizing census data have demonstrated the relative preponderance of youth among migrants in the cityward flow of population in the United States. The 1935-40 data make it possible to study age differentials in receiving centers by direct means. Table 2 presents the median ages of nonmigrants and mi-

TABLE 2. Median Ages of Urban Males and Females in the Census South, by Migration Status and Race: 1940

Race and Sex	Non-migrants	Migrants			
		Total	Urban	Rural-nonfarm	Rural-farm
Males					
Total	31.6	29.1	30.4	27.8	25.6
White	32.1	29.2	30.5	27.9	25.5
Nonwhite	30.3	27.9	29.3	27.4	25.8
Females					
Total	32.0	27.6	28.8	26.0	24.0
White	32.8	27.7	29.0	26.1	24.0
Nonwhite	30.0	25.7	27.0	25.1	24.0

Source: U. S. Bureau of the Census, *Sixteenth Census of the United States: 1940. Population, Internal Migration, 1935 to 1940, Age of Migrants* (Washington: Government Printing Office, 1946), Tables 11, 12, 12a, and 12b.

grants classified by race and sex in the urban South in 1940. From these figures it is evident that migrants were considerably younger than nonmigrants in southern cities. Among males the median age of all migrants was 29.1 years as compared with that of 31.6 years for nonmigrants. Among females the corresponding median ages were 27.6 and 32.0. Similar differences set apart migrants and nonmigrants irrespective of race and sex. However, in both sex groups, the spread between the median ages of the migrants and nonmigrants was somewhat larger for whites than for nonwhites; and for both races, this difference was almost twice as great for females as for males, female migrants being younger than male migrants. The median ages of the nonmigrant males and females were approximately the same.

Comparison of the median ages of the migrants indicates that those residing on farms in 1935 were youngest, those from urban centers were oldest, and those from rural-nonfarm territory were intermediate. This pattern prevailed with minor variations among all race and sex groupings. The actual median ages may be read from Table 2. It will be observed that the median ages of the migrants from urban areas, although consistently the highest of the three groups, were in all cases considerably lower than those of the corresponding nonmigrants. This supports the thesis that migration from farm areas usually takes place at the age when individuals are in the process of leaving home and going to work. Migration between urban centers, on the other hand, probably is more frequently associated with the search for job advancement or better pay and is consequently less likely to be related to a particular age or stage of development.

A detailed comparison of the age distributions of the nonmigrants and the migrants reveals that the latter are disproportionately concentrated in the young, vigorous years. Among males, for example, the age class 20 through 34 years included 42.9 percent of the migrants but only 27.4 percent of the nonmigrants. Among females, corresponding percentages were 45.4 and 29.0. On the other hand, the nonmigrants had relatively greater representations in the age classes under 20 and over 35 years.

Although the migrants of each residential group were found disproportionately in the young adult years when compared with the nonmigrants, the migrant groups differed significantly from each other in age make-up. In general, the migrants from farm areas were concentrated in the younger adult ages while those from urban areas were least numerous in these ages. Migrants from rural-nonfarm areas were intermediate in this respect. The ages from 18 through 24 years included 26.4 percent of the males from farms, 20.3 percent of those from rural-nonfarm territory, and 15.1 percent of those from urban centers. In the ages from 30 through 54 years, on the other hand, the male migrants from urban centers had the heaviest representation, those from rural-nonfarm areas an intermediate status, and those from farms the least representation. The age distributions of the migrant groups in all race and sex categories varied in a similar manner. The evidence is clear that migrants from farms were youngest and from urban areas were oldest.

These age differentials have important implications for southern cities. The relative youthfulness of the migrants means that they are in a position to make the maximum contribution to the economy of the receiving centers. Large numbers of the migrants from farms are just at the age to begin their work careers. Conversely, relatively few of the migrants are in the extreme age groups which would make them economically dependent or likely to require welfare assistance. Moreover, since the migrants are concentrated within ages which have high age-specific fertility rates, their contribution to population growth is significant. The presence of these young adult migrants sustains urban birth rates.

Sex.—Sex ratio differentials have been one of the most frequently studied aspects of the selectivity of cityward migration. The evidence seems conclusive that females are over-represented among migrants to urban centers. To this preponderance of female migrants is usually attributed the high femininity of American cities, a distinctive demographic characteristic. In 1950, for example, preliminary data indicate that the sex ratios among native whites were 93.5 in the nation's urban areas and 110.2 in rural-farm sections. Final tabulations for the census South reveal corresponding sex ratios of 93.8 and 107.8.

Although females outnumbered males among all migrants resident in the urban South in 1940, the sex ratio of the migrants was nevertheless substantially higher than that of the nonmigrants. This differential is apparent from the sex ratios for the population aged 5 years and over, shown in Table 3. The sex ratio among all migrants was 96.2 compared with that of 89.6 for nonmigrants. It will be noted that this difference, while prevailing among both races, was very small among nonwhites. However, for the migrants taken as a whole, the sex ratio in both races was higher than that in the corresponding nonmigrant categories.

TABLE 3. Sex Ratios for the Urban Residents of the Census South, by Migration Status and Race: 1940

Race	Non-migrants	Migrants			
		Total	Urban	Rural-nonfarm	Rural-farm
Total	89.6	96.2	98.5	93.0	92.0
Standardized *	. . .	97.9	99.2	95.6	95.3
White	91.4	97.8	99.9	94.1	94.2
Standardized *	. . .	99.1	100.2	96.5	97.7
Nonwhite	84.7	85.8	86.6	85.1	85.4
Standardized *	. . .	89.6	90.1	89.7	88.2

* Standardized sex ratios are standardized on the age distribution of the non-migrant population for the respective races.

Source: U. S. Bureau of the Census, *Sixteenth Census of the United States: 1940. Population, Internal Migration, 1935 to 1940, Age of Migrants* (Washington: Government Printing Office, 1946), Tables 11, 12, 12a, and 12b.

Age differences between the migrants and nonmigrants were not responsible for this sex ratio differential. It prevailed even after the sex ratios of the migrant groups were standardized.[13] The standardized ratios are those which would have prevailed if the migrant groups had had the same age distribution as the nonmigrants. As is shown in Table 3, in every case the difference between the migrant and nonmigrant sex ratios is increased by this standardization process. Therefore, the age structure is *not* responsible for the differences. It is, however, partly responsible for the fact that the differences between the two migration categories are not greater.

That the migrants should have a higher sex ratio than the nonmigrants is somewhat surprising but not necessarily contrary to generally accepted evidence on sex differentials. In all cases there were more females than males in the migrant groups. Moreover, the differentials with which this analysis is concerned are those in the receiving centers whereas most of the selectivity studies have concentrated on differentials in the sending areas. Especially for the migration from rural areas, there is no question of its being

13. See Freedman, *op. cit.*, p. 43.

selective of females when compared with nonmigrants in the areas of origin which are characterized by high sex ratios. In evaluating these differentials, another factor of significance is the very low sex ratio prevailing in the urban South.

Several studies have indicated that the sex ratio of cityward migrants is lowest in the upper adolescent and young adult age groups.[14] This definitely seemed to be the case for migrants to the urban South. In the ages from 14 through 24 years the sex ratio was lower for every migrant group of both races than for the corresponding nonmigrants. It was the relatively higher sex ratios among the migrants in the age classes above 25 years which pushed their total sex ratios above those of the nonmigrants.

Comparisons indicate that females were relatively more numerous among the migrants from rural areas than among those from urban areas. This difference held true for both whites and nonwhites. Among the former the sex ratios for urban, rural-nonfarm, and rural-farm migrants were 99.9, 94.1, and 94.2 respectively. The corresponding ratios for nonwhites were 86.6, 85.1, and 85.4. This pattern of differentials is in accord with other analyses which have found the selection of females to be most pronounced in the cityward migration from nearby rural areas. Again, age standardization indicates that these sex ratio differentials are not due to age differences among the various migrant groups.

Education.—In our society the educational status of the individual is generally accepted as a reliable index of his preparation for contemporary living. The maximum premium is placed on formal education in urban communities where problems of adjustment are conceded to be complex and challenging.

In general, migrants in southern cities in 1940 were found to be better educated than nonmigrants. This is apparent from the information relative to years of schooling completed by persons 25-34 years of age, the only educational data made available by the 1935-40 migration materials (Table 4). Among males, the median years of schooling reported by all migrants to the urban South was 12.1 compared with 9.1 for nonmigrants. Corresponding medians for females were 12.1 and 9.7. Proportionately more of all

14. *Ibid.*, p. 42; and Dorothy Swaine Thomas, *Research Memorandum on Migration Differentials* (New York: Social Science Research Council, 1938), pp. 55-69.

TABLE 4. Median Years of Schooling Completed by the Urban
Residents of the Census South, by Migration Status and Sex: 1940

Sex	Non-migrants	Migrants			
		Total	Urban	Rural-nonfarm	Rural-farm
Males	9.1	12.1	12.4	10.0	8.4
Females	9.7	12.1	12.3	12.1	9.1

Source: U. S. Bureau of the Census, *Sixteenth Census of the United States: 1940.*
  Population, Internal Migration, 1935 to 1940, Social Characteristics of
  Migrants (Washington, Government Printing Office, 1946), Tables 14
  and 15.

migrants, male and female, as compared with nonmigrants, had
finished high school or had completed four or more years of
college. On the other hand, fewer of them had completed less than
five years of schooling. The evidence seems conclusive that in 1940
the formal education of migrants as a whole was superior to that
of nonmigrants in the urban South.

Important educational differentials, however, set apart the three
major migrant groups. For both sexes, migrants from urban areas
had the most schooling whereas those previously residing on farms
fell below nonmigrants. Migrants from rural-nonfarm areas occupied an intermediate status in this regard. Among males the median years of school completed was 12.4 for urban migrants, 10.0
for those from rural-nonfarm areas, and 8.4 for those from farms.
The corresponding medians for females were 12.3, 12.1, and 9.1.
Comparison of the migrant groups in terms of percentage finishing
high school, graduating from college, or completing less than five
years of school yields the same relative standing. This pattern is in
general accord with the differences in educational opportunity and
attainment known to characterize the major residential areas. Farm
migrants were considerably below the nonmigrants, whereas the
other two migrant groups ranked definitely above the nonmigrants
in educational attainment.

These differentials suggest that migration has a somewhat mixed
impact upon the composite educational status of the southern urban
population. In general, migrants have had the effect of raising the
average educational level. They have contributed disproportionately large numbers of college graduates and others with relatively

high formal education to the region's cities. However, it is not here possible to balance the influence of incoming migrants against that of the migrants who departed from these cities. To a very large extent, the urban migrants to southern cities represent losses to other urban centers of the region. Thus, those with the highest educational attainment would have little if any net favorable impact upon the urban South considered as a whole. The migrants from rural-farm areas, on the other hand, represent net additions for the most part to the region's urban population. As far as their contribution to the educational level of the urban South is concerned, these data give no basis for optimism. Farm migrants were substantially lower than nonmigrants in terms of formal education in 1940. However, insofar as the migrants from nonfarm areas represent net additions to the South's cities, the general urban educational level is thereby raised.

Occupation and Social Class.—The contribution of cityward migrants to the urban economy is more adequately reflected by their occupational distribution than by any other single index. Their fields of employment will indicate the nature of the economic adjustment migrants have made in the new urban environment.

By using the Edwards' socio-economic scale, differentials in specific occupational categories between migrants and nonmigrants and among the major migrant groups were explored. Following Freedman's procedure, attention is also directed to migration differentials with respect to two broad aspects of occupational distribution by grouping the categories into more general classes. One aspect is concerned with the functional nature of the occupational activity and another with the social status reflected by the various occupations.[15]

15. For his use of this method, see Freedman, *op. cit.*, pp. 26-27, 53-59. The functional analysis is implemented by grouping the several occupations in the Edwards scheme into two classes, the service-production occupations and the physical-production occupations. Among the former are included professional and semi-professional workers; proprietors, managers, and officials; clerical, sales, and kindred workers; domestic service workers; and other service workers. The physical-production occupations include craftsmen, operatives, and laborers. The service-production occupations, generally considered to be more typically urban, are devoted primarily to the serving of people or controlling their activity. The physical-production occupa-

In the urban South in 1940 all male migrants, as compared with nonmigrants, were markedly over-represented among professionals and clerical workers but were relatively less numerous among craftsmen, operatives, domestic and other service workers, and laborers (Table 5). In general, the male migrants were more concentrated in the service-production occupations. They were less numerous than nonmigrants, on the other hand, in every one of the physical-production occupations. The service-production occupations provided jobs for 56.8 percent of the employed male migrants but for only 48.5 percent of the nonmigrants. These differentials, viewed in terms of status, indicate that the migrants were disproportionately found in the white-collar occupations. To be specific, 47.2 percent of the male migrants were employed in the white-collar occupations as compared with only 37.3 percent of the nonmigrants. The evidence seems conclusive that the male migrants as a whole in the southern cities were disproportionately concentrated in the service-production and white-collar occupations, especially the professional and semi-professional category.

The three major types of male migrants in the urban South differed substantially from each other and from the nonmigrants in occupational distribution. It is apparent from Table 5 that the urban migrants, as compared with the other migrant groups and the nonmigrants, were relatively most numerous in the professional, proprietory, and clerical occupations and least numerous among operatives, domestic and other service workers, and laborers. The representation of the nonfarm migrants in the various occupations in general ranked between those of the urban and farm migrant groups. The farm migrants, in comparison with the two other migrant groups and the nonmigrants, had relatively the fewest

---

tions, as the name implies, primarily involve the processing and production of physical goods.

The approach to social status, admittedly a rough one, is afforded by grouping the white-collar occupations of the Edwards scale into one class and all the other categories into another class. The white-collar occupations are professional and semi-professional workers; proprietors, managers, and officials; and clerical, sales, and kindred workers. In general, these occupations represent a relatively high status group while the class of other occupations is composed for the most part of low status workers, sometimes referred to as blue-collar workers.

TABLE 5. Occupation of Employed Urban Workers in the Census South, by Migration Status and Sex: 1940

Sex and Occupation *	Non-migrants	Migrants			
		Total	Urban	Rural-nonfarm	Rural-farm
Males	100.0	100.0	100.0	100.0	100.0
Professionals	5.9	11.9	14.0	10.9	3.4
Proprietors	13.8	13.7	16.4	10.9	6.1
Clericals	17.6	21.6	24.6	18.8	12.7
Craftsmen	16.8	15.4	15.1	16.6	14.8
Operatives	20.3	18.1	14.8	22.3	26.6
Domestics	1.3	0.7	0.6	0.7	1.3
Service workers	9.9	8.9	8.0	9.2	12.7
Laborers	14.4	9.7	6.5	10.6	22.4
Service production	48.5	56.8	63.6	50.5	36.2
Physical production	51.5	43.2	36.4	49.5	63.8
White-collar	37.3	47.2	55.0	40.6	22.2
Blue-collar	62.7	52.8	45.0	59.4	77.8
Females	100.0	100.0	100.0	100.0	100.0
Professionals	9.9	18.8	19.9	20.6	12.4
Proprietors	3.6	3.0	3.8	2.4	1.4
Clericals	25.7	28.7	33.6	26.6	16.2
Craftsmen	0.7	0.5	0.6	0.4	0.4
Operatives	16.5	11.3	9.2	11.6	17.3
Domestics	29.9	21.1	17.2	20.8	34.1
Service workers	11.8	14.7	14.1	15.8	15.5
Laborers	1.9	1.9	1.6	1.8	2.7
Service production	80.9	86.3	88.6	86.2	79.6
Physical production	19.1	13.7	11.4	13.8	20.4
White-collar	39.2	50.5	57.3	49.6	30.0
Blue-collar	60.8	49.5	42.7	50.4	70.0

* The occupational categories used in this table represent abbreviations of the following categories (as employed by the U. S. Bureau of the Census), respectively: Professional and semi-professional workers; Farmers and farm managers, proprietors, managers, and officials; Clerical, sales, and kindred workers; Craftsmen, foremen, and kindred workers; Operatives and kindred workers; Domestic service workers; Service workers, except domestic; Farm laborers and foremen, laborers.

Source: U. S. Bureau of the Census, *Sixteenth Census of the United States. Population, Internal Migration, 1935 to 1940, Economic Characteristics of Migrants* (Washington: Government Printing Office, 1946), Tables 9 and 10.

representatives among professionals, proprietors, clerical workers, and craftsmen. On the other hand, they were relatively most numerous among operatives, domestic workers, other service workers, and laborers.

Male urban migrants were more concentrated in the service-production occupations while the male rural-farm migrants were relatively least numerous in these occupations. Specifically, 63.6 percent of the urban migrants, 50.5 percent of the rural-nonfarm migrants, and 36.2 percent of the farm migrants as compared with 48.5 percent of the nonmigrants were employed in the service-production occupations. It thus will be noted that in terms of the broad functional nature of their occupations, the male nonfarm migrants closely resembled the nonmigrants. The urban migrants, on the other hand, were especially prominent in the service-production occupations whereas the farm migrants were found disproportionately in the physical-production occupations.

A comparison of occupational distributions of the major types of male migrants from the standpoint of social status also reveals some fundamental differentials (Table 5). The urban migrants were concentrated in the white-collar occupations while the farm migrants had relatively the smallest representation in these occupations. The actual percentages were 55.0 for urban migrants, 40.6 for nonfarm migrants, and 22.2 for farm migrants, compared with 37.3 for nonmigrants. The balance of each group was employed in the so-called blue-collar occupations. The male urban migrants were of the highest status among the migrant groups and clearly of higher status than the nonmigrants. The male farm migrants, on the other hand, were of lowest status among the migrant groups and of lower status than the nonmigrants. The higher status of all migrants as compared with nonmigrants may be attributed primarily to the relatively high status of the urban migrants although nonfarm migrants ranked slightly above the nonmigrants.

Female migrants, as compared with nonmigrants, were disproportionately employed in the professional, clerical, and other service occupations. Their relative concentration was particularly marked in the professional category. On the other hand, they were relatively under-represented among proprietors and managers, operatives, and domestic workers. In terms of their functional roles, the female migrants were somewhat more concentrated in the service-production occupations than were the nonmigrants, the percentages being 86.3 and 80.9, respectively. From the standpoint of status considerations, the female migrants were relatively more numerous in the white-collar occupations than were the nonmigrants. These occupations provided employment for 50.5 percent of the migrants as compared with only 39.2 percent of the nonmigrants. Thus, considered as a group the female migrants in comparison with nonmigrants contributed disproportionately to those occupations primarily providing service for people and to those generally having higher status.

Significant differentials are disclosed by comparing the occupational distribution of each of the female migrant groups with one another and with that of the nonmigrants. Despite variations, the major migrant groups were more concentrated in the professional category and in other service work than were nonmigrants. The concentration of urban and nonfarm migrants in the professional and related occupations was especially marked. On the other hand, female farm migrants, as compared with all other migrants and the nonmigrants as well, were most concentrated among operatives and domestic workers, but least numerous among proprietors, managers, and craftsmen. In general, the female urban migrants were most concentrated in the service-production occupations, followed in order by nonfarm migrants, nonmigrants, and farm migrants. The percentages were 88.6, 86.2, 80.9, and 79.6, respectively. In terms of status, urban migrants ranked highest with 57.3 percent of its females in white-collar occupations, followed by nonfarm migrants (49.6), nonmigrants (39.2), and farm migrants (30.0). The evidence is clear that farm migrants contribute disproportionately to the physical-production occupations and to the lower status service occupations.

CONCLUSIONS AND IMPLICATIONS

What conclusions emerge from our study? In the last decades southern cities grew rapidly, greatly aided by the incoming tide of humanity from the region's farms. The agricultural areas of the South, prolific and limited in absorption capacity, sent much of their outflow to cities outside the region. More and more it seems that new arrivals in southern cities come from cities, denoting a change in the peopling of the urban South. Little change in cities selected was evident between 1935-1940 and 1949-1950.

Here, it seems from the census data, are the principal kinds of people who have recently been moving into the cities. Migrants were more likely to be white than colored; they were much younger than those who stayed at home; and they were better educated and held more white-collar jobs. Migrants from farms were younger, included more females, and held more blue-collar jobs than other migrants. In the main, migrants to cities were already more like city people in those traits held desirable for employment. Migrants from other cities, however, ranked the highest, followed by those from rural-nonfarm areas. Farm migrants, who rank lowest in education and job attainments, furnish the one large stream of net additions to the cities. As such they largely define the problem of assimilation in the growing cities of the New South. To a large degree the future of southern cities and thus the quality of life in the South will depend on the contributions of these newcomers to the urban scene.

CHAPTER FIVE

Peopling the City: Fertility

ROBERT M. DINKEL

T HE BASIC QUESTION of this chapter is: what has happened to fertility in the South [1] under the impact of urbanization? The general conclusion—if it may be announced before it is demonstrated—is that the South from 1910 to 1950 decreased its fertility more rapidly than the rest of the nation. This convergence toward lowered birth rates differed in degree among important groups in the social structure: white-collar workers, in particular, had higher rates of declining fertility in the South than in other regions. Although the general trend in fertility was downward, the facts indicate that birth rates will remain high enough in the region to yield positive rates of natural increase and to furnish additional population if industrial and commercial development can provide employment in the South.

Fertility trends differed greatly during the two periods, 1910-1940 and 1940-1950.[2] Changes from 1910 to 1940 can be listed as follows: (1) Fertility in the South in 1910 was 19 percent higher and in 1940 16 percent higher than in the nation. (2) The South's

1. The South in this analysis includes the usual 13 states plus Maryland, Delaware, and West Virginia.

2. Data from the 1910 and 1940 censuses on number of children ever born will be relied upon principally in the analyses of this chapter. These data permit estimates of change over a 30-year period and furnish sufficient detail to allow control over several variables that influence fertility—variables that often cannot be held constant, because the necessary information has not been obtained or has not been published. These data on number of children ever born, furthermore, show changes in size of completed families for the older age groups, thus avoiding some of the problems that arise in connection with postponement of births or from other factors which affect the spacing of children.

rural fertility was from one-quarter to one-half higher than its urban fertility in 1910, and from one-third to two-thirds higher in 1940. (3) Southern Negroes in 1910 had a fertility rate from 5 to 13 percent higher and in 1940 from 2 to 4 percent higher than that of southern whites. (4) The over-all picture of an increase in the rural-urban differential was accounted for mainly by the older age groups of whites of the South and the United States, but such increase does not portray accurately the experience of the rural-nonfarm Negroes of the South nor of the youngest age groups of the region and nation. (5) The decrease in the white-nonwhite fertility differential of the South was determined specifically by all age groups of the rural-nonfarm residents and by the older age groups of the rural-farm and urban residents. (6) Rural-nonfarm nonwhite residents of both region and nation had particularly high rates of fertility decrease. (7) There was a definite movement among rural residents of the South toward the lower fertility levels of the rural residents of the nation only when the universe considered was all white women 15 to 74 years of age.

The decade 1940 to 1950 [3] featured a reversal of the downward trend in fertility that had persisted in this country for more than a hundred years.[4] The stimulus of war conditions plus recovery from the economic depression of the 1930's sent the United States crude birth rate in 1947 to a high of 25.8. This rate was more than 50 percent above the all-time low of 16.6 for 1933 and was higher than that of any year since 1915. Between 1947 and 1950, there was a recession of approximately 10 percent in the crude birth rate; but this decline was halted by war in Korea and in the following three years fertility again moved upwards, reaching in 1953 a height almost equal to that attained in 1947. This upsurge in fertility after 1940 has been accounted for in part by increased

3. A limited use is made in this and the following paragraph of data for the United States and its regional, residential, and racial subdivisions for the period from 1940 to 1953. These data provide partial validation of the trends that were found in the detailed analyses for the period from 1910 to 1940. Similar examination of the age, racial, rural-urban, and occupational subgroups within the South for the later period would be desirable, but must await publication of the 1950 census volume on fertility.

4. Fertility rates for the nineteenth century are given in P. K. Whelpton, "Geographic and Economic Differentials in Fertility," *Annals of the American Academy of Political and Social Science,* 188 (November 1936), pp. 37-55.

marriage rates with subsequent increases in first- and second-order births. Its duration for more than 10 years and some evidence of an expansion in the number of third- and fourth-order births, however, suggest the possibility of permanent change in the patterns of family size prevalent in the 1930's.[5]

During this period, 1940-1950, differences in rates of change of regional, rural-urban, and racial fertility were consistent with the hypothesis of convergence used in this study to describe trends in southern fertility under the influence of urbanization. Convergence was clearly manifested in comparison of 1940 with 1947 fertility rates since groups of relatively high fertility had the lowest percentage increase. Thus the South increased its fertility only 22 percent, while other regions had increases ranging from 34 to 42 percent. Residents of rural-farm areas had only a 12 percent increase, while rural-nonfarm residents showed an increase of 25 percent and urban residents an increase of 47 percent. Nonwhites had an increase of 28 percent compared with 33 percent for whites.[6] This clear-cut picture of convergence, however, was maintained from 1947 to 1950 only in the case of the South in comparison with other regions. In other comparisons, urban fertility declined slightly more than rural, and nonwhite fertility continued to increase while white fertility decreased. The net changes between 1940 and 1950 diminished appreciably the difference between southern and non-southern and between rural and urban fertility, but left relatively unchanged that between white and nonwhite fertility.[7]

5. Crude birth rates and some fertility rates for the years from 1915 to 1953 may be found in the following publications of the U. S. Department of Health, Education, and Welfare, Public Health Service, National Office of Vital Statistics: *Vital Statistics—Special Reports:* "Births and Birth Rates in the Entire United States, 1909-1948," Vol. 33, No. 8, September 29, 1950; "Summary of Natality Statistics, United States, 1950," Vol. 37, No. 7, May 19, 1953; "Births by Age of Mother, Race, and Birth Order, United States, 1950," Vol. 37, No. 13, November 27, 1953; and *Monthly Vital Statistics Report:* "Annual Summary for 1952, Part 1," Vol. 1, No. 13, June 8, 1953; and "Provisional Statistics on Births, Marriage Licenses, and Deaths for September 1953," Vol. 2, No. 9, November 18, 1953.

6. U. S. Department of Commerce, Bureau of the Census, *Current Population Reports*, "Population Characteristics," Series P-20, No. 18, June 30, 1948.

7. U. S. Department of Health, Education, and Welfare, Public Health Service, National Office of Vital Statistics: *Vital Statistics—Special Reports:* "Births by Race and by Urban and Rural Areas," Vol. 36, No. 4, June 13,

I. FERTILITY IN THE URBANIZED SOUTH

The effect of urbanization upon fertility is not necessarily limited to urban places. Urbanization can be viewed as a shift of population from rural to urban centers, increasing the proportion of the total population having relatively low fertility; it can also be viewed as a diffusion of values typical of urban centers to smaller urban places and rural areas, thus lowering village and farm birth rates and narrowing the rural-urban differential in fertility.

The first viewpoint restricts analysis to a determination of the differential in rural-urban fertility with an estimate of the effect of a higher percentage of urban population on the fertility of the region. It is important to make this analysis separately for whites and Negroes since their cultures and consequently their fertility can reasonably be assumed to differ.

With the second viewpoint, analysis is broadened to a consideration of fertility changes in important divisions of both urban and rural social structures of the South with a comparison of their fertility before and after the change with corresponding groups in the nation. Here we seek to determine the rate of decline in the South, the extent to which fertility declined in different parts of the southern social structure, and the degree to which such changes have brought the South into line with fertility of regions previously urbanized. This latter procedure should afford some indication of the eventual realignment of southern fertility levels and differentials under the influence of the whole process of urbanization.

The second point of view will be taken in this chapter. Its development will be organized around certain hypotheses: (1) Southern fertility has declined in both rural and urban areas with the intensification and diffusion of urban values. (2) The South, having begun the process (largely completed in other regions) of adjusting fertility to urban values, is becoming more and more like the rest of the nation in its patterns of family size. (3) Rural-urban fertility differentials have narrowed as a result of this process of urbaniza-

1951; "Summary of Natality Statistics, United States, 1950," Vol. 37, No. 7, May 19, 1953; and "Births by Age of Mother, Race, and Birth Order, United States, 1950," Vol. 37, No. 13, November 27, 1953.

tion. (4) Negroes in the past because of their rural background responded slowly to the social forces associated with the small-family pattern, but are now rapidly adopting urban values and are decreasing the differential between their fertility and that of whites. (5) Families with husband employed as a white-collar worker have decreased in size more than families with husband employed in other occupational groups. (6) Finally, although urban fertility in the South has fallen below replacement levels, rural fertility is still sufficiently high to provide for the continued growth of the region.[8]

These propositions will serve as the framework of the analyses in the following sections of this chapter. Some are already well established, while others deserve further investigation because of conflicting evidence and inadequate data. It is desirable, therefore, to begin with a review of some of the literature to ascertain the status of some of these propositions as a result of the research of the last twenty or thirty years.

It is clear, first of all, that fertility declined in all regions almost continuously from the early part of the nineteenth century to the third decade of the twentieth.[9] Equally clear is the fact that urban populations are less fertile than rural.[10] Regional differentials have also been generally found, with the South having the highest fertility rates.[11] The convergence of regional rates was forecast as early as 1934 by Lorimer and Osborn, who held that it would

8. Detailed analysis of the data for the period from 1910 to 1940 necessarily focusses upon decreases in fertility since the trend had been downward without major interruption from the beginning of the nineteenth century. It is still too early to determine whether the change from 1940 to 1953 in the direction of this trend will persist and keep urban fertility above replacement levels for an indefinite time or whether in the near future net reproduction rates for cities will fall again below 1,000.

9. P. K. Whelpton, "Geographic and Economic Differentials in Fertility," *loc. cit.;* and P. K. Whelpton and C. V. Kiser, "Trends, Determinants, and Control in Human Fertility," *Annals of the American Academy of Political and Social Science,* 237 (January 1945), pp. 112-122.

10. United Nations Economic and Social Council, *Economic and Social Factors Affecting Fertility, Findings of Studies on the Relationships Between Population Trends and Economic and Social Factors* (Provisional revised report submitted by the Secretariat, 24 April 1951), p. 17.

11. Rupert B. Vance, *Research Memorandum on Population Redistribution Within the United States* (New York: Social Science Research Council, 1938).

result from the further spread of contraceptive information and devices among the geographic areas of the country that had relatively high birth rates.[12]

Although considered sound, the prediction of convergence has not been tested. Has it already taken place? Through what particular process has this development occurred? Instead, efforts have been directed to probing within the regional groupings to determine the various factors which account for fertility differentials. Landis in this connection has stated that the relationship between reproductive rates and geographic region is much less direct than that between rural and urban areas.[13] Thompson has demonstrated that regional rural differences are due in large part to different proportions of the population found at various levels of living.[14] Vance went further along this line of research by attempting to measure the comparative influence of rural-urban distribution, nativity and race distribution, age structure, and age-specific birth rates in accounting for the relatively high fertility of the Southeast region.[15]

There has been some disagreement concerning the Negro-white differential in fertility. In 1938, Hauser stated that the fertility of the Negro is higher than that of the white in rural places and lower than that of the white in urban places.[16] On the other hand, Vance in 1945 reported that net reproduction at all ages is highest among the Southeast's white women and next highest among its Negroes.[17] Thompson in 1942 noted that it is reasonable to expect that a larger proportion of Negroes than of whites will continue to have birth rates characteristic of rural people for several decades and

12. Frank Lorimer and Frederick Osborn, *Dynamics of Population* (New York: Macmillan Company, 1934), pp. 13-18 and 341.

13. Paul Landis, *Population Problems* (New York: American Book Company, 1948), p. 99.

14. Warren S. Thompson, "Differentials in Fertility and Levels of Living in the Rural Population of the United States," *American Sociological Review*, 13 (October 1948), p. 534.

15. Rupert B. Vance, *All These People* (Chapel Hill: University of North Carolina Press, 1945), p. 77.

16. Philip Hauser, Differential Fertility, Mortality and Reproduction in Chicago, 1930 (unpublished doctoral dissertation, University of Chicago, 1938), pp. 15-17.

17. Vance, *All These People*, p. 77.

that, even in the farm population, it appears that the birth rate is declining faster among whites than among Negroes.[18]

Further uncertainties arise over the nature of trends in rural-urban and in class differentials. Woofter has noted a narrowing of the rural-urban differential, pointing out that this may have resulted from migration trends rather than from any fundamental change in the two fertility levels.[19] This same trend in the rural-urban differential was found for Canada by Enid Charles in her recent analysis of census materials for that country.[20] Conflicting reports likewise have been made of class changes, with majority opinion holding that a decrease in this differential is due to an increase in family size in the topmost class.[21]

Revision of earlier findings appears necessary in view of current increases in birth rates. "It has been suggested that two processes working in opposite directions have contributed to the movement of births in recent years, namely on the one hand a continued reduction in the proportion of persons not practising family limitation and an increase in the efficiency of family limitation, and on the other hand an increase in the size of family among certain groups where the practise of family limitation is well established. . . ." [22] More specifically, Kiser found in his analysis of data from the Current Population Survey of the Census Bureau for the period 1940-1947 that there has been a narrowing of regional, rural-urban, race, and class differentials because of increasing fertility of groups with the lowest birth rates.[23]

18. Warren S. Thompson, *Population Problems* (New York: McGraw-Hill Book Company, 1942), pp. 128-129.

19. T. J. Woofter, "Trends in Rural and Urban Fertility Rates," *Rural Sociology*, 13 (March 1948), p. 9.

20. Enid Charles, *The Changing Size of the Family in Canada* (Ottawa: Dominion Bureau of Statistics, Eighth Census of Canada 1941, Census Monograph #1, 1948), p. 138.

21. Lorimer and Osborn, *op. cit.*, p. 200; Clyde V. Kiser, *Group Differences in Urban Fertility* (Baltimore: The Williams and Wilkins Company, 1942), pp. 163-164; Margaret Hagood, "Changing Fertility Differentials Among Farm-Operator Families in Relation to Economic Size of Farm," *Rural Sociology*, 13 (December 1948), pp. 363-373; and Clyde V. Kiser and P. K. Whelpton, "Social and Psychological Factors Affecting Fertility: IX. Fertility Planning and Fertility Rates by Socio-Economic Status," *The Milbank Memorial Fund Quarterly*, XXVII (April 1949), 188-244.

22. United Nations Economic and Social Council, *op. cit.*, p. 62.

23. Clyde V. Kiser, "Fertility Trends and Differentials in the United

II. SOUTHERN FERTILITY DIFFERENTIALS, 1910-1940

The review made above of current research indicates the need for further understanding of what is happening to fertility in the South. Three questions can be answered for 1910 and 1940 from the data on number of children ever born per 1,000 women 15 to 74 years of age: [24] (1) How does urban fertility differ from rural in the South and in the United States? (2) How does white fertility differ from nonwhite in the South and in the United States? (3) How does southern fertility differ from United States rates? They will be answered not only for the total population of each group but also for the several racial and residential subdivisions of interest in this chapter, since differences found for the total groups may be averages of very heterogeneous components of the social structure. Thus, the rural-urban comparison will be broken down by color, the white-nonwhite by residence, and the South-United States difference by both color and residence.

This section is intended, then, to establish the size of residential, color, and regional differentials in 1910 and 1940 as bench marks for further analysis. A preliminary answer will be obtained to the question of what basic stocks and class groups are increasing their proportions in the regional and the national population. Intensive treatment of the problem of trends, however, will be reserved for a subsequent section.

Rural-Urban Fertility

Numerous studies have established the fact of high rural fertility.[25] The index numbers of Table 1 show by color the size of

States," *Journal of the American Statistical Association*, 47 (March 1952), pp. 37-48.

24. The data used and the definitions of terms come from the 1940 census volumes on fertility. See U. S. Bureau of the Census, *Sixteenth Census of the United States: 1940. Population: Differential Fertility, 1940 and 1910. Fertility by Duration of Marriage* (Washington: U. S. Government Printing Office, 1947).

25. A. J. Jaffe, "Urbanization and Fertility," *American Journal of Sociology*, 48 (July 1942), pp. 48-60; Kingsley Davis, *The Population of India and Pakistan* (Princeton: Princeton University Press, 1951), pp. 70-73; T. J. Woofter, "Trends in Rural and Urban Fertility Rates," *loc. cit.*

the rural-urban differential in 1910 and 1940 for the South and the United States.[26] Rural fertility was in all subgroups substantially higher than urban fertility. This difference increased during the 30-year period except for rural-nonfarm nonwhites.

In 1910, white fertility in the South and the United States was about one-quarter higher in the rural-nonfarm and about one-half higher in the rural-farm than in the urban population. For non-

TABLE 1. Percent Rural Fertility Was of Urban Fertility in 1910 and 1940 by Color for the United States and the South

Area and Color	1910		1940	
	United States	South	United States	South
All Classes				
Urban	100	100	100	100
Rural-nonfarm	128	132	131	134
Rural-farm	152	156	167	169
Total	121	135	119	131
Whites				
Urban	100	100	100	100
Rural-nonfarm	125	128	131	135
Rural-farm	148	154	165	170
Total	118	133	118	132
Nonwhites				
Urban	100	100	100	100
Rural-nonfarm	146	138	138	132
Rural-farm	170	159	175	166
Total	140	138	128	131

Source: Computed from data in U. S. Bureau of the Census, *Sixteenth Census of the United States: 1940. Population: Differential Fertility 1940 and 1910: Standardized Fertility Rates and Reproduction Rates*, pp. 8-10.

whites, this rural-urban difference was about 20 percent greater than for whites in the nation and from 5 to 10 percent greater than for whites in the South.

In 1940, white and nonwhite fertility in both region and nation was approximately one-third higher for the rural-nonfarm group and about two-thirds higher for the rural-farm group than for

26. Urban fertility in each of the several regional and color subdivisions of the data is taken as 100 percent and rural-nonfarm and rural-farm fertility are expressed in relative terms. Thus if urban fertility were 1,250 children ever born per 1,000 women and rural-farm fertility were 1,640 children ever born per 1,000 women, the respective index numbers would be 100 and 131.

the urban population. Nonwhites in 1940 were in about the same position as whites with respect to rural-urban differences. This was due to a 6 to 8 percent decline in their urban-rural-nonfarm differential and to a much smaller increase in their urban-rural-farm differential than that experienced by whites.

White-Nonwhite Fertility

The problem of white-nonwhite fertility is for the South, first of all, simply a question of whether Negroes or whites have more children ever born per 1,000 women 15 to 74 years of age. This aspect of the problem is implicit in Warren Thompson's statement that Negroes have responded much the same as whites to forces that determine family size.[27] Changes in the proportion of nonwhites in the South have been due in the past mainly to the Negroes' higher mortality.[28] As mortality of the two groups becomes similar,

TABLE 2. Percent Nonwhite Fertility Was of White Fertility in 1910 and 1940 by Rural-Urban Residence of Woman for the United States and the South

Color of Woman by Area	1910		1940	
	United States	South	United States	South
Total				
Whites	100	100	100	100
Nonwhites	123	109	113	104
All Classes	102	103	101	101
Urban				
Whites	100	100	100	100
Nonwhites	103	105	104	104
All Classes	100	101	100	101
Rural-nonfarm				
Whites	100	100	100	100
Nonwhites	121	113	110	103
All Classes	103	104	101	100
Rural-farm				
Whites	100	100	100	100
Nonwhites	118	109	110	102
All Classes	103	102	101	101

Source: Computed from data in U. S. Bureau of the Census, *Sixteenth Census of the United States: 1940. Population: Differential Fertility 1940 and 1910: Standardized Fertility Rates and Reproduction Rates*, pp. 8-10.

27. *Population Problems*, p. 147.
28. Vance, *All These People*, pp. 347-350.

interest will be increasingly focussed on the subject of differential fertility.

The size of the white-nonwhite differential in 1910 and 1940 is shown in Table 2 for the South and the United States by rural-urban residence of women. The index numbers indicate that southern nonwhites had higher fertility than southern whites in 1910 and 1940. In urban areas, the differential was small at the time of the earlier census and remained almost the same during the next 30 years. In rural areas, on the other hand, the differential was substantial in 1910 but decreased considerably by 1940.

In urban places, racial differences in fertility were 5 percent or less in both the nation and region at the time of both censuses. In rural areas, the difference in 1910 was about 20 percent in the United States and 10 percent in the South, but by 1940 it had shrunk to about 10 percent in the nation and to 3 percent or less in the region. These reductions brought differences between whites and nonwhites in the rural South to the same low level as in the urban South, but left the rural areas of the United States with about twice the difference found in the nation's urban areas.

Regional Fertility

Southern fertility in the twentieth century has been substantially higher than fertility in the rest of the nation. Several analysts of this differential believe that it has arisen out of the lag in the industrialization and urbanization of the South, pointing to the fact that other regions had as high or higher fertility during the first half of the nineteenth century.[29] In this interpretation it is assumed that the South will go through a similar shift from rural to urban economy and in so doing will approximate the fertility rates of other areas. There is, however, still some question as to whether regional differences, based on such structural factors as proportions of rural-urban population, racial composition, and age distribution, will be eliminated entirely as the South gains industrial maturity.

In Table 3 the size of the South-United States fertility differential in 1910 and 1940 is indicated by color for rural and urban divisions

29. See Robert Dinkel, Regional, Rural-Urban and Occupational Fertility Trends in the United States, 1910 to 1940 (unpublished doctoral dissertation, University of North Carolina, 1950), pp. 7-11, 80-108, 190-243, and 266-269.

of the population. These index numbers indicate that southern fertility was 19 percent higher than national fertility in 1910 and was 16 percent higher in 1940. No color and area specific component of

TABLE 3. Percent Southern Fertility Was of United States Fertility in 1910 and 1940 by Rural-Urban Residence of Woman for Whites and Nonwhites

Area	1910			1940		
	All Classes	Whites	Nonwhites	All Classes	Whites	Nonwhites
Total	119	119	105	116	116	108
Urban	106	105	107	105	104	105
Rural-nonfarm	110	108	101	107	107	101
Rural-farm	109	109	100	107	107	100

Source: Computed from Data in U. S. Bureau of the Census, *Sixteenth Census of the United States: 1940. Population: Differential Fertility 1940 and 1910: Standardized Fertility Rates and Reproduction Rates,* pp. 8-10.

the southern population, however, had in 1910 more than 9 percent higher fertility or in 1940 more than 7 percent than the same color and area specific component of the population of the United States. This means that over 50 percent of the difference in the South's fertility compared with the nation's was due to different percentages of race and residential groups. In particular, the higher percentage of rural residents in the South accounted for most of the higher birth rate.

III. CHANGE AND PROCESS IN SOUTHERN FERTILITY

The preceding section was designed primarily to assess at two points in time the size of the rural-urban, white-nonwhite, and South-United States fertility differentials. Some information on trends was obtained through comparison of the size of the differentials in 1910 and 1940. The data indicated an increase in the rural-urban differential and decreases in the white-nonwhite and South-United States differentials.

These trends will now be examined in greater detail using the more dynamic approach of rates of change. As general background for this task, the percentages of decline for the South and the United States will be examined by color and by rural-urban residence. Next will come an analysis of age-group rates of fertility decrease to see whether there was a consistent trend or a series of diverse movements toward expansion or contraction of the differences associated with residence, color, and region. Finally, change in the South and in the nation will be broken down by occupational groups to see whether regional trends can be accounted for in any substantial measure by particular groups of workers.

Fertility Decline, 1910-1940

Percentage decreases for the South and the United States are presented in Table 4 by color and by rural-urban residence. Fertility among women in 15 to 74 years of age declined 29 percent in the region, 27 percent in the nation. All residence and color subgroups likewise had substantial decreases in fertility, ranging from 18 to 30 percent. Since the region and nation did not differ by more than 2 percent in any of these subdivisions, further description of these data will be given below only for the South, the area of primary interest.

TABLE 4. Percent Decrease 1910-1940 in Number of Children Ever Born to Women 15 to 74 Years of Age by Color of Woman and by Rural-Urban Residence for the South and the United States

Area	United States			South		
	All Classes	Whites	Nonwhites	All Classes	Whites	Nonwhites
Total	27	26	32	29	28	31
Urban	26	26	26	27	27	27
Rural-nonfarm	24	23	30	26	23	30
Rural-farm	19	18	24	21	19	24

Source: Computed from Data in U. S. Bureau of the Census, *Sixteenth Census of the United States: 1940. Population: Differential Fertility 1940 and 1910: Standardized Fertility Rates and Reproduction Rates*, pp. 8-10.

In the urban South the number of children ever born declined 27 percent from 1910 to 1940. Urban whites and nonwhites showed no difference in percentage decrease. In the rural South, fertility declined from 19 to 30 percent, depending upon farm or nonfarm residence and upon color. The white rural-farm women were at the lower end and the nonwhite rural-nonfarm women were at the upper end of this range of decrease in fertility.

The percentages of Table 4 necessarily are in general agreement with the trends noted in the preceding section since they are derived from the same data. Cast in the more dynamic form of percentage decline in number of children ever born, however, Table 4 suggests perhaps more clearly that the increase in the rural-urban differential was largely the result of the relatively slow rate of decline of the white rural-farm group while the narrowing of the white-nonwhite differential was the result of the relatively high rate of decline in the fertility of the rural nonwhite group. There are also shown in high relief comparatively high rates of fertility decrease of the nonwhite rural-nonfarm residents of both the region and the nation.

Age-Group Analysis of Trends in Fertility Differentials

The purpose of this section is to analyze the trends noted above in residence, color, and regional differentials for consistency throughout the time period for which there are data. It is necessary first to determine what time period the data cover. Here it is accurate only in a limited sense to refer to the decline in southern fertility shown in Table 4 as having occurred from 1910 to 1940 because the data of this table based on number of children ever born were influenced by changes in birth rates from about 1850 to 1940. This fact is evident from consideration of Table 5, which shows for the specific age groups of both the 1910 and 1940 census samples the probable time period of the last century during which these women were bearing their children.

In effect, Table 5 indicates there are 20 samples of fertility experience covered by the data of the 1910 and 1940 censuses. These samples are of separate, if somewhat overlapping segments of the 90-year period from 1850 to 1940. A comparison of any age group of the 1910 census with the same age group of the 1940 census shows change over a 30-year period.

Ten such rates of change can be computed, but in the case of five the women involved were less than 40 years of age at the time of the census inquiry and thus might not have completed their families. In these cases, the rates of fertility change are subject to the question of proper interpretation. Use of these rates to estimate

TABLE 5. Historical Period During Which Age Groups of 1910 and 1940 Census Samples Probably Were Childbearing and Maximum Number of Years of Exposure to Childbearing at Time of Census

Age Group	1910 Census Sample		1940 Census Sample	
	Period of Childbearing	Maximum Years of Exposure	Period of Childbearing	Maximum Years of Exposure
15-19	1905-1910	5	1935-1940	5
20-24	1900-1910	10	1930-1940	10
25-29	1895-1910	15	1925-1940	15
30-34	1890-1910	20	1920-1940	20
35-39	1885-1910	25	1915-1940	25
40-44	1880-1910	30	1910-1940	30
45-49	1875-1905	30	1905-1935	30
50-54	1870-1900	30	1900-1930	30
55-64	1860-1895	30	1890-1925	30
65-74	1850-1885	30	1880-1915	30

trends in family size is questionable since the shift to smaller families would show up only in high-order births, normally procreated at an older age than these women had attained. Moreover, shifts in the spacing of children might lead to larger differences in the incompleted than in the completed families. If these rates are used for the purpose of estimating trends in fertility differentials, such difficulties are lessened.

Rural-Urban Differentials

Reduced rural and urban fertility from 1850 to 1940 is shown by the age groups of Figure 1 for whites and nonwhites in the South and for whites in the United States. Percentage decrease in fertility among the older age groups indicates earlier trends; among the younger, more recent trends.

The data show a greater decline in urban than in rural fertility. The consequent widening of the rural-urban differential has already been noted. What is new, however, is the indication that this change in fertility by residence was the net result of diverse movements among the age groups and between whites and nonwhites.

The over-all picture of an increase in the rural-urban differential is accounted for mainly by the older age groups of whites of the South and the United States. Such increase does not portray ac-

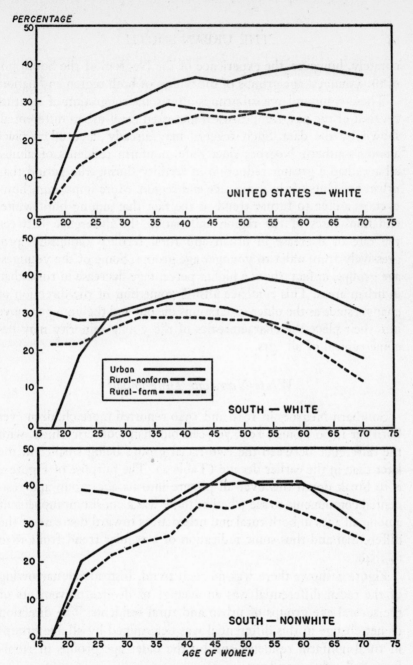

PERCENTAGE

UNITED STATES — WHITE

Urban
Rural-nonfarm
Rural-farm

SOUTH — WHITE

SOUTH — NONWHITE

AGE OF WOMEN

Figure 1. Percent Decrease (1910 to 1940) in Number of Children Ever Born to Rural and Urban Women 15 to 74 Years, by Age of Women, for the United States and the South

(Source: Computed from data in U. S. Bureau of the Census, *Sixteenth Census of the United States: 1940. Population: Differential Fertility 1940 and 1910: Standardized Fertility Rates and Reproduction Rates,* pp. 8-10.)

curately, however, the experience of the Negroes of the South nor of the youngest age groups of the whites of both region and nation.

These color and age subgroups offer some suggestion of a future reversal of the past trend toward increased rural-urban differentials shown by the data. Such reversal may already have taken place among southern Negroes since rural-nonfarm residents of almost all ages had a greater reduction in fertility during the period than urban residents of the same race and region. More important, however, as a clue to future trends is the fact that among both whites and nonwhites of the region and nation the difference between the rate of decrease in urban and rural fertility diminishes progressively from older to younger age groups. Some of the youngest age groups, in fact, show a higher percentage decrease in rural than in urban areas. This evidence affords some hint of the direction of change, since as the older generations die out and the younger move into their place the characteristics of the young minority may become typical of all ages.

White-Nonwhite Differentials

Southern Negroes in 1910 and 1940 reported more children ever born per 1,000 women 15 to 74 years old than southern whites, with the difference between the two racial groups being smaller in the later than in the earlier decade (Table 2). The purpose of Figure 2 is to break down this over-all picture into its age-group and residential components to see whether there was a consistent movement among all ages in both rural and urban areas toward decrease of the differential and thus some indication of a regular trend from 1850 to 1940.

Figure 2 shows there was no such trend. Instead the narrowing of the racial differential was an average of diverse movements of the several age groups of urban and rural residents. The direction of net change in this differential was determined by all age groups of rural-nonfarm residents and by the older age groups of rural-farm and urban residents.

The question of whether the data suggest a future reversal of the trend toward a decrease in the white-nonwhite differential cannot be answered readily from the data of Figure 2. The residen-

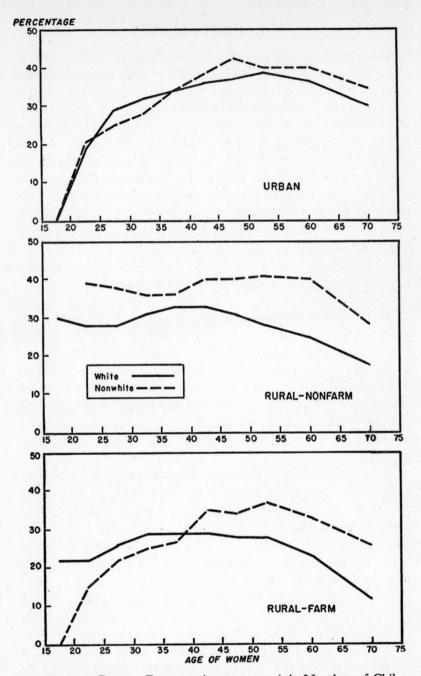

Figure 2. Percent Decrease (1910 to 1940) in Number of Children Ever Born to White and Nonwhite Southern Women 15 to 74 Years, by Age of Women, and by Rural-Urban Residence

(Source: Computed from data in U. S. Bureau of the Census, *Sixteenth Census of the United States: 1940. Population: Differential Fertility 1940 and 1910: Standardized Fertility Rates and Reproduction Rates*, pp. 8-10.)

tial groups vary in their evidence on this point. Rural-farm women were definitely moving in such a direction since the younger age groups showed greater reductions in white than in Negro fertility. Rural-nonfarm women, on the other hand, offer no suggestion of such a change in trend since among all age groups the reduction in fertility was higher for nonwhites than for whites. Urban residents give some indication of the same pattern of change as that shown by the rural-farm women. Whites and nonwhites, however, had such similar rates of fertility decrease throughout the entire age range that this pattern may have been shaped by minor forces. It may in fact be due to random factors and thus may disappear quickly under the impact of new circumstances.

South-United States Differentials

The differential between the fertility of the South and of the nation was shown in Table 3 to have been 19 percent in 1910 and 16 percent in 1940. Subgroups of the region and nation differed less and had smaller gross reductions in their differences during the 30-year period. The greater difference between total populations than between corresponding color and residential subgroups of the total populations is due to one simple fact. The region has a higher percentage of the more fertile subgroups in its social structure than does the United States.

This section explains change in regional differentials by a breakdown of the data by age group. The analysis (Figure 3) is made only for white women according to rural-urban residence. Such restriction and subdivision of the data eliminate the influence of racial composition, rural-urban distribution, and age structure upon regional differences, and expose that part of the total trend due to change in age-specific fertility rates of whites.

Figure 3 indicates that the whites of the South and the nation will probably further reduce the difference between their fertility. This change may take place at an accelerated rate compared with that between 1910 and 1940. The inference is based on the fact that southern white women of rural areas had progressively higher rates of reduction in their fertility with decrease in age, whereas white women of rural areas of the nation had progressively lower rates

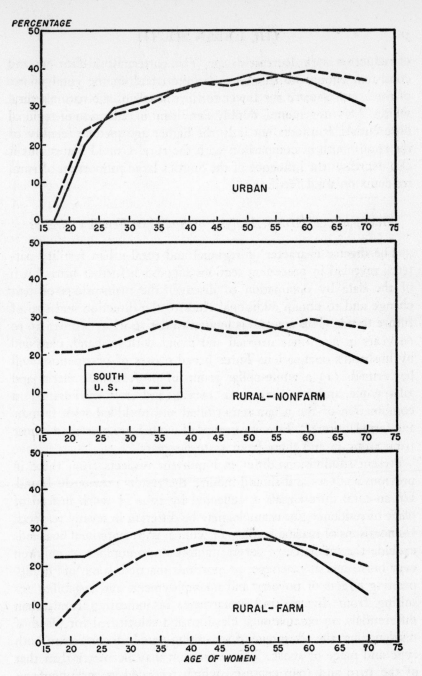

PERCENTAGE

URBAN

SOUTH ———
U. S. - - - -

RURAL—NONFARM

RURAL—FARM

AGE OF WOMEN

Figure 3. Percent Decrease (1910 to 1940) in Number of Children Ever Born to White Women 15 to 74 Years, of the South and the United States, by Rural-Urban Residence

(Source: Computed from data in U. S. Bureau of the Census, *Sixteenth Census of the United States: 1940. Population: Differential Fertility 1940 and 1910: Standardized Fertility Rates and Reproduction Rates*, pp. 8-10.)

of reduction with decrease in age. This patterning is clear-cut and consistent enough to suggest a definite trend among rural whites of the South toward the lower fertility levels of the nation's rural whites. This movement is doubly significant in reduction of regional differentials. It affects not only the higher age-specific fertility of the rural South in comparison with the rural United States, but it also decreases the influence of the South's large proportion of rural residents on total fertility.

Occupational Group Analysis of Southern Fertility Trends

The diverse character of regional and rural-urban fertility patterns revealed in preceding sections suggests a further breakdown of the data by occupation to discover the mainsprings of past change and to obtain additional clues to the direction and size of future trends. This analysis is limited to native white women 20 to 69 years of age, once married and living with husband, classified by husband's occupation. Three broad classes of occupations will be formed: (1) a white-collar group of professionals, clerks and salespeople, and proprietors; (2) service and craft workers; (3) a combination of the urban semi-skilled and unskilled with farmers and farm laborers.[30] Two age groups of women are presented—those from 20 to 44 and those from 45 to 69 years.

Present subdivisions differ in important respects from those in previous analyses and should modify the results previously found. Urban-rural differentials as reflected by type of work instead of place of residence, for example, may be different in several respects. Comparisons of marital fertility of women with employed husbands exclude the influence of several factors upon number of children ever born: age at marriage, proportions married, some of the depressing effects of poverty and unemployment, and instability resulting from divorce and remarriage. In indicating rural-urban differentials, an occupational classification substituted for place of residence has the advantage of separating people according to both type and place of work. This separation may be better than that of the 1910 and 1940 censuses, which recorded as rural-nonfarm residents those families living in suburbs of large cities. Certainly

30. See Table 6 for a more exact statement of the occupations included in these three groups.

suburbanites are more urban than rural in attitudes, values, and interests.

Clearly the rate of fertility decrease varied with occupational group in the South (Table 6). White-collar workers had a substantially sharper decline than urban unskilled, urban semi-skilled, and rural workers. No trend, however, can be observed since younger women had about the same rates of reduction in fertility by occupational class as older women. A comparison of southern experience with that of other regions perhaps can be made more readily through the data of Figure 4 for the nine occupational groups for which the Census Bureau gives information.

Among the older women, the South differed from the North Central and Western regions in percentage decrease of fertility only in the case of the white-collar group of professionals, clerks and salespeople, and proprietors. The greater reduction in fertility by these southern workers, however, was not large. A more significant difference is found in comparison of these three regions with the Northeast. In this comparison, northeastern women 45 to 69 years are found to have had for all occupational groupings of their husbands a lower rate of fertility reduction than the South, North Central, and West.

Among the younger women, the South differed markedly from the other three regions in having had a relatively high percentage decrease in fertility among all occupational groups. This regional difference was slight in the case of rural workers and urban laborers, moderate in the case of operatives, craftsmen and service workers, but large in the case of the white-collar group of professionals, clerks and salespeople, and proprietors.

The data of Table 6 and Figure 4 indicate an accelerating decrease of the South-United States differential and an accelerating increase of the rural-urban differential. These findings deviate some from those for women 15 to 74 years of age obtained in previous tables and charts. They are not in agreement with the probable reduction in the rate of increase and the possible eventual reversal of the rural-urban differential suggested by the data of Figure 3. They also are at variance with the source in Figure 1 of the narrowing of the South-United States differential. In the earlier sections this narrowing was attributed to the white women of the rural South, whereas in this section it has been associated with wives

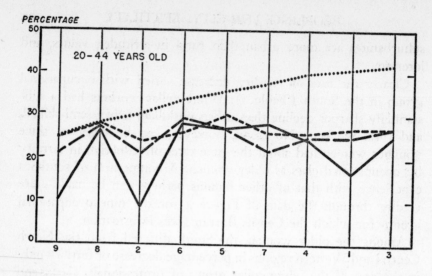

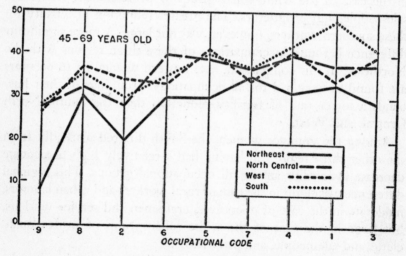

9—Farm laborers and foremen
8—Laborers, except farm and mine
2—Farmers and farm managers
6—Operatives and kindred workers
5—Craftsmen, foremen and kindred workers

7—Service workers
4—Clerical, sales, and kindred workers
1—Professional and semi-professional
3—Proprietors, managers, and officials

Figure 4. Percent Decrease (1910 to 1940) in Number of Children Ever Born to Native White Women 20-44 and 45-69 Years with Unbroken Marriages, by Occupation of Husband and by Region, with Rates Standardized for Duration of Marriage

(Source: Computed from data in U. S. Bureau of the Census, *Sixteenth Census of the United States. Population: Differential Fertility 1940 and 1910: Fertility by Duration of Marriage*, pp. 199-208.)

TABLE 6. Percent Decrease 1910 to 1940 in Number of Children Ever Born to Native White Women of Selected Age and Occupational Class by Region *

Region	Age Groups 20-44 Years Old Occupational Group **			Age Groups 45-69 Years Old Occupational Group **		
	A	B	C	A	B	C
Northeast	22	27	20	31	32	24
North Central	26	24	25	39	38	32
West	27	28	26	38	39	34
South	41	37	30	43	39	32

* Women of unbroken marriages and with rates standardized for duration of marriage.
** Occupational Group:
  A. Professional and semi-professional workers; proprietors, managers, and officials, excluding farm; and clerical, sales, and kindred workers.
  B. Craftsmen, foremen, and kindred workers and service workers.
  C. Operatives and kindred workers; laborers, except farm and mine; farmers and farm managers; and farm laborers and foremen.

Source: Computed from data in U. S. Bureau of the Census, *Sixteenth Census of the United States: 1940. Population: Differential Fertility 1940 and 1910: Fertility by Duration of Marriage*, pp. 184-193 and 199-208.

of husbands in white-collar occupations, who presumably are mainly urban residents.

These divergent findings are probably due to the fact that different groups were subjected to analysis. Further unravelling of these complexities depends upon analysis of change among foreign-born whites and among native whites of different marital and employment status than that of the women considered in Figure 4. White-collar workers of rural residence may have different fertility from those living in urban places. Such clarification, however, is beyond the scope of the present study.

IV. POPULATION GROWTH AND REPLACEMENT

Section II analysed for 1910 and 1940 the extent of fertility differences between (1) rural and urban residents of the South, (2) whites and Negroes of the South, and (3) the South and the United States. Section III was concerned principally with trends in these differentials. The first approach was a static one, in its comparison of levels of fertility among important groups in the region. The second approach was more dynamic, dealing with degrees of change occurring among these groups during the 30-year period. Relative change shown in Section III indicated shifts in fertility differences, revealed the particular groups of the social structure that account for such shifts, and suggested the future status of fertility levels and differentials. It is the purpose of this section to examine these trends in terms of population growth and replacement in the South.

Growth of Southern Population With Urban Development

The South's urban fertility in 1940 was only 5 percent higher than the nation's; its rural fertility was only 7 percent higher (Table 3). Total southern fertility, however, was 16 percent higher. Greater fertility for the total group than for its residence subdivisions is due simply to the fact that the South has a higher percentage of the high fertility group—namely, rural residents. The South, it is suggested, will approximate national fertility only as its rural-urban balance approaches that of the nation.

What would be the effect of such a shift on the southern fertility rate, on the rate of decline in fertility, and on the size of the southern population? Table 7 suggests an answer to these questions. It shows, first of all, that the South in 1910 had 49 percent of its

TABLE 7. Southern Women 15 to 74 Years Old and Number of Children Ever Born by Rural-Urban Residence According to 1940 Census and According to Certain Assumptions Regarding Number and Distribution of Southern Population in 1940 if Urbanization of the South from 1910 to 1940 Had Not Occurred

	Percent Rural-Urban Distribution		1940 Census			1940: Assumption A			1940: Assumption B		
Area	Women 15-74 1910	Women 15-74 1940	Women 15-74 Years *	Children Ever Born *	Fertility Rate	Women 15-74 Years *	Children Ever Born *	Fertility Rate	Women 15-74 Years *	Children Ever Born *	Fertility Rate
Urban	26	42	5,291	8,189	1548	3,271	5,063	1548	2,300	3,560	1548
Rural-nonfarm	25	24	2,955	6,223	2106	3,145	6,624	2106	2,211	4,657	2106
Rural-farm	49	24	4,334	11,576	2671	6,164	16,465	2671	4,334	11,577	2671
Total	100	100	12,580	25,998	2066	12,580	28,152	2238	8,845	19,794	2238

*Hundreds of Thousands
Assumption A: Total population of women 15-74 years, color distribution, and fertility rates of 1940 census and rural-urban distribution of 1910 census.
Assumption B: Total rural-farm population of women 15-74 years, color distribution, and fertility rates of 1940 census and rural-urban distribution of 1910 census.

Source: Computed from data in U. S. Bureau of the Census, *Sixteenth Census of the United States: 1940. Population: Differential Fertility 1940 and 1910: Women by Number of Children Ever Born*, pp. 210-213.

total population classified as rural-farm; in 1940, only 24 percent. This change is accounted for by an increase from 26 to 42 percent of the total population living in urban places. The rural-nonfarm group had approximately the same percentage of the regional population in both decades.

Here migration is clearly responsible since (1) the rural birth rate was higher than the urban birth rate and (2) farm residents had a lower death rate than city dwellers. Without migration of this magnitude, it seems reasonable that either (1) people would have been dammed up on southern farms, or (2) the flow of migrants would have been deflected to northern centers, or (3) changes in birth and death rates would have brought the rate of natural increase into approximate balance with the level of social and economic development characteristic of the South in 1910.

The first assumption made in Table 7 is that southern population would have grown from 1910 to 1940 as shown by the census, but that its rural-urban distribution would have remained as in 1910. In this event, women 15 to 74 years of age would have totaled 12½ million in 1940 as shown by the census, but 3¼ million instead of the actual 5¼ million would have resided in urban places. Rural population under this assumption would have included about 9 1/3 million of these women instead of the 7¼ million listed by the 1940 census. Given the same rural and urban fertility rates of that time, this different distribution of women would have resulted in approximately 28 million instead of 26 million children ever born. The fertility rate for the whole South in terms of number of children ever born per 1,000 women 15 to 74 years of age would have been 2,238 instead of 2,066. Since the 1910 rate was 2,882, the decline in southern fertility so measured would have been 22 percent instead of 29 percent.

Since southern farms might not have been able to accommodate the increased number of women 15 to 74 and the additional children born under this first assumption, it seems reasonable to assume that the number of women 15 to 74 who were rural-farm residents was the same as shown by the 1940 census, while the distribution of the total population by residence was that of 1910. In this case, there would have been about 2,200,000 women 15 to 74 years of age in rural-nonfarm areas and about 2,300,000 in urban places. With the residence fertility rates shown by the 1940 census, the number of children ever born would then have been only 19,800,000 instead of the 26,000,000 indicated by the census. Since the residence fertility rates and the proportion of the total population in each residence group would be the same as in the first assumption, fertility in this case would also have declined only 22 instead of 29 percent.

Under both of these assumptions, it is clear that urbanization increased the rate at which southern fertility declined. This greater rate of decrease through urbanization, however, does not mean that there are today fewer people in the South as a result of this process. There probably are more, in that industry and trade developed and provided more employment for the natural growth of the rural population than could have been afforded by southern farms under the old rural economy, had it been preserved. Under the second assumption—the more likely of the two—urbanization resulted in an increase of over 3 million women 15 to 74 years of age living in the South and of over 6 million children ever born to southern women.

Population Replacement in the South

Southern fertility rates thus declined substantially from 1910 to 1940 although southern population increased in numbers during this period. Urbanization has been given credit both for the decrease in family size and for the growth in total southern population by providing work opportunities for children born in the region. Has fertility declined so far in the South as to suggest impairment of the region's ability to provide sufficient workers for continued growth in urban opportunities?

The significance of fertility differentials and trends in terms of population replacement is reflected in Table 8 in terms of intrinsic rates of natural increase. These rates, based on number of children under 5 years, indicate "current" fertility rather than "lifetime" fertility shown by number of children ever born.

In 1905-1910 and in 1935-1940 urban residents of the South had intrinsic birth and death rates insufficient for replacement of the population of urban places (Table 8). Rural residents during both periods had adequate intrinsic rates of increase. Rural-farm women exhibited increases of nearly 3 percent per year in the first period

TABLE 8. Intrinsic Rate of Natural Increase and Intrinsic Birth and Death Rates, by Color, for the South and United States, Urban and Rural, 1905-1910 and 1935-1940

Residence Group by Color	United States			South		
	Natural Increase	Birth Rate	Death Rate	Natural Increase	Birth Rate	Death Rate
1905-1910						
All Classes						
Whites	10.1	26.0	15.9	18.6	35.3	16.7
Nonwhites	10.1	34.6	24.5	13.9	38.0	24.1
Total	10.1	26.9	16.8	17.1	36.0	18.9
Urban						
Whites	−0.9	19.4	20.3	−4.6	21.6	26.2
Nonwhites	−21.6	16.3	37.9	−20.8	19.6	40.4
Total	−2.3	19.2	21.5	−9.5	20.8	30.3
Rural-nonfarm						
Whites	14.8	28.5	13.7	18.5	33.7	15.2
Nonwhites	12.1	34.4	22.3	13.4	35.1	21.7
Total	14.3	29.2	14.9	16.9	34.1	17.2
Rural-farm						
Whites	24.2	36.5	12.3	28.1	42.4	14.3
Nonwhites	26.1	47.2	21.1	27.6	48.1	20.5
Total	24.5	38.1	13.6	27.8	44.0	16.2
1935-1940						
All Classes						
Whites	−1.5	14.7	16.2	5.2	18.7	13.5
Nonwhites	4.4	22.1	17.7	8.0	24.5	16.5
Total	−0.7	15.5	16.2	6.0	20.2	14.2
Urban						
Whites	−11.0	10.2	21.2	−12.0	10.1	22.1
Nonwhites	−13.9	12.3	26.2	−15.3	12.2	27.5
Total	−11.4	10.3	21.7	−12.8	10.6	23.4
Rural-nonfarm						
Whites	5.3	18.5	13.2	7.5	19.9	12.4
Nonwhites	6.7	22.8	16.1	6.0	22.0	16.0
Total	5.3	18.9	13.6	7.2	20.4	13.2
Rural-farm						
Whites	16.3	26.2	9.9	19.1	28.3	9.2
Nonwhites	26.1	38.2	12.1	26.3	38.0	11.7
Total	18.2	28.1	9.9	21.4	31.0	9.6

Source: U. S. Bureau of the Census, *Sixteenth Census of the United States: 1940. Population: Differential Fertility 1940 and 1910: Standardized Fertility Rates and Reproduction Rates*, pp. 22-23.

and over 2 percent in the later period. Low mortality as well as high fertility contributed to this high rate of replacement.

Southern Negroes in both periods had higher intrinsic birth and death rates than whites of the region. The color balance in terms of intrinsic rates changed, however, during this 30-year period because the great reduction in Negro mortality brought it to the low levels achieved earlier by whites. Whites had higher replacement rates in 1905-1910; Negroes occupied this position in 1935-1940. Differences between these two southern groups were not large during either period, however.

A comparison of the South with the United States serves to demonstrate the higher rate of natural increase in the region. The differences have their origin in the different proportions of residence and color groups found in the total population. The point of chief interest, however, is the fact that in both 1905-1910 and 1935-1940 the urban population of the South had higher negative rates than the nation—in the earlier period because of higher mortality, and in the later because of both high mortality and low fertility.

V. CONCLUSION

The theme of this chapter is that the continued diffusion of urban values throughout the regions of the nation has lowered fertility generally, with greater decline among areas and classes of relatively high birth rates. Convergence in fertility trends was expected in our analysis (1) between the South and the rest of the nation, (2) between rural and urban residents, and (3) between whites and nonwhites. Such convergence has been found, but within the framework of both increasing and decreasing fertility. During the period of decrease, convergence occurred through greater decline among the groups with higher fertility. During the period of increase, however, convergence occurred by higher rates of increase among groups with the lowest levels of fertility.

The hypotheses of this chapter, generally speaking, have been supported by the data used to test their validity. Southern fertility has definitely become more like that in the rest of the nation. Both rural-urban and white-nonwhite differentials have narrowed since 1910 although this process has not been consistent throughout the 40 years. Furthermore, the evidence supports our contention that white-collar workers during periods of fertility decline have tended to have the highest rates of decrease in family size. And, finally, there is no doubt that rural fertility has remained high enough to replace whatever losses southern cities will have if their birth rates fall below the values at which they are able in the long run to maintain their own numbers. The only hypothesis requiring major revision is the first one predicting continued decline of fertility in southern rural and urban areas. The trend, indeed, was downward from 1910 to 1940, but the upsurge in birth rates from 1940 to 1947 and the fluctuations around a high fertility from 1947 to 1953 give no certain clue as to whether the decline has been halted or whether it will be resumed in the near future.

The failure of southern cities as early as 1905-1910 to replace their numbers over a generation gives meaning to the analysis of levels, differentials, and trends. This problem of low urban fertility invites continued comparison with the rest of the nation to obtain perspective on regional changes and to secure clues from national trends as to what may happen. Increases in the birth rate since 1940 have to some extent taken the sharp edge off our concern over population replacements. We should remember, however, that even in 1947, when birth rates were at their peak, net reproduction rates for cities of the nation were not much above replacement levels. Furthermore, some increases in urban birth rates during the 1940's probably are accounted for by births to families recently migrated from rural areas since they still retained some values of the places from which they had come.

It seems for the time being that the process of peopling the southern cities is somewhat lightened by recent reversals of the downward trend in fertility. That the rural South will be able to continue its replenishment of cities is suggested by the potential rate of natural increase of about 2 percent per year among the rural-farm people shown by 1935-1940 data. After 1940 increases in birth rates were substantial in urban areas as well. Optimism, however, may be tempered by the caution that failure to continue economic development in the South will probably be reflected in reduced birth rates. As the population advances in education and social well-being, the impact of depression in reducing fertility would, no doubt, be even greater.

Part Two

ORGANIZATIONAL ASPECTS
OF SOUTHERN CITIES

Introduction

I N THE PRECEDING CHAPTERS, attention was directed to the emergence and growth of cities in the South. The next four chapters are concerned with the product of this urbanization process, that is, with cities themselves. More specifically, the following chapters give emphasis to the city as a social organization whose parts are mutually dependent and whose relation to its setting or environment is also one of interdependence. It has been impossible, of course, to present anything like an exhaustive treatment of urban organization even for one city—much less for the South! However, the four chapters of Part Two deal with four especially significant aspects of urban organization and action.

The interdependence of cities and their hinterlands, of smaller cities and metropolises, is traced by Vance and Smith in Chapter 6. This original inquiry—clearly related to the authors' previous work and to that of Gras, McKenzie, and Bogue—leads to the conclusion that in the South as elsewhere man and his works are being drawn into closer relations with central cities. Vance and Smith point out, however, that southern metropolises need not become the kind of vast, highly dense, and unattractive concentrations which Geddes and Mumford have called "megalopolis." A balance of the urban and rural ways of life is socially and economically possible. At the same time the authors skeptically observe that such a balance has often been advocated but rarely achieved.

Following the account of the "external" relations of cities presented in Chapter 6, attention is directed in the next chapter to their "internal" relations. Demerath and Gilmore, beginning with an examination of general economic functions as these relate to socio-physical forms, summarize what is known of the intra-urban ecology of southern cities. The region's urban ecology is found to be distinguished by the prevalence of small cities, bi-racially populated and sharply segregated in housing as well as in other facilities. In the larger cities, a changing social structure is seen to have its physical corollaries, though with a time lag. And while Negro society, especially in the larger cities, now has numerous social classes not unlike the white, urbanization and the achievement of higher levels of living do not in themselves entail less racial segregation. As long as housing is racially segregated, the authors note, public service facilities such as schools, health centers, parks, and settlement houses must also be segregated in most instances for administrative efficiency if for no other reason. It is probable that such usages in the long run will be affected more by changes in the Negro class structure than by decisions of the courts.

Whereas Chapters 6 and 7 both emphasize the socio-physical or ecological aspects of urban organization, Chapters 8 and 9 deal with two different though related "social orders," namely, class and conformity. Clearly involved in these analyses are changes and contrasts in social values and beliefs, morals and customs. Though no organization of human life, ecological or otherwise, is possible without a value element, this element is apt to be especially conspicuous in matters of class and criminality.

Changes in the South's class structure and social values are described by Kaufman in Chapter 8 as a third major aspect of the region's emerging urban life. Though first-hand studies are few and detailed substantiation is missing, it seems clear that different rewards are being differently distributed as a concomitant of urbanization. By the same token it is also evident that the traditional social hierarchies and related values of the old South are no more. Industrialization and urban concentration together appear to be reshaping the class and value structures of the South so that they resemble more and more those of the non-South.

Though the social changes attendant on urbanization be many, they are by no means smooth. The conflicts and aggressions endemic in southern urban society are seen reflected in the striking contrasts between rates of crime in the South and non-South as analyzed in Chapter 9 by Porterfield and Talbert. In an analysis which will appear controversial to some readers, these authors find much higher rates of crime in 43 southern cities larger than 50,000 compared with 43 non-southern centers of the same size. As between the southern cities, moreover, Porterfield and Talbert find great differences in crime rates which, contrary to popular belief perhaps, cannot be accounted for either by the number or percentage of Negroes in given urban populations. The comparative "mal-integration" of these southern cities, as indicated by their higher crime rates, involves more, it seems, than racial cleavages alone. The fact remains, however, that among the disadvantaged and those whose aggressions are tolerated or encouraged by sizable groups, urban Negroes are disproportionately represented in the South.

Seen as a kind of deviant behavior, the "excessive" criminality of the urban South is one more evidence perhaps of the breakdown of the traditional way of life and the failure as yet to develop, for numerous southerners, a rewarding and socially acceptable substitute. Changes in the arrangements of people and place, and changes in matters of social hierarchy undoubtedly reflect shifts in respect to aspirations, values, and beliefs. It may well be that the hiatus between present needs and existing organizational facilities is greater in the urban South than in other sections of the country. Unquestionably, present-day urban organization is already vastly different from that of an earlier and more rural South. Are we not also witnessing a *reorganization* which over the next fifty years will yield an even more different way of life in the urban South?

CHAPTER SIX

Metropolitan Dominance and Integration

RUPERT B. VANCE AND SARA SMITH

Viewed in the national context, southern metropolises are small; they came late upon the scene and they developed on the edge of the great industrial concentration in the Northeast and Middle States. Except for their recent rapid growth, they are unremarkable cities. Human ecologists and students of urbanism in the United States have had little reason to study them. Viewed in the southern context, however, these metropolises are important because the functions which are concentrated in them exert an organizing influence upon the economic and social structure of the communities in their hinterlands. This chapter will be an exploratory attempt to trace the pattern of metropolitan dominance and integration in the South, the myriad nets of intercity relationships which extend from the smallest southern village through the larger cities to the super-metropolises outside the region.

Writers from the time of Aristotle have been aware of the influence of the great city upon its hinterland; but even now so little is known about the dynamics of this influence that metropolitanism must be defined descriptively. It is of course one aspect of the urbanization process. Urbanization in its minimal meaning is the concentration of population and human activities at focal points in space. This concentration proceeds in two ways simultaneously: the multiplying of the points of concentration and the accompanying increase in the size of the individual concentrations. With an increase in both number and size of the city-units, there comes about a territorial division of labor which can be described in much the same way as any division of labor. As differentiation of function develops, communities do not grow in accidental fashion but in terms of the strategic services they develop in relation to each other and to the primary sustenance activity of the area. Functional differentiation here as in other situations creates the necessity for some hierarchy of control; the city which by fortunate location or historical accident becomes the place where the institutions of control center tends to become the largest city—the metropolis— and its sphere of influence, the metropolitan community or region. Whereas urbanization may refer to any aspect of population ag- glomeration, metropolitanism should be reserved for the organiza- tional component that great cities impose upon the urbanization process. Any city with a large population is usually referred to as a metropolis, but it may be well to point out that while all metrop- olises are large cities, not all large cities are metropolises. Popula- tion size is a concomitant; function is the keynote.

N. S. B. Gras, the economic historian, has named the economy of the modern world "metropolitan economy" because of the crucial part played by the great cities in organizing and integrating the world's commercial, financial, and communication arrange- ments.[1] The first of the modern super-agglomerates—the capital markets of the world—developed around the North Sea in London, Berlin, and Paris; the second, for the Americas, grew up along the New York-Chicago axis; and the third developed in the Far East, dominated by Tokyo and Shanghai.[2] World War II has retarded the growth of the first and the third, but the New York-Chicago axis has continued to increase in importance.

As Gras explains, "A metropolitan economy is the organization of producers and consumers mutually dependent for goods and services, wherein their wants are supplied by a system of exchange concentrated in the large city, which is the focus of local trade and the center through which normal economic relations are established and maintained."[3] Implied in this definition are lines of integration tying the central city to other metropolitan centers outside its re- gion. Gras also emphasized the necessity of a sizeable and produc- tive hinterland; there must be a "respectful" distance from other great cities.

1. N. S. B. Gras, *An Introduction to Economic History* (New York: Harper and Brothers, 1922).
2. Giles A. Hubert, "A Framework for the Study of Peripheral Economic Areas," *Journal of Farm Economics*, XXVIII (August 1946), 807-808.
3. *Op. cit.*, p. 186.

The development of the metropolitan center, according to Gras, has four successive and overlapping phases. The first, and probably the basic one, is the *organization of the market*. The second is the *development of industry*, which in the nineteenth century gave such dramatic impetus to population concentration, centering wealth and power in the cities and adding greatly to the primary market function. The third phase, which is closely related to market organization and industrial development, is the *organization of transportation and communication facilities*. The fourth is the *development of financial organization*, the banking and corporate control within the metropolis which is necessary to make the region more independent and without which it will not attain economic maturity. These four developmental stages need not be described as a sequence; they are also a classification of the broad economic functions of the metropolis—distribution, manufacturing, transportation-communication, and finance. If we knew the exact balance and interrelationship of these required for a city to become a true metropolis, we would be closer to a real understanding of metropolitanism and would not be limited to a descriptive definition.

The classic study of the metropolitan community as it evolved in the United States is that by the human ecologist, R. D. McKenzie. This study, published twenty years ago, was the first empirical examination of the new "city regionalism" which, as McKenzie said, ". . . differs from the regionalism of former times in that it is the product of contact and division of labor rather than of mere geographic isolation." [4] McKenzie used the bio-social language of ecology to describe the competitive struggle among great cities for dominance and the adjustment process by which those that lost out in the process tended either to become integrated to the dominant metropolis by specialization or to die out, a symbiotic competition for survival similar to that in plant and animal "communities."

McKenzie showed that the particular spatial pattern of the dominant center and its dependent integrated communities in the United States owes much to the organization of modern transportation and communication, which has centralized the control of all types of

4. R. D. McKenzie, *The Metropolitan Community* (New York: McGraw-Hill, 1933), p. 113.

commodity handling in the larger cities.[5] The axiate spiderweb pattern of city location in most of the nation was laid down in the era of rail transport. Motor transportation, it appears, has not created a new spatial ordering of metropolises but has opened up hinterlands in such a way as to increase interdependence between the central city and its surrounding towns.[6] In a similar way air transport may now be tightening the integration among the dominant centers by providing an improved communication mode—the rapid transit of key personnel.

Location in relation to transportation may give one city initial advantage as a distribution point or industrial site. The larger its population becomes, the larger its local market, and thus the greater its competitive advantage.[7] In the twentieth century it is not so much industrial development that leads to population growth as it is a concentration of what McKenzie calls "center work," highly specialized distributive and control activities.[8] Once this concentration has begun, it becomes in itself an important factor in creating more concentration. As McKenzie says, ". . . once a city becomes established as a regional distributing center, its banking, transportation, and other facilities compel new concerns to select it for their point of operation. This cumulative process is one of the chief factors in explaining the recent rapid growth of many . . . cities." [9]

These statements of Gras and McKenzie have never been challenged; they have remained in the literature for years as illuminating but untested hypotheses. In 1949, however, Don J. Bogue took Gras and McKenzie's theory as the basis for a statistical analysis of the structure of the metropolitan community and established beyond doubt the *fact* of metropolitan dominance.[10] By an ingenious statistical method he found that cities over 100,000 in population (which

5. R. D. McKenzie, "Dominance and World Organization," *American Journal of Sociology*, XXXIII (July 1927), 30.

6. McKenzie, *The Metropolitan Community*, pp. 7, 93.

7. R. D. McKenzie, "The Rise of Metropolitan Communities," in *Recent Social Trends in the United States, Report of the President's Research Committee on Social Trends*, I (New York: McGraw-Hill, 1933), 455.

8. McKenzie, *The Metropolitan Community*, pp. 53, 89.

9. *Ibid.*, p. 164.

10. Don J. Bogue, *The Structure of the Metropolitan Community: A Study of Dominance and Subdominance* (Ann Arbor: University of Michigan Press, 1949).

he arbitrarily called "metropolises" without considering their
economic function) exert a consistent pattern of influence on the
distribution of population and sustenance activities in the area
surrounding them. This influence is direct for a certain distance,
roughly for the retail delivery area or the commuting zone; but
most of the influence is indirect and is closely related to the role
played by the surrounding cities and towns in mediating the controls of the central city.

Dominance therefore, according to Bogue, can be understood
only if one relates it to subdominance—successful competition of
those hinterland communities which accept the conditions imposed
by the dominant city.[11] Here is the empirical proof for Gras's
dictum that the keynote of the metropolitan economy is the functional interdependence of city and hinterland and for McKenzie's
analogy of the metropolitan region to a symbiotic "community,"
an organismic whole of differentiated parts. From Bogue's work it
is also possible to learn much about the effects of the size of the
metropolis and of distance from it on the spatial distribution of
population and activities related to dominance and subdominance.
Unfortunately his statistical size classes lifted the cities from their
specific areal context, making it impossible to apply his findings
directly to the metropolitan organization of any one geographical
region like the South.

In drawing the lines of metropolitan dominance and integration
in the South, the writers feel that it is better at the present state
of knowledge to be tentative and discursive. Any statistical findings
should be overlaid wih evidence about the cities from history,
geography, and applied economics. Certainly the first questions
to be answered are *how much* and *what kind* of metropolitan
development can one expect to find at the mid-twentieth century in
the South?

GENESIS OF THE PATTERN

In colonial America, where the most important urban function
was to get raw materials into the channels of world trade, the
larger cities were ports. The early struggle for metropolitan dominance was carried on between Boston, Philadelphia, and New York.

11. *Ibid.*, p. 18.

Boston led in population until 1750; in 1760 Philadelphia passed Boston, and by 1790 New York had passed Boston. Of the five cities of 8,000 or more population in the Census of 1790, only two—Baltimore and Charleston—were southern. Baltimore, gateway city to the South, offered some competition to New York's position at the end of the eighteenth century, but was soon relegated to secondary importance along with Boston and Philadelphia. Logically, Charleston with its fine harbor should have been a national contender against New York, but the collapse of Charleston's plan for a railroad to reach the rich resources of the Mississippi Valley finally forced it out of the running. Interestingly enough, New York's most serious rival in the 1800's was New Orleans, the only town in the United States with comparable inland water connections. In the steamboat period this city flourished even though its imports never equalled New York's. The outcome of the Civil War, however, settled the question. Since then, although New Orleans has often ranked as the nation's second port in tonnage, it has never risen to be a top-level metropolis. Once the east-west railroads had tapped the Mississippi Valley for New York, her ascendancy was assured. New Orleans had not felt the need of railways. Now the difference in the economic positions of New Orleans and Chicago can be gauged by the number of railroads entering each of the cities.

While it is impossible to determine when the pattern of metropolitan dominance was finally laid down in this country, once the New York-Chicago axis was formed, the supremacy of the northern metropolises over the southern was assured. It is doubtful that any of the southern cities could have won pre-eminence after the early nineteenth century, growing as they did under the shadow of the great.

In the ante-bellum plantation South there were four types of urban communities besides the sea ports—river ports, state capitals, county seats, and rural hamlets—all of which were small.[12] The early ocean ports were strictly limited by the size of the sustentation area they could count on with the prevailing mode of inland transportation. This led to the establishment of trading posts at the

12. *The South in the Building of the Nation. VI: Economic History, 1865-1909* (Richmond: The Southern Historical Publication Society, 1909), 607.

head of navigation, the fall line of the rivers. The list of these towns carries many familiar names: Richmond, Columbia, Augusta, Macon, Columbus, Montgomery, Selma. When river transport waned, many of these places continued to grow as markets. They were often the cotton collecting places and sometimes the state capitals.

It should not be forgotten that the patterning of urban location in the South took place under the domination of the cotton economy. Whereas financial control centered in several futures markets and in points of export like New Orleans, the actual buying, collecting, and storing of cotton was spread among many small communities around railroad stations, cotton gins, and crossroad stores. This resulted in very few large cities and many towns of even size rather than the sharply competitive grading of population in an industrialized area. In the reorganization of the cotton industry after the Civil War, the same trend can be noted. Thus in South Carolina the number of towns grew from 16 in 1860 to 493 in 1880; yet only three of the towns in 1880 had as many as 4,000 people.[13]

Because cotton was for so long oriented to world trade, the railroad network may not have had quite as determinate an effect on the actual territorial location of cities in the South as it did in the great interior of this nation, but rail transport has had a great influence on the factors which have caused some cities to grow and others to languish. In the early days, just where the tracks were laid made a difference; later the difference came in the way the freight rate structure was organized. In many cases railroads followed the river transportation routes and merely reinforced the positions of the fall line cities and ports. Sometimes the railroads changed the lines of integration. There was no national policy in railroad building and no national network was envisaged. Cities possessed of capital and local enterprise tried to make rail connections and to capture trade, leaving many gaps that were later remedied by captains of industry who functioned as system builders and consolidators. Thus in 1860 between the Baltimore and Ohio in the East and the Louisville and Nashville there was a 700-mile vacuum where not a single railroad cut across the Appalachians

13. E. Merton Coulter, *The South During Reconstruction* (Baton Rouge: Louisiana State University Press, 1947), p. 253.

to tie southern trade with the Middle West. The scheming of all the Atlantic coastline cities from Richmond to Savannah to be the terminus of such an east-west railroad is lost in history.[14] As the main rail lines did develop, they ran north and south along the Piedmont and truncated the hinterlands of the Atlantic coast cities, relegating these ports forever to second place and bringing the life-blood of trade to the market cities of the interior.

The gateways to Europe, the ports, were no longer as important as the rail gateways to the North and Middle States. An example of the bitter rivalry among cities to capture the southern trade was the railroad building feud between Louisville and Cincinnati in the 1870's. Louisville tried to interfere with Cincinnati's efforts to keep her position when the river trade was seized by the railroads by refusing to let her use the Louisville and Nashville and by blocking in the Kentucky legislature Cincinnati's request for a right of way for the railroad she wished to build to Chattanooga. A threat of Congressional action gave Cincinnati her chance in 1872; and when that railroad was completed in 1880, the great Appalachian barrier was finally pierced. Not only did Cincinnati get a good share of the trade from the South, but freight rates to the Middle West were reduced as much as 20 percent.[15] The location of gateway cities like Cincinnati and Richmond later became even more strategic when the regulations of the Federal Government on freight rates set them within Official Territory, the area of lower rates.

As any region develops its own productivity and economic complexity, the locus of metropolitan development shifts from the "gateway" cities to those in the interior which the German theorists have called "central place" cities. This began to happen in the South before 1860 in the organization of distribution laid down by the railroads. It is in this trend that we see the beginnings of the phenomenal development of the two great regional metropolises, Atlanta first and later Dallas.

Here is the genesis of Atlanta:

... In 1843 it was a railroad station on a hilltop in central Georgia. It was given rail connections with the seacoast in 1845. In 1850 it had a population of 2,372; in 1860, 9,554; in 1870, 21,789. ... [Located] on the broad interstream area of the Piedmont, to the south of the rough

14. *Ibid.*, p. 236.
15. *Ibid.*, p. 238.

mountain and gorge lands of the Southern Appalachians and opposite low-grade gaps across these highlands, it was central to most of the Southeast. Atlanta could have been a few score miles north, south, east or west of its present location and still be the active Atlanta that it is; but the placing of the southern terminus of the first railroad in northern Georgia, the Western and Atlantic, fixed its location and it became a crossroads of railroads in early 1850's when a line was built northwestward from Augusta and another from Atlanta to Montgomery.[16]

A depot for supplies and a seat of manufacturing for the Confederacy, Atlanta rose from its wartime destruction to become a central point in the main currents of traffic and the regional capital for national distributors.

Dallas in the Southwest, as Parkins points out, resembles Atlanta in its location and development. Growing up on broad flat plains in one of the most fertile sections of the Southwest, Dallas reached 10,000 population by 1880 and entered the census classification of cities over 100,000 in 1920. After Atlanta's old cotton lands had reached their maximum production, the lands of Dallas's sustenance area continued in their prime, and the riches of oil from under those soils did far more than cotton to make Dallas a major distribution center.

A city becomes a metropolis, writes Gras, ". . . when most kinds of products of the district concentrate in it for trade as well as transit, i.e., when these products are paid for by wares that radiate from it and when the financial transactions involved in the exchange are provided by it." [17] Thus far in discussing the historical development of the southern metropolises, we have paid attention to trade and transit. Now we must consider what manufacturing can mean to a city. The most dramatic example of the rise of an industrial center to metropolitan status is that of Birmingham. In 1870 it was a cotton field in which two railroads happened to cross, 167 rail miles from the thriving trade center, Atlanta. In 1876 pig iron was first made and in 1879 the Pratt mines of coking coal were opened. It was not until 1888 that Birmingham saw its first ton of steel run through the furnaces. The town then contained about 26,000 people. Today Birmingham is the South's one center of

16. Almon E. Parkins, *The South: Its Economic and Geographic Development* (New York: John Wiley and Sons, 1938), p. 461.
17. *Op. cit.*, p. 294.

heavy industry, has the largest amount of capital invested in manufacturing in the Southeast, and is the region's largest labor employment center. Coal, iron, limestone, cast iron pipe, steel and local manufactures have contributed to the city's position. Because of its manufacturing activities, Birmingham can be its own best market. Without this backlog of local buyers it could not have risen to metropolitan importance so close to Atlanta.

A consideration of the locational pattern of southern industry, however, makes Birmingham's centralization the exception rather than the rule. The well-chronicled recent movement of industry into the South has come about at a time when the combination of hydro-electric power and motor transport has permitted location in the areas around urban centers rather than in them. Bogue proved that if a metropolis can encourage industry within a radius of 45 miles it has the same effect for metropolitan dominance as location within the central city.[18] McKenzie's insight—that it is not production so much as the "center work" of production that fosters urban growth—is nowhere better proved than in the development of Charlotte in an area where industrial plants are scattered over the countryside.

Only within recent years has the South pulled far enough out of its colonial economy to develop much financial organization within the region. Most important in this connection has been the effect of a legislated change—the establishment of the Federal Reserve system in 1914, which provided 12 regional cities with bankers' banks in which reserves against deposits were to be kept. The selection of these centers was on the basis of the "flow of trade" and the urban connections of the small town banks. Whatever mistakes the decision-makers made have been obliterated by the fact that once a city became a regional capital of finance, the flow of trade actually went its way. Federal Reserve cities have had increases in bankers' balances with some repatriation of funds from the New York money market. This has meant lowered interest rates for these communities, a factor which seems of special importance in the higher order distribution (wholesale trade) which is central to metropolitan function. It is also agreed that the system has made for greater elasticity of credit in the movement of regional crops and products and that, as a result, the smaller cities have

18. *Op. cit.*, p. 183.

been tied more closely to the selected financial centers. In the South this has meant a closer tie with Richmond, Atlanta, and Dallas within the region of our study and with St. Louis and Kansas City on its northern edge. The Federal Reserve Branch cities which channel this integration for the South are listed by districts in Table 1.

TABLE 1. Federal Reserve Banks and Branches for the South

RICHMOND	ATLANTA	DALLAS	ST. LOUIS	KANSAS CITY
Charlotte	Birmingham	El Paso	Little Rock	Oklahoma City
	Jacksonville	San Antonio	Louisville	
	Nashville	Houston	Memphis	
	New Orleans			

In all this fragmentary historical evidence of the genesis of the pattern may be found the answers to the question posed earlier: *how much* and *what kind* of metropolitan development may one expect in the South of 1950? It is evident that southern metropolises, no matter how rapidly they are now growing, will be smaller than the giants of the New York-Chicago axis because in all specialized functions they are subdominant to these super-metropolises (as in fact is the whole nation). Any change in their general position in the metropolitan hierarchy is unlikely, for it is in the nature of dominance that once it is gained it reinforces itself and sets down a remarkably stable pattern. Meanwhile modifications in the balance of power will continue as the South moves toward economic maturity. The location of industry may modify the kind of constellation these southern cities make when they are considered as a regional unit; but a glance at any map shows that here are no huge industrial satellites crowding the greater cities. Instead there have grown up a number of well-spaced, fairly evenly populated, middle-sized centers which should have considerable autonomy over their surrounding areas, the pattern set down by the market towns of the old agricultural economy.

THE PRESENT-DAY PATTERN

A second important question concerns the individual cities: which of the larger ones may be considered metropolises in 1950 and how do they rank in the dominance they exert? The writers have explored this question with a simple statistical technique which is their own but which is grounded in the suggestions of the theorists and in prior research.

In reviewing the methods used in determining the metropolitan centers of the United States, we find that except for one British geographer, writers have been content to name the Federal Reserve Bank cities and the cities where the Branch Banks are located. Actually this may be as good a rough classification as any simply because financial organization tends to set a capstone on the distributive and control functions crucial to dominance. Gras limited his list of metropolises to 11 of the Federal Reserve cities—the metropolises of the South, therefore, being Richmond, Atlanta, and Dallas. McKenzie, interested in the territorial limits of metropolitan regions, used the circulation areas of great city newspapers as his single index. The basis of his list of metropolises was the Federal Reserve Bank and Branch cities with an occasional Branch city omitted and others added to follow newspaper areas. In the region of our interest, Knoxville was the only addition to the list of Bank and Branch centers (Table 1) and San Antonio was omitted.[19]

The close relation of these banking centers with wholesale trade has already been pointed out. The market research carried on by the Department of Commerce in the 1920's named as southern wholesale trade centers all the Bank and Branch cities, adding to them only Knoxville and Chattanooga for the Southeast and Fort Worth for the Southwest.[20] The definitive mapping of trade areas done under the NRA in the early 1930's used the Federal Reserve sub-districts, adjusted somewhat to geographical barriers, lines of transport, etc., as wholesale trade areas.[21] This juxtaposition of bankers' banks with specialized distribution seems to point to the heart of metropolitan dominance. In fact, Dorothy Hope Tisdale, in a statistical analysis of the factors involved in urbanization, found the correlation between the higher-order distributive factor (wholesale trade) and the growth of very large cities to be about twice as high as between such growth and the lower-order distribution

19. McKenzie, *The Metropolitan Community*.
20. U.S. Department of Commerce, *Market Data Handbook* (Washington, D.C.: Government Printing Office, 1927).
21. Robert A. Dier, *Natural Areas of Trade in the United States* (Washington: Office of NRA, Division of Review, February 1936).

(retail trade) and production.[22] Bogue found that wholesale sales per capita in the metropolitan centers were seven times those of the hinterland, a degree of concentration far greater than in the other basic sustenance activities he investigated—retail trade, services, and manufacturing.[23]

Dickinson, the British geographer, in his attempt to outline metropolitan regions independent of the Federal Reserve districts, centered his method on the volume of wholesale trade per capita, which he weighted with the volume of manufacturing and two ingenious indices: warehousing space and the number of branch offices listed in Thomas's *Register of Manufacturers*. He came out with a smaller list than McKenzie and with two orders of magnitude. Atlanta and Dallas with Fort Worth were top-level; Birmingham, Jacksonville, Louisville, Memphis, New Orleans, Richmond, and Houston were the secondary metropolises.[24] This has been the most sophisticated attempt to differentiate the true metropolises from the other large cities; but it is twenty years old.

The meager research that has been focused on this problem is perhaps as helpful in pointing out what *not* to do as in providing positive suggestions. There is no question that the most important index to metropolitan status is the concentration of wholesale trade, but it seems that efforts to mark off the areal limits of dominance by either trade or the closely associated newspaper circulation has meant too literal a tie to territory for the different contingencies on space involved in metropolitan influence. In certain specialized functions the whole United States may well be the hinterland of one city. On the level of consumer buying, the trade area marked off with pins on a map makes sense, but not for the complexities of economic structure. For this reason no attempt will be made here to outline the area of dominance of each city as has been done heretofore. The assumption is that the extent of influence will be at least crudely reflected in the volume of the activity in the central city. It seems better to use several indices than a single index if for no other reason than the tradition of "safety in numbers." It also

22. Dorothy Hope Tisdale, Urbanization: A Study of Population Concentration in the United States and its Relation to Social Change (unpublished doctoral dissertation, University of North Carolina, 1942), p. 129.

23. *Op. cit.*, p. 173.

24. Robert E. Dickinson, "Metropolitan Regions of the United States," *Geographical Review*, XXIV (1934), 278-286.

seems advisable not to *assume* that the Federal Reserve Bank and Branch cities are the metropolitan centers before investigating their influence. Nor should it be assumed that the largest cities are necessarily the metropolises; here we should use Gras's insight that the size of certain functions and not the size of the population is crucial.

To rank southern cities in their metropolitan function, six indices related to dominance have been selected. The first is *Wholesale Sales* (*1948*). The second, *Business Services Receipts* (*1948*), concerns the most specialized type of service which is used by larger concerns, defined in the census as including advertising, consumer credit, adjustment and collection agencies, news syndicates, mailing lists, machine rental and repair, telephone answering, etc. In a sense this measures the degree of specialization, the premise being that the metropolis is the most specialized community of its area and thus the least typical.[25] The third, taken from Dickinson, *Number of Branch Offices*, is an excellent index of the channeling function Gras stressed in his definition. All of the first three factors stress high-level distribution, specialization, and control; and in the construction of the rank-score from the six indices, they are weighted two to one. (The statistical findings of Tisdale and Bogue substantiate this.) The remaining three indices, each with a weight of one, are *Retail Sales* (not a metropolitan specialty but an index of size), *Bank Clearings* (used as an index of business activity which also reveals the presence of Federal Reserve Banks), and *Value Added by Manufacturing* (the most sensitive index of the volume rather than the type of industrial activity). Except perhaps for Bank Clearings of Federal Reserve cities, these last three indices reflect the gross underpinnings a city has for building its market and amassing wealth.

The 29 metropolitan areas of the South which contain central cities of 100,000 and over were chosen as the most likely candidates for metropolitan status. They were ranked according to the six indices. So that their relative positions in each factor would be strictly comparable, z-scores using the standard deviation were constructed for each index; those of the first three indices were weighted by two; the weighted z-scores (actually accurate rank-scores) were converted to make all of them positive numbers,

25. Bogue, *op. cit.*, p. 61.

added, and then divided by six to arrive at an average rank-score for *Metropolitan Function*. This score for each of the 29 metropolitan areas can be seen by consulting the first column of Table 2. To point up the difference between size of metropolitan function and population size, a similarly constructed rank-score for size of

TABLE 2. Cities of Over 100,000 in the South, Ranked by Metropolitan Function

City	Rank Score on Metropolitan Function	Rank Score on Size
SECOND ORDER METROPOLISES		
Atlanta	9.91	6.67
Dallas	9.71	6.38
THIRD ORDER METROPOLISES		
Houston	8.10	7.43
New Orleans	7.36	6.77
Memphis	6.62	5.67
Louisville	6.43	6.18
Birmingham	5.94	6.07
SUBDOMINANTS with METROPOLITAN CHARACTERISTICS		
Richmond	5.34	4.83
Fort Worth	5.24	5.00
Oklahoma City	5.02	4.81
* Miami	4.90	5.71
Charlotte	4.80	4.11
Jacksonville	4.79	4.70
Tulsa	4.60	4.40
Nashville	4.59	4.79
Little Rock	4.54	4.09
* San Antonio	4.48	5.75
* Norfolk-Portsmouth	4.42	5.28
El Paso	4.38	4.12
SUBDOMINANTS		
Tampa-St. Petersburg	4.18	5.26
Chattanooga	4.11	4.38
Knoxville	3.84	4.88
Shreveport	3.62	4.00
Mobile	3.54	4.29
Savannah	3.46	3.87
Corpus Christi	3.30	3.94
Montgomery	3.25	3.79
Baton Rouge	3.25	3.90
Austin	3.19	3.92

* Miami because of its resort function and San Antonio and Norfolk-Portsmouth because of military installations probably rank somewhat higher than their basic metropolitan function would place them. They are essentially Subdominants.

population is given in the second column. The relation of these two factors for each city is shown in simple graphic form in Figure 1.

The most certain finding yielded by this method is that Atlanta and Dallas with similar scores on metropolitan function stand head and shoulders above the other cities. There is no doubt about their being the regional capitals. These two cities have been classified as Second Order Metropolises, with the idea that the First Order Metropolis has a nation-wide sphere of influence. A glance at Figure 1 will show that the selection of the Third Order Metropolises might be questioned. Houston, New Orleans, Memphis, and Louisville rank high enough to be considered dominant cities of this class. The question is whether one should include Birmingham and not the Federal Reserve city, Richmond. The evidence of the indices taken singly points to a decline in Richmond's metropolitan function. Only in Bank Clearings and Value Added by Manufacturing does it rank within the first nine cities; its proximity to Baltimore, Philadelphia, and New York means subdominance in many functions. It may be too that the remarkable emergence of Charlotte is infringing on the hinterland of Richmond. Certainly Richmond's metropolitan position must be considered more marginal than it has been in the past.

Class III, which has been named Subdominants with Metropolitan Characteristics, includes a number of smaller cities which have important distributive and control functions over considerable area and which have the balance in specialization associated with metropolitanism: Richmond, Fort Worth, Oklahoma City, Charlotte, Nashville, Little Rock, and on the geographic fringe, El Paso. Although their scores were fairly high, consideration of their distorted size and specialization should remove Miami, the resort city, and San Antonio and Norfolk-Portsmouth, areas of military installations, to Class IV as Subdominants. It should be noted, however, that Norfolk-Portsmouth is a strong center of wholesale trade and might well qualify for Class III. Class IV is residual as far as metropolitan function is concerned. What is interesting here as well as in Class III is the evenness of the scores. One wonders if there may be very little difference between these urban centers and some of the industrial and distribution centers with populations between 50,000 and 100,000: Roanoke, Winston-Salem, Greensboro, Columbia, Macon—to name a few. In fact, if one looks at the 22 cities

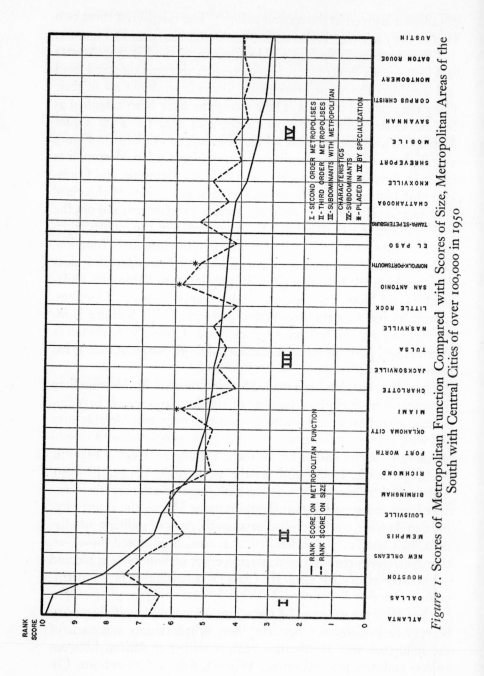

Figure 1. Scores of Metropolitan Function Compared with Scores of Size, Metropolitan Areas of the South with Central Cities of over 100,000 in 1950

that have been classified as Subdominants, their independence is striking; not one is a really dependent satellite.

Worthy of note here is the high rank of Fort Worth in metropolitan characteristics. Only 33 miles from Dallas, it has managed by organizing the hinterland to the north and west to resemble in dominance a traditional metropolis like Richmond. Dallas and Fort Worth taken together surpass all the cities of the Southeast in their potential. Houston, startling in its rapid development, has taken command as the specialized point of export for the rich oil industry of Texas and Oklahoma. From the day its inland ship channel cut off the growth of Galveston, Houston has offered New Orleans strong competition as a gulf port. Houston has played its important role without blocking the continual development of Dallas and Fort Worth, illustrating again the values of specialization among metropolises. Here an examination of the difference in the import-export trade of New Orleans and Houston would probably explain how they manage to live together.

It seems that we can place some confidence in this method of selecting the metropolitan centers of the region because the seven cities which qualified—Atlanta, Dallas, Houston, New Orleans, Memphis, Louisville, and Birmingham—are the only ones which have qualified in *every* other attempt to delineate metropolises. The most significant finding, however, is that the pattern of dominance in the South is not nearly as marked as the pattern of strong subdominance. Here we may have caught the emerging urban configuration of the twentieth century. Southern cities are growing in the time of hydro-electric power and motor and air transport. The nation is under the shadow of the kind of air attack that may force some modification of the nineteenth century concentration in the Northeast. The division of labor that is being worked out in the Piedmont of the Carolinas does not involve heavy industry; but it bears watching, as does the little city of Charlotte which already is more of a metropolis than some larger rivals. And of course Charlotte cannot be understood unless one considers its interdependence with Greenville, Winston-Salem, High Point, Greensboro, etc.

In Figure 2, the constellation of cities has been moored to territory so that it is possible to trace the major lines of integration. The great Appalachian barrier set the spatial pattern early in the

South's history. Transportation lanes run south to north, toward New York in the east and toward Chicago west of the mountains. The Dallas-Fort Worth metropolitan region is oriented to the Chicago-New York axis through St. Louis and Kansas City. On this map-like diagram, one can also see the vacuum out of which Memphis was able to carve a hinterland. The orientation of the South's great ports—like Houston and New Orleans—to intercoastal traffic is indicated by the broken lines.

THE METROPOLIS AND ITS HINTERLAND

Metropolitan regionalism involves more than the relation of dominance and subdominance among great cities. In the organization of its hinterland, the metropolis extends its sway through subdominant centers to the smallest hamlet and rural homestead within its orbit. In the New South as elsewhere, the metropolis is related to its region in the way it integrates communities of different size, position, and function. Here each center plays a distinct and necessary role and the region itself can be thought of as a constellation of communities.[26]

What processes have been operating here and what changes have occurred in the South within the recent period? As elsewhere, men, activities and products are being drawn into closer relations with central cities and transportation has brought rural life more under the dominance of the metropolis. Warren Wilson once drew the radius of the farm trade center, the basic unit in this hierarchy, as the distance of a day's team haul. The extension of this radius by means of the auto, truck, and hard-surfaced highway created a new pattern of market and service areas. Rural people are tied in with more trading centers and have a wider element of choice and variety; the remaining centers have a broader population base and appear more closely related to one another and to dominant metropolitan centers than they did three decades ago.

For the smaller rural centers the problem at times, as H. C. Nixon points out, has seemed to be one of survival. In a Louisiana study T. Lynn Smith found that trade centers less favorably situated in regard to trade and transportation had been smothered out of

26. Radhakamal Mukerjee, *Social Ecology* (New York: Longmans, Green and Company, 1945), p. 87.

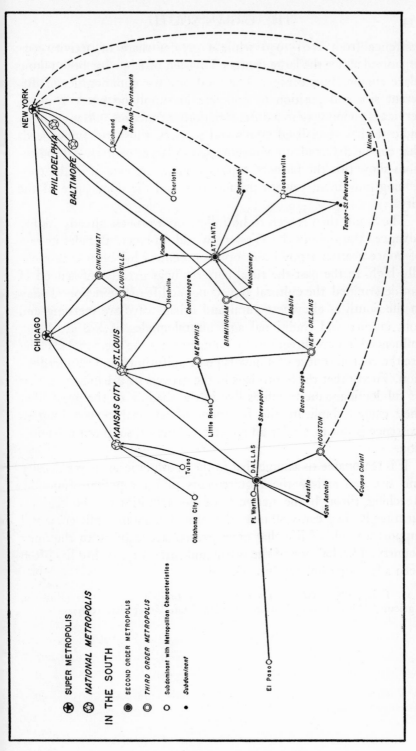

Figure 2. Metropolitan Organization of the South, with Orders of Dominance and Major Lines of Integration

SUPER METROPOLIS

NATIONAL METROPOLIS

IN THE SOUTH

SECOND ORDER METROPOLIS

THIRD ORDER METROPOLIS

Subdominant with Metropolitan Characteristics

Subdominant

existence from 1901-1930 while a greater share of activity was organized about the large centers. Division of labor has been taking place among these centers. The tendency for communities of different size and position to compete in supplying every type of service is giving way to a differentiation of function.[27] Many studies indicate that specialized goods and services, those satisfying needs that can be deferred, are concentrated in larger centers. All indications show that the farmers' trading centers are caught in the continuing movement toward urbanization and the dominance of the city.

The South then is seen to be following a process already highly advanced throughout the Western world. In recent decades its rate of concentration around metropolitan centers has been exceptionally high. In the past the rural patterns have greatly influenced, if not determined, the cultural and economic life of the region. Today in the South as elsewhere rural and urban ways are merging and folk culture and traditional agricultural modes of life are being influenced in new directions by contacts with the metropolis. Cities are the central source of a new type of uniformity and standardization. To say that the South lags in the process of urbanization, that its subdominant metropolises live in the shadow of the great, that they cannot duplicate the functions of national centers long in existence is not to render an adverse verdict on southern urbanization.

It is reasonable to assume that in the South cities of lesser density and size can satisfy the requirements of metropolitan function. Reaching through the network of communities to the region's farmsteads, they can well meet the tests of economic efficiency and support a mode of life that gives greater accessibility to the open country. This balance of the urban and rural ways of life has often been advocated but rarely achieved.

27. T. Lynn Smith, *Farm Trade Centers in Louisiana, 1901-1931* (Bulletin, Agricultural Experiment Station, Louisiana State University, 1936).

CHAPTER SEVEN

The Ecology of Southern Cities

NICHOLAS J. DEMERATH AND
HARLAN W. GILMORE

THE ARRANGEMENTS of people—their groupings, institutions, activities, and artifacts—on the land and in time constitute the subject matter of human ecology. With reference to urban places, these arrangements may be analyzed *between* cities (together with their respective hinterlands) as Vance and Smith have done in the preceding chapter. Or, as we shall attempt to do here, ecological phenomena may be studied *within* particular urban areas. From the former comes an "inter-urban" or regional ecology and from the latter comes an "intra-urban" ecology. In both instances, ecological arrangements constitute an important dimension of urban organization.

Like all products of man, cities originate and change in response to human needs, the needs of persons and groups. In relation to human needs cities get their dynamic and their *raison d'être*. Consequently, among the most fundamental questions to be raised in respect to cities are the questions of function: What do cities do? How do they do it? What human ends or needs are served? What is the consequence of one activity for another? Nothing like definitive answers to these questions are possible on the basis of present scientific knowledge. Some general clues or "hunches" may be derived from economic data and common observation, and to these we turn for evidence of the unknown as much as for the known.

THE FUNCTIONS AND "GOODNESS" OF SOUTHERN CITIES

One of the more obvious things about southern cities is that they "do" different things. They tend to specialize in certain activities and, accordingly, get their reputations and their renown. That is, cities get tagged and stereotyped so that certain functions and related physical characteristics, events, or customs are immediately brought to mind at the mere mention, say, of New Orleans, Miami, Birmingham, Memphis, Atlanta, or Tuscaloosa. Just as cities are commonly differentiated according to what they do as units in a larger economy and society, so are they compared according to the range and quality of functions and facilities which they offer their residents. The southerner who has "been around," or who is nostalgic for his favorite city, likes nothing better than a lively discussion of which city has the better hotels, restaurants, night clubs, houses, parks, offices, hospitals, schools, and physicians, for example.

Viewing the activities of southern cities a little more systematically, one can distinguish two sets of functions according to their range and extent. First, one observes *general urban functions* serving both country and city people, rural and urban residents alike. These are the functions through which southern people even in the more remote Louisiana bayous, Tennessee coves, and Florida glades come to participate in the world economy and the urban civilization of the West and, increasingly, the world. These are the ties that bind together far-flung metropolitan regions, as well as smaller urban areas and hinterlands, in the patterns of integration and dominance so well described by Vance and Smith in Chapter 6. They include: (1) wholesale distribution, (2) retail distribution, (3) manufacturing, (4) mining, (5) specialized and higher education, (6) specialized medical care, (7) urban recreation, (8) resort and retirement. In addition, southern cities perform four "headquarters" functions whose importance is far greater than their employment figures indicate: (9) transportation, (10) finance, (11) communication, and (12) government.

Second, one can also identify *local urban functions* that serve directly only those who reside in cities and their daily commuting areas: (1) employment, (2) residence, (3) retail shopping, (4) local government, (5) religious affiliation, (6) ordinary health-welfare-recreation-education, (7) heat-light-water-waste disposal, (8) local transportation, (9) informal associations, and (10) civic identity. This second set of urban functions stands in mutual dependence with the first. Without the economic base provided by the performance of one or more general functions, no city can long exist. In this sense local functions depend on the general functions. On the other hand, the performance of general functions is impossible without personnel and facilities whose needs are served by local functions.

Local and general functions are not easily distinguished within given cities. That they may be so distinguished, however, Hoyt and others have demonstrated on the basis of economic statistics for a few northern cities.[1]

Harris has developed a scheme for classifying American cities of more than 10,000 population according to their most important economic activity or function, determined by employment statistics. His nine categories parallel our general functions, except for the addition of "diversified," and the omission of finance, communication, government, and medical care, none of which bulk large enough employment-wise, presumably, to constitute a useful category for purposes of his classification. Applied to the cities of Odum's Southeast, a tabulation of Harris's data gives the distribution shown in Table 1.[2]

It should be noted that the South does have cities of all types as classified by Harris. However, only one-fourth (26 percent) of the cities were classed as manufacturing towns and only one city had mining as its dominant function. The vast majority of the cities reflect the fact that the South has been dominantly an agricultural region and the cities of the region get their livelihood by performing merchandising, transportation, governmental, and educational

1. H. Hoyt, *The Economic Status of the New York Region* (New York: Regional Plan Association, 1944).

2. C. D. Harris, "A Functional Classification of Cities in the United States," *Geographical Review*, 33 (January 1943), pp. 86-99.

"Diversified" means employment in manufacturing, wholesaling, and retailing is less than 60 percent, 20 percent, and 50 percent respectively of the total employment in these activities. (In such cities manufacturing and mechanical industries generally contain between 25 percent and 35 percent of the gainful workers.) The principal criterion of "Manufacturing—Dominant" is that employment in manufacturing equals at least 74 percent of total employment in manufacturing, retailing, and wholesaling. In the case of "Manufacturing—Secondary," manufacturing employment equals at least 60 percent of total employment in manufacturing, retailing, and wholesaling. Other definitions and criteria detailed in Harris's article are omitted here to save space.

TABLE 1. Southeastern Cities of more than 10,000 Population in 1940
Classified by Predominant Economic Activity; General
Location and Examples

Type of City	Number	Percent	General Location and Examples
TOTAL	146	100.0	
Diversified	35	24.0	Scattered inland: Richmond, Columbus, Nashville, Little Rock
Manufacturing			Highland area between coastal plain and
Dominant	19	13.0	mountains in Virginia, N. C., S. C.,
Secondary	19	13.0	Ga., Ala.: Thomasville, North Carolina
Retailing	18	12.3	Scattered inland: Shreveport
Educational	13	8.9	Scattered: Baton Rouge, Durham, Athens, Tuscaloosa
Transportation	12	8.3	Mostly on coast plus rail centers inland: Mobile, New Orleans, Norfolk, Monroe, La., Meridian, Miss.
State capitals	11	7.4	Scattered: Raleigh
Resort-Retirement	10	6.8	Coasts, mountains: Palm Beach, Miami, Biloxi, Hot Springs
Wholesaling	8	5.6	Scattered: Hopkinsville, Wilson, Suffolk
Mining	1	0.7	West Virginia: Morgantown

functions. If Harris had included smaller cities in his study, these
types undoubtedly would have been still more evident. Even so,
it is clear that southern cities do differ from each other in major
economic functions and fewer southern cities have manufacturing
as their dominant function than is true of cities in some other sections of the country. The major economic function certainly bears
a relation to the occupational composition of the population and
probably to numerous other social and ecological characteristics.
Thus, since southern cities differ considerably from each other in
these major functions, we may conclude that there is no "one and
only" ecological pattern for the southern city.

Though one may quarrel with the classification of some cities—
like Baton Rouge and Durham—and though numerous questions of
greater discrimination can be phrased, this classification of southern
cities by general economic functions points the way to a much
better understanding of the ecology of different cities than we now
have. This will become apparent when we turn to considerations
of ecological pattern and process.

Before leaving the consideration of urban functions, we would mention another line of research dealing particularly with local functions and in some instances pertaining to southern cities. It is often argued that some cities are "better places to live" than others. As frequent observations in this vein confirm, "better" or "worse" refers typically to the range and quality of employment opportunities, housing, retail stores, government services, schools, recreation facilities, and the rest of the local urban functions and related facilities which we have already noted.

Social scientists have begun to collect the facts and measure such differences. Here it is impossible to treat the details of these investigations, but we would call attention to some of the more suggestive observations of southern cities. Thorndike, attempting to measure the "goodness" of 117 cities (over 30,000 population in 1930) in terms of 10 major indices, found that southern cities ranked lowest, with Augusta and Columbus, Georgia, High Point, North Carolina, and Charleston, South Carolina, at the bottom.[3] Roterus investigated "well-being" and the effects of population growth and non-growth. Nashville, Chattanooga, Fort Worth, and New Orleans were included in a group of nine cities which had a moderate rate of growth and enjoyed certain advantages over non-growing cities.[4] Spengler, using 1930 census data, found that while the rural South is an important seedbed of future population, a disproportionate share of the population increment was to be found in counties lying within 25-mile radii of southern cities with populations of 100,000 or more. This milieu was not suited "to bring out the potentialities of the human product." Much of it included inferior land described earlier by the National Resources Board as "too poor to provide adequate family living and support public institutions and services." [5] Hawley's analysis of 1935 Census of Business data points to some of the determinants of "good" and "bad" places to live. Income is the most important variable; the higher the income, the greater the "volume" of urban services.

3. E. L. Thorndike, *Your City* (New York: Harcourt, Brace, 1939).

4. V. Roterus, "Effects of Population Growth and Non-Growth on the Well-Being of Cities," *American Sociological Review*, 11 (February 1946), pp. 90-97.

5. J. J. Spengler, "Population Problems in the South—Part II," *Southern Economic Journal*, IV (July 1937), 1-27.

The presence of manufacturing on a large scale, however, was found associated with poor urban services.[6] It is not known what relation these differences bear to ecological patterns; but it would be no surprise if cities which rank low on the Thorndike Scale, for instance, have more housing in slum areas than those which rank high on the scale.

THE VARIETY OF SOUTHERN CITIES:

FORM AND FUNCTION

It is a well-known principle of science that function depends on structure and vice versa. To discharge its functions, to meet the needs of people in its service area, every city must possess an appropriate ecological structure or form. This structure consists of a physical order and a related social order seen in physical dimension. Buildings, streets, open spaces, tools, machinery, and equipment, their sites and locational relationships are the elements of the *physical order*. That these elements must be articulated is a prerequisite set by societal requirements, on the one hand, and by considerations of natural environment on the other. It is this articulated natural and man-made physical environment that constitutes the physical order of every city.

The *social order*, which in physical dimension is a component of ecological structure, is composed of concrete persons located, related, differentiated, and using material equipment in physical space to meet human needs according to cultural design. Physical and social orders are mutually dependent: each imposes limitations on the other, and each depends on the other. By no means *all* of social order or "social structure" is here conceived as part of ecological structure. On the contrary we refer only to those phenomena which have location in physical space as a significant datum, such as economic activities or residential segregation by race, a subject we shall consider later.

Little is known scientifically about the modes of relationship between these physical and social orders. The pioneer work of Merton, Festinger, and Kuper in studying relations between neighbors as these are affected by the site plans of various housing projects is

6. Amos Hawley, "An Ecological Study of Urban Service Institutions," *American Sociological Review*, 6 (October 1941), pp. 629-639.

worthy of note in this connection.[7] And Hughes' observations regarding the spatial aspects of institutions point toward still another mode of relationship between physical and social orders, physical space and "social space." [8]

Despite ignorance of the particulars of physical-social relatedness, we have some knowledge of the general connections between urban functions and ecological structures. Just as common observation discloses that southern cities "do" different things, so do we observe that cities "look" different in some respects and alike in others. The local functions through which cities do their "housekeeping" are quite uniform in many ways. Physical plants, tools, and locational relations are likewise very much the same from one city to another. So uniform are they in fact that an urban dweller on a cross-country tour feels relatively at home in any town he passes through. It is a rare town that is different enough in any of its local functions and facilities, particularly in its downtown sections, to attract attention. Where such differences do occur, as in the French restaurants of New Orleans, they are apt to be tourist meccas, known far and wide, and thus facilitate a general function.

Distinctive ecological structures are more often linked with the general functions by which cities earn their living, as it were, rather than with local functions. Manufacturing cities differ from college towns. Birmingham with its coal and steel complex symbolized by Vulcan's statue is a vastly different city from New Orleans with its port and its past. So do Thomasville and its furniture differ from Chapel Hill and its University. The "company town," often a city without municipal government or a specialized area within a city (as in Greensboro or Columbia, for example), is the manufacturing product *par excellence*. Built for industrial workers, owned and operated by a single company, these sometimes urban phenomena—so important in an earlier period of southern industry—are slowly disappearing. Where they are absorbed by

7. R. K. Merton, "The Social Psychology of Housing," in *Current Trends in Social Psychology* (Pittsburgh: University of Pittsburgh Press, 1948), pp. 163-217; L. Festinger, S. Schachter, and K. Back, *Social Pressures in Informal Groups* (New York: Harper, 1950); L. Kuper et al., *Living in Towns* (London: Cresset Press, 1953).

8. E. C. Hughes, "The Ecological Aspects of Institutions," *American Sociological Review*, 1 (April 1936), pp. 180-189.

growing cities nearby, they leave their imprint ecologically long after company ownership has passed.

Miami's resort function has stamped its ecology unmistakably as hotels, apartments, restaurants, night clubs, dog tracks, etc., have mushroomed in a semi-tropical coastal setting not exactly to nature's advantage. In recent years, however, as Miami has become more diversified, more specialized sections have developed in the metropolitan area and Miami Beach has probably become more and more "the" center of the tourist trade. New Orleans is stamped by its port activity and, related thereto, by the heterogeneity of its people—quite conspicuous in a homogeneous South whose ethnic and racial monotony is relieved only by the Negro.

Similarities no less than differences in ecological structures are also attributable to predominant general functions. The large diversified cities like Atlanta, Dallas, Richmond, and Nashville resemble one another in office buildings, hotels, theaters and auditoriums, the arrangement of specialized areas, and in other matters noted subsequently. So do the port cities (Jacksonville, Mobile, Norfolk, Wilmington, Charleston, New Orleans) and railroad centers (Monroe, Meridian). Other cities with the same predominant activity display similar ecological structures.

The dominant type of southern city has been and still is the small city, and it has a more or less distinctive ecological structure. Important as these small cities are in the South's economy, and desirable as they may be to their citizens and to city planners, they have been almost entirely neglected by students of urban ecology. Ecological researches have dealt principally with larger cities and rural communities.

So far as its source of livelihood is concerned, the small city is more frequently and to a greater degree a one-function town than is the large city. Most of the South's small cities are mercantile and service centers for surrounding agricultural areas, educational centers, government seats, factory towns, or mining towns. Numerically speaking, the mercantile and service cities are perhaps the most typical. Until the coming of the automobile and all-weather highway about thirty years ago, these towns functioned as the collection and shipping centers for the agricultural commodities produced for export in their rural hinterlands, as the retail shopping centers of these rural areas for semi-durable and luxury goods, and as wholesale centers for staple commodities like groceries and work clothing. They were comparatively diversified.

With the coming of the automobile and all-weather road, the retail merchandising function of these small cities became more and more important. Many of these towns have also gained importance as centers for various professional and skilled services. At the same time, of course, the automobile has also meant the eclipse of many small centers whose functions were relegated in large part to other cities which have grown and flourished consequently. Towns that had been made by the railroad were undone by the automobile. Prior to the automobile, furthermore, there was a relatively complete concentration of business in the central business district of these small cities. In recent years considerable dispersion has occurred, just as in the big and new cities.

THE PARTS OF SOUTHERN CITIES AND
HOW THEY CHANGE

By far the greater number of ecological studies deal with ecological structure in non-functional terms. Considerations of change and process, like considerations of function, also tend to be treated incidentally or neglected altogether. Studies of southern cities are no exception. They have followed in the conceptual and methodological footsteps of orthodox ecology and the "Chicago School." The "revisionists" have had little perceptible influence as yet on southern city research.[9] The studies nevertheless contain reliable if incomplete descriptive accounts of the structural features of a number of southern cities which permit a certain amount of comparative analysis, particularly in the few instances where the hypotheses of orthodox ecology have been examined.

No ecological hypothesis has attracted greater attention among investigators than the *concentric zone* hypothesis, suggested by

9. By "Chicago School" we refer to the earlier formulations and methods of ecology as they were developed and applied by R. E. Park, E. W. Burgess, to some extent R. D. McKenzie, and others associated with the Department of Sociology at the University of Chicago. By "revisionists" we refer to M. A. Alihan, *Social Ecology* (New York: Columbia University, 1938); Walter Firey, *Land Use in Central Boston* (Cambridge: Harvard University Press, 1947); and others who call for a more sociologistic ecology and who are critical of earlier naturalistic ("symbiotic") emphases.

Hurd in 1911 and later detailed by Burgess. Accordingly, cities are said to expand from the center outward, and the several areas of segregated and specialized land use and activities tend to form a pattern of concentric circles or zones. From (1) the central business district outward, there is (2) the zone in transition (or interstitial area) with wholesaling, slum housing, and light manufacturing, (3) the zone of "respectable" workingmen's homes and heavy manufacturing, (4) high-class apartment and better residence zones, and (5) the suburban or commuters' zone.[10] Questions of empirical generalization as to the "parts" of cities, their regularity and patterning, are thus raised without direct reference, however, to the underlying dynamics of urban development which may best be conceived perhaps in functional terms. Although this hypothesis has been examined for a few of the larger cities in the South and in the border states, no comparisons of the structures of different types of cities, classed functionally or otherwise, are possible from the literature. Nor are comparisons possible between cities at the same stage of development, another important variable.

Gilmore observes that in the case of New Orleans, within the limits imposed by the natural barriers of river and swamp, the drainage system, and altered transit facilities, the city has been assuming "the more usual" concentric zone pattern since 1917, whereas previously New Orleans displayed a "T" shaped configuration.[11] Hoyt cites Baltimore, particularly before 1904, as a good example of this sort of growth and pattern—"central growth," as he calls it. At the same time he observes that New Orleans has also grown radially, expanding along the bend of the Mississippi until 1906, and between 1906 and 1929 flinging out "radial bands of growth" toward Lake Pontchartrain and establishing a few settlements across the river from the main body of the city.[12]

These and other observations, based on a variety of historical

10. For references to source material for this and other hypotheses and concepts of city pattern as well as change and process, see such texts in "urban sociology" as, for example, N. P. Gist and L. A. Halbert, *Urban Society*, 3rd. ed. (New York: Thomas Y. Crowell, 1948), pp. 95-204.
11. Harlan Gilmore, "The Old New Orleans and the New: A Case for Ecology," *American Sociological Review*, 9 (August 1944), pp. 384-394.
12. H. Hoyt, *The Structure and Growth of Residential Neighborhood in American Cities* (Washington: U. S. Government Printing Office, 1939), p. 100.

maps and additional information for scores of American cities, including a few in the South and the border states, enabled Hoyt to substantiate Ernest Fisher's more comprehensive axial or *sector hypothesis.* While axial growth along transit routes of relatively greater speed and efficiency was recognized in the Hurd-Burgess concentric circle idea, it remained for Fisher and Hoyt to give it emphasis and at the same time point out that the concentric and axial forms of growth and patterning are *not* mutually exclusive. That is, there may be axial growth to isolated nuclei [13] on the periphery. This growth, moreover, may precede or occur coextensively with the appearance of zones in concentric arrangement. Also, zones are seen to develop as the areas between axes and sectors are built up and coalesce. Hoyt presents for five dates in each case sequential maps of New Orleans, Baltimore, Dallas, and the border cities of Charleston, West Virginia, and Washington, D. C.—all illustrating Fisher's theory. Throughout his analysis Hoyt emphasizes the "effects" of different forms of surface transportation, of the automobile and all-weather road, on the internal structure of cities.

In no region do cities show the effects of the automobile and truck more clearly than in the South, where most of the cities have undergone their greatest development during the gasoline age. Here as nowhere else except perhaps on the Pacific coast and in the western mountain states, cities continue to expand along highway axes while great interstitial land areas remain undeveloped either because of natural barriers or, more frequently, as a corollary of the stage of economic development.[14] It may be that the railroad and urban "maturity" produced concentric zones, whereas the automobile and urban "immaturity" produce patterns more accurately described by the sector hypothesis. One sees in southern cities about what Davie observed in the cities he studied: (1) a central business district, (2) commercial land use along radial streets

13. C. D. Harris and E. L. Ullman have worked out the *multiple nuclei hypothesis*, having observed that many cities are built around several discrete nuclei instead of a single center. This seems to be merely a variation of Fisher's idea. See their "The Nature of Cities," *Annals of the American Academy of Political and Social Science*, 241 (November 1945), pp. 7-17. Their three hypotheses of spatial structure, however, are quite original.

14. As Vance has observed, southern *inter-city* ecology reflects not only the automobile and truck, but electric power and the railroad as well. See R. B. Vance, *All These People* (Chapel Hill: University of North Carolina Press, 1945).

and in sub-centers, (3) industry near water, rail (and automotive) transport, (4) low-grade housing near industrial and transportation areas (and in the urban fringes), (5) first- and second-class housing anywhere else. We cannot agree with Davie, however, that the search for a single theory of urban growth and structure should be discouraged.[15]

The component areas of southern cities—variously designated and defined as "districts," "neighborhoods," "land use areas," and "natural areas"—have been described in scores of investigations. The larger cities with survey-minded welfare agencies, planning commissions, and college sociology departments like Nashville, Birmingham, Dallas, and Atlanta have received the bulk of this attention. Most of these area studies have had a practical purpose. Nevertheless, compared with other kinds of urban studies where the domination of practical considerations seems to have been a great deterrent to the advance of scientific theory, a greater proportion of these studies seems to have some theoretical relevance, although in the fashion of ecological orthodoxy already noted.[16] As yet they have been little used in building empirically sound ecological theory. Nor have we found it possible to do more than state a few of the major generalizations here.[17]

From these studies it is evident that the most extensive data on the sub-areas of large cities of the South, as elsewhere in the United States, are census tract data. Analysis of tract data and various rates of deviant behavior have led to the not surprising conclusion that southern cities have their areas of delinquency, slum housing, concentrated mental illness, poor health, and "bad environment" just as cities elsewhere. It seems clear that southern cities have residential

15. M. R. Davie, "The Pattern of Urban Growth," in G. P. Murdock (ed.), *Studies in the Science of Society* (New Haven: Yale University Press, 1937), p. 161.

16. Sara E. Smith, The Sociological Adequacy of a Group of Southeastern Urban Studies (unpublished master's thesis, University of North Carolina, 1947).

17. Blackwell, Brooks, and Hobbs have brought together the bulk of this information in an action-oriented study made by the Institute for Research in Social Science for The Presbyterian Church in the United States. The Appendices contain useful abstracts of the literature on southern communities, rural and urban, much of which has never been published—theses, local surveys, and the like. G. W. Blackwell, L. M. Brooks, and S. H. Hobbs, Jr., *Church and Community in the South* (Richmond: John Knox Press, 1949).

segregation by socio-economic class, just as cities elsewhere. They have areas of relatively new and expensive residences, areas of second-hand homes, and areas of extremely dilapidated residences. Likewise, they have their transition zones and slums. Delinquency, dependency, mental disease, and other pathologies also show the expected distribution. In brief, it does not seem that southern cities differ from other American cities in these patterns. Most of these quantitative studies are of larger cities, of course, and little is known about this type of ecological pattern in small towns and cities either in the South or elsewhere.

The ethnic homogeneity of southern cities is such that specialized ethnic areas or "cultural islands" have developed less frequently than in the more heterogeneous cities of the North and West. New Orleans' French Quarter, Tampa's Ybor City, the Greek settlement at Tarpon Springs, the Portuguese in Gulf Coast cities, Mexican districts in Texas—all are well-known exceptions to the rather monotonous Negro and Anglo-Saxon white pattern. The literature on this aspect of southern urban ecology is therefore sparse, although as yet it is far from exhaustive. Davis has described Mexican settlements in Dallas with particular reference to mobility, and Sutker has observed the changes in Jewish community life in Atlanta.[18] Neither of these studies, however, probed the life and culture of their specialized areas with greater success than Asbury's popular book on the New Orleans French Quarter.[19]

Offsetting the homogeneity of ethnic composition is the growing heterogeneity of occupations and the accentuation of class differences in southern cities, particularly those affected directly by industrialization. As Heberle has noted, the effects in terms of hierarchy (as well as status differentiation) are in all essentials the same as elsewhere, according to the observations of the Lynds, Mills, and others. The major differences in the South are due to the late beginning of industrialization and the presence of large num-

18. E. C. Davis, Little Mexico: A Study of Horizontal and Vertical Mobility (unpublished master's thesis, Southern Methodist University, 1936); and Solomon Sutker, The Jews of Atlanta: Their Social Structure and Leadership Patterns (unpublished doctoral dissertation, University of North Carolina, 1950).

19. H. Asbury, The French Quarter (New York: A. A. Knopf, 1936). Lyle Saxon's books likewise contain much that is informative, though romanticized, on New Orleans places and people.

bers of Negroes. The old independent middle class of cotton merchants, bankers, small manufacturers, and other small businessmen and professionals is being superseded by a smaller and economically more powerful class of larger manufacturers and executives of big corporations. At the same time a broad layer of clerical and supervisory technical personnel is being recruited largely from the white lower middle class; and a permanent, more or less hereditary class of white factory workers is perhaps becoming separated by widening social distances from middle and upper strata. These distances are emphasized (and symbolized) by ecological segregation into class- and status-designated residential areas.[20]

While the ecological aspects of Negro-white segregation have been described in comparatively great detail, nothing like the full range of ecological consequences of the South's changing social structure has been treated. Heberle makes the general observation that factory workers, not only in company towns but in multi-industry cities as well, live together in crowded and less desirable areas, whereas the wealthy have moved from downtown locations to the periphery, leaving blighted areas behind and invading Negro and other low income areas at the fringes.[21] The Stones and Price in Dallas observed "the civic structure" had been weakened by the flight of the "leading citizens" to the suburbs where they lived apart from white-collar workers and laborers who, in turn, were residentially segregated from one another.[22] Hunter has described the "location" of the power-wielding elite in a large southern metropolis, both in respect to residence and office space. He found a clustering of power personnel in one residential area and professional personnel in another area.[23] Irion, studying neighboring in Dallas, divided the city into nine areas according to class. Variations in the amount of neighboring were found. He found neighboring in Dallas predominantly a lower middle class phenomenon, followed in order by the upper middle class, the upper class, and the lower class. Differences in the patterns of neighboring be-

20. R. Heberle, "A Sociological Interpretation of Social Change in the South," *Social Forces*, 25 (October 1946), pp. 9-15.

21. *Ibid.*

22. H. A. and K. H. Stone and D. K. Price, *City Manager Government in Dallas, Texas* (Chicago: Public Administration Service, 1939).

23. Floyd Hunter, *Community Power Structure* (Chapel Hill: University of North Carolina Press, 1953), pp. 8-25.

havior were also observed between classes as well as between different ethnic groups.[24]

While there are many other investigations of class and "caste" in southern cities, either as primary or secondary phenomena, few have any particular ecological slant. Subsequently, however, as we look at the process of segregation, we shall refer to several studies that might almost as well have been presented at this point.

Of such, then, is the regularity and patterning of southern cities. But what of their changes in time, the processes that modify those arrangements of people, activities, and artifacts that we term ecological structure? In urban forms we see the products, the still photographs, of change and process, ". . . the tendency in time toward special forms of spatial and sustenance groupings of the units comprising an ecological distribution."[25] But just as permanence and change are everywhere joined, so they are in the ecology of cities. Although process considerations inevitably creep into the most static pictures of urban form, they are not in the foreground of attention in such studies. While many ecologists believe the study of processes to be ecology's most important task, such phenomena have received little attention. Lacking verified and precise empirical generalizations concerning the sequence of events in urban development, and with many a priori assumptions discredited, there are no impressive scientific theories of ecological change. The concepts and principal hypotheses available deserve attention nonetheless inasmuch as they are the best tools we have at hand. Let us examine them as they have been applied in the few instances to southern cities.

Southern cities, like all grouped settlements, represent concentration, the massing of human beings and their utilities in more or less delimited areas where nature or man has made conditions favoring the satisfaction of their needs.[26] Concentration is especially

24. C. Irion, A Study of Neighboring in Dallas (unpublished master's thesis, Southern Methodist University, 1940).

25. R. D. McKenzie, "The Scope of Human Ecology," in E. W. Burgess (ed.), The Urban Community (Chicago: University of Chicago Press, 1926), p. 172.

26. In the definition of concentration and the other processes we have relied on A. B. Hollingshead, "Human Ecology," in R. E. Park (ed.), An Outline of the Principles of Sociology (New York: Barnes and Noble, 1939), pp. 98-104.

noticeable in connection with more recently developed industrial plants requiring large sites often at a distance from other areas of concentration for reasons of health and safety, but with housing nearby for their own workers—for example, the synthetic rubber plants and aircraft factories in Texas, chemical plants in the Virginias and Carolinas, the refineries of Louisiana and Texas, the Bell plant at Marietta, Georgia.

The "overspill" or dispersion from old to new areas of urban concentration has rendered the definitions of cities in terms of political boundaries more and more useless for practical purposes. By 1950 the Census Bureau had recognized 53 "standard metropolitan areas" in the South. By 1950 results of concentration and dispersal were such that the Census Bureau used whole counties to delineate metropolitan areas. Other urban places await only official recognition to go into the metropolitan county or district class, and virtually all cities of more than 10,000 population have long since burst their legal-political seams.

Some measure of the extent of recent urban concentration (viewed regionally and with reference to the rural population) and dispersion (viewed in terms of internal urban structure) is gained by a 1947 census sample survey of the growth (1940 to 1947) in selected metropolitan districts, including 10 in the South. While the central cities are not distinguished from their districts, we know that the greater proportion of urban increment generally has fallen outside central cities in the fringe and suburban areas. The percent increases in the southern and border state metropolitan districts that were sampled were as follows: Atlanta, 13 percent; Baltimore, 25 percent; Birmingham, 23 percent; Dallas, 25 percent; Memphis, 21 percent; New Orleans, 11 percent; Norfolk-Portsmouth-Newport News, 43 percent; San Antonio, 31 percent; St. Louis, 16 percent; and Washington, 33 percent.[27] Whitney has also pointed out that gains in the rural-nonfarm population between 1930 and 1940 were primarily an aspect of urban growth and dispersion. Concentration near urban places, particularly near those of metropolitan size, occurred to an extent which makes the rural-

27. Bureau of the Census, *Current Population Reports*, "Population Characteristics of Metropolitan Districts, April 1947," Series P-21, No. 35.

nonfarm designation misleading.[28] This has gone on in the South as well as elsewhere both before and since 1940.

Centralization, like concentration, is a basic urban process; it is the integration of human beings and facilities around pivotal points at which interaction occurs most frequently. These pivotal or focal points—like retail shopping centers, tobacco markets, city halls and amusement centers—are located where lines of transportation and communication converge. Centralization has been described as a "temporary form of concentration." The distinction between the terms is none too clear, and they tend to be used interchangeably. (Hoyt apparently wants to reduce the confusion by simply using the term "concentralization"!) In any case, centralization is of course found in southern cities, and along with it, *decentralization,* often confused with dispersion. Call it one thing or the other, "the suburban trend" has reached the South.

Especially since 1940 the dispersion to the suburbs and to the urban fringe has proceeded apace. Municipal officials and central city taxpayers are haunted by the same specters that have stalked cities in the North for many years: higher service costs, lower property values, and lower tax revenues. Even by 1940—a long way back as urbanization has occurred in the South—23.5 percent of the residents of southern metropolitan districts lived in the suburbs, slightly more than the 22.4 percent in the Midwest. This was by no means as great as the 49.2 percent in the metropolitan districts of the older industrialized New England and Middle Atlantic states, or the 30.1 percent living outside central cities in the West, where cities are even newer than in the South.[29] More detailed observation of the suburban trend has been recorded for Augusta and Austin; and in the case of Greenbelt, Maryland, we have a general picture of social life in a planned community which turned out to be a dormitory suburb.[30]

28. V. H. Whitney, "Rural-Urban People," *American Journal of Sociology,* LIV (July 1948), 48-54.
29. C. D. Harris, "Suburbs," *American Journal of Sociology,* XLIX (July 1943), 1-13.
30. Georgia W. P. A., *Population Mobility: A Study of Family Movements Affecting Augusta, Georgia, 1899-1939* (Federal Works Agency, Official Report, No. 165-1-34-53, 1942); Bureau of Research in the Social Sciences, *Population Mobility in Austin, Texas, 1929-1931* (Austin: Univer-

Though by no means "abnormal" in the evolution of cities, and in some respects a highly desirable trend, dispersion can also wreak considerable havoc. Where outlying areas are developed too rapidly, poor planning—or no planning at all—is the accompaniment. Indeed, over-dispersion rather than over-concentration may well be the greatest obstacle to humane urban living in the South. Already inferior in their institutional facilities and municipal services, southern cities are promised scarcely any improvement by excessive and poorly planned dispersion. The redistribution of land uses within city limits would be desirable in older areas, and of course careful articulation of new areas with old through effective zoning and subdivision regulation is necessary if the costs of dispersion and decentralization are not to get out of hand. As Chapin observes in Chapter 13, unfortunately city planning has only begun and cities lack the legal and fiscal powers needed to control a trend already far along.

The tendency toward dispersion is evidently much more pronounced in some cities than in others and it probably takes different patterns depending on the type of city and natural setting. One of the first observed effects of the automobile era on cities was the tendency of residential areas to spread over a wider area. R. D. McKenzie presented data showing the prevalence of this tendency nearly two decades ago. Unless complicated by other forms of dispersion, this residential dispersion seems to follow a pattern of relatively contiguous development. This is recognized in the formula used by the Bureau of the Census to determine the boundaries of metropolitan districts. It is based on contiguous residential settlement of a specified minimum density with only small unoccupied intervening areas allowed for.

While this pattern of residential dispersion was underway, the automobile and other local rapid transit developments seemed to be concentrating more than ever the luxury, quality, and specialty merchandising into the central business section. And there is even yet less evidence of a dispersion of these functions than of almost any others. Therefore, cities which are primarily retail centers are

---

sity of Texas, 1941); W. H. Form, The Sociology of a White Collar Suburb: Greenbelt, Maryland (unpublished doctoral dissertation, University of Maryland, 1944).

likely to experience residential dispersion but little else. This is probably also true of transportation cities where the major business enterprises tend to stay concentrated around the port facilities or the railroad intersection.

On the other hand, as noted above, the tendency of industries to seek "solitary" suburban location seems to be getting greater and greater. Many of these plants with their workers' villages locate so far from the city that they are outside the metropolitan district as presently defined, and in many cases it is difficult to say whether or not they should be sociologically considered a part of the city. For example, Baton Rouge has a number of refineries and other oil-based industries so located. Also it is the state capital and the seat of Louisiana State University. On a basis of the employment indices which he used, Harris [31] classed it as a political and educational center. However, the people of Baton Rouge consider it primarily an industrial center; and that both the people of Baton Rouge and of these remote industrial suburbs consider themselves part of the community was evidenced several years ago by the voluntary formation of a planning commission including representation from the City of Baton Rouge and a number of other political jurisdictions to draw up a metropolitan plan for this area. Had these industrial areas been included in the data on the basis of which Harris made his classification, he very likely would have categorized that city differently. Indeed, when these areas were included in the city, the census figures showed a jump in population from 34,719 in 1940 to 125,629 in 1950. Of a similar nature but more extreme, Vance found that in the textile and furniture manufacturing section located in the Piedmont area of North Carolina there is a constellation of industrial towns, constituting an urbanized area with no clearly dominant center.[32]

Manufacturing is one of the big economic developments taking place in the South and, more than any other economic function, it has produced a dispersed ecological pattern. However, as stated before, manufacturing developments are very unequally distributed over the South. Some cities have had no such development and others have had so little that it has not significantly changed their

31. C. D. Harris, "A Functional Classification of Cities in the United States," *loc. cit.*
32. R. B. Vance, *op. cit.*

basic ecological patterns. Thus, while New Orleans has had some industrial development, the major changes taking place in the ecological pattern as described by Hoyt and by Gilmore do not seem to be those typical of industrial developments and are not attributed by either author to industrial growth. But in the case of Baton Rouge, ninety miles away, more or less the opposite seems to be the case.

THE ECOLOGY OF RACE IN SOUTHERN CITIES

One of the most clearly distinguishing characteristics of southern cities is of course the bi-racial composition of their populations. Racial heterogeneity is not an unusual characteristic of large cities. Rome and most of the other large cities past and present have counted in their populations large numbers of people of diverse races and cultural backgrounds. Similarly, the large northern and eastern cities of the United States drew population from many lands, and immigrant colonies have been part of their ecological pattern. With few exceptions southern cities are relatively unique in having only two racial groups of significance, whites and Negroes. The whites to a high degree are native southerners and so are the Negroes. Both are steeped in a tradition of race relations which dates from the slave era. The cities, like the rural areas, developed social patterns in keeping with the basic tenets of these traditions.

The proportion of Negroes in the population of southern cities varies greatly from city to city, but in many cities it is one-third or more of the total. Few towns in the South have a "pure" white or a "pure" Negro population, and these few know the southern tradition so well that they know what the pattern would be if members of the other race were present. Although these patterns are changing, the bi-racial populations plus the deeply ingrained race relations traditions still constitute a fundamental element of urban organization in the South. By the same token, segregated residence by race is one of the most universal ecological characteristics of southern cities.

Small southern cities probably display a higher degree of residential and institutional segregation along racial lines than do the larger cities, especially those which have grown rapidly in recent years. To be sure, segregation in the small city is modified by the "back-yard" arrangements of white-Negro residences, a pattern which has survived from an earlier day of low-wage domestic servants close at hand to their white employers. Small city segregation is modified too by a few culturally approved patterns of association in certain work situations where the whites, however, are in superordinate roles. Thus some observers have been led to the conclusion that there is "less" segregation in smaller and older cities than elsewhere. Yet it would seem only in the large and comparatively new cities, functionally typed as diversified or manufacturing, that one finds the occupational structure and related class-caste distinctions sufficiently altered in fundamental respects to produce real change in segregation patterns now or in the future.

These features of small city layout have been described in three social anthropological studies by Dollard, Powdermaker, and Davis and Gardner.[33] Though these investigators do not use ecological concepts, certain structural features are reported as the authors describe the settings for their researches.

Powdermaker, dealing with a fictitiously named town of some 3,000 people in the Yazoo-Mississippi Delta, observes that the city is by no means an entity distinct from its environs; rather it is fused with the countryside that focuses on it. Daily in-and-out movements of people may be observed that are not unlike the "routinization" observed within large cities. The business district is grouped in a four blocks square, and running out from it in three directions are the streets on which whites live. On the fourth side, separated by the railroad tracks which roughly divide the town according to color, live the Negroes in a district known as "across the tracks." There are no trolleys or bus lines. Opposite the four business blocks is the courthouse dominating its neighbors, the city hall and a red brick jail across the street. The well-kept lawn around the courthouse is the only green around the treeless and grassless business district. The courthouse steps serve as an informal social center along with the drug stores. The business establishments are those found in any small American town. While there is a small Negro

---

33. John Dollard, *Caste and Class in a Southern Town* (New Haven: Yale University Press, 1937), pp. 1-16; Hortense Powdermaker, *After Freedom* (New York: Viking Press, 1939), chap. I; Allison Davis and Burleigh Gardner, *Deep South* (Chicago: University of Chicago Press, 1941).

business center, the bulk of Negro buying is done in the white stores.

Powdermaker observes no white slum in "Cottonville." Poor whites reside in country slums, both on and off the plantations. She comments on what, to her, is the "suburban homogeneity" of the town dwellings of whites, "uniformly neat and snug." She declares, "It is perhaps typical of the South that the worst over-crowding, the most acute undernourishment, the most dirt, are found in the country rather than in town. This holds true for both races, but more strikingly for whites. . . ." [34] This may be true of most small retailing centers close to commercialized farming areas; we doubt that it is true of other cities. Certainly some of the worst housing in Louisiana, Georgia, and Tennessee, for example, is occupied by whites in New Orleans, Atlanta, and Nashville. This is also true of non-southern states and cities.

Davis and Gardner emphasize the symbolic aspects of segregation in "Old Town," a city of about 10,000 people (of whom one-half are Negroes) and the trade center for the large cotton plantations that surround it. They point out that spatial separation is used to symbolize the separate and subordinate status of the Negro. Negro and white residential areas are not segregated by law; but although Negroes live throughout the city, even in cabins along the bayous and back alleys of the choice districts, there are several large concentrations of Negro residents, although not without some white residents. In these, only the through streets are paved, others are poorly drained and maintained, street lights are few or absent. Many districts have no sewerage systems. They write,

In essence, this means that the Negroes generally occupy the least desirable residential areas and receive only a minimum of public services and improvements. Only whites of the lowest social status live in these neighborhoods, and in the white mind they become symbolic of the Negro's inferior status. [35]

That the patterns of residential segregation by race observed in small cities is by no means atypical of the South is attested by several ecological investigations. The scattered Negro residences

34. Powdermaker, op. cit., p. 11.
35. Davis and Gardner, op. cit., p. 22.

described by Davis and Gardner resemble what others have called "marble caking" or "the back-yard residence pattern." This pattern is commonly regarded as a survival of the years before "the servant problem" was a matter of such extensive concern and when most Negro dwellings were either servants' quarters in the rear of white homes or shacks along the streets where low-income whites lived also. Johnson notes,

In more recent years there are large proportions of whites who are not wealthy enough to have servants and larger numbers of Negroes who are above the servant level. The accommodation to racial proximity has persisted, and Negroes live in any section of town where they can secure a dwelling, whether on the street or in the rear of a dwelling; and living in the rear carries no obligation to the white owner other than the rent. Frequently both front and rear houses are owned by persons other than the occupants.[36]

Such residential arrangements are found in many cities besides Charleston, where Johnson thought it "somewhat unique": for example, in New Orleans, Memphis, and in smaller cities like Chapel Hill and the "Old Town" mentioned above. The "marble cake" or "back-yard" pattern of scattered and comparatively little concentrated residence seems especially characteristic of older cities in which accommodation to racial proximity in residence is part of local tradition. Though such patterns are found in northern cities or in newer cities in the South, it is not clear whether they exist as relatively stable structural arrangements or merely reflect a stage in an invasion cycle.

In newer cities like Tulsa, Durham, Miami, and many others, the extent of residential segregation of the races appears much greater. Here, according to Johnson and Weaver, there is a concentration of Negro residence which approaches "complete segregation." The separation may be marked by a railroad track, as it was in Powdermaker's community, by a stream, or by some other fixed barrier. Here too segregation by class within "the isolated community" of Negroes, as Johnson terms it, is at a minimum. Durham, for example, he finds has some of the best and some of

36. C. S. Johnson, *Patterns of Negro Segregation* (New York: Harper and Brothers, 1943), p. 9.

the worst Negro dwellings in the South along one paved street, the main thoroughfare for Negroes there.[37] Actually, there is also definite class segregation of Durham's Negro residences. We believe this may be found in other southern cities too. And as we suggested in the previous discussion of smaller cities, the existence of greater segregation is questionable in more diversified, larger, and newer cities. Residential propinquity in surviving "back yard" patterns does not necessarily entail social relationships. On the other hand, the improved occupational status and class position of many Negroes in more diversified cities prepare them for associating with similarly situated whites, particularly in city political groups, as we have already seen in the South.

The most prevalent pattern of Negro-white residential segregation in southern and border cities appears to be "the urban cluster," as Johnson calls it. Most cities of the South contain at least one large Negro area with smaller areas scattered around the city in clustered (or nucleated) arrangement. The core area is almost certain to be located near the center of the city in the oldest section. As described by Frazier, it is the same kind of area often inhabited by whites. The residences are typically old, not owned by the occupants, out-of-date, depreciated, difficult to keep in repair, and hard to acquire for either higher grade residential or other uses. The land may have speculative value for another use and the tax rate is high. For the owners who make little effort to maintain, modernize, or pay the taxes, such properties are often highly lucrative investments rapidly "turned" at tax sales. Such is the downtown slum area observed in cities like New Orleans, Birmingham, Atlanta, Memphis, and others in the 100,000 and over class.[38]

Although more attention has been paid to the forms of segregation than to the process, some general observations on the dynamics of residential segregation by race are reported. Johnson declares that the acquisition of residence sites by Negroes "has been observed to follow the cycle described by Burgess: (1) the initial penetration or invasion, (2) mild or violent reaction, (3) influx of newcomers and exodus of the old residents, (4) climax marked by

37. *Ibid.*; see also R. C. Weaver, *The Negro Ghetto* (New York: Harcourt, Brace, 1948).
38. E. F. Frazier, *The Negro in the United States* (New York: Macmillan, 1949); and Johnson, *op. cit.*

achievement of a new equilibrium or stability." [39] While complete residential segregation is never found, it is fundamental to other forms of segregation as well as to discrimination. Just as residence generally is a determinant of the service areas of institutions, segregated residence is an especially important factor in the differential access of Negroes and whites to the facilities and services of recreation, education, public transportation, hotels and restaurants, employment and trade, professional and governmental services.

Woofter's investigation of seven northern and nine southern cities led him to observe that each city had a physical pattern of residential segregation determined by (1) the percentage of Negroes in the total population, (2) attitudes of people toward segregation, (3) the rate of expansion of business and manufacturing areas, and (4) the distribution of areas where property is within the economic means of Negro families—a condition which seems to us to be more a "result" than a "determinant" comparable to the other factors. [40] Woofter's attempt to identify the factors in segregation is more satisfying, however, than Johnson's rather vague assessment in terms of ". . . social and economic selection, direct operation of racial sanctions, internal pull and cohesion of a community . . . those impersonal forces operating in the growth of a city." [41]

Weaver, with his emphasis on the production of housing for Negroes and the operation of restrictive covenants in cities of the North and border states, identified eight "principal instruments" used to hem Negroes and other colored minorities into "too little space": (1) community, neighborhood, and individual opposition to colored neighbors; (2) race restrictive housing covenants; (3) agreements, practices, and codes of ethics among real estate practices; (4) neglect of the Negro market by private builders and sources of finance; (5) the fear of local government officials that more and better housing for Negroes will bring more Negro migrations; (6) local political action to restrict Negroes to given areas; and (7) the development of exclusive one-class neighborhoods. [42]

39. C. S. Johnson, *op. cit.*
40. T. J. Woofter, *Negro Problems in Cities* (New York: Doubleday, Doran and Co., 1928).
41. C. S. Johnson, *op. cit.*
42. R. C. Weaver, *op. cit.*, p. 211.

Although sociologists will detect a certain overlapping, conceptual inadequacy, and lack of vigor in Woofter's and Weaver's analyses of the dynamics of segregation, at least these authors have dealt with this crucial aspect of the phenomenon.

Weaver and Johnson are of the opinion that residential segregation has not been carried as far, Negro residence is not as concentrated, and the impediments to new Negro housing are not as great in southern cities as in northern cities. Johnson feels that

In the South the location of many Negro homes near places of employment (as domestics) has established a large degree of tolerance of Negro neighbors, and it is frequently possible for Negroes to purchase and improve property. Moreover, in many cities of the South Negroes have preceded white populations in sites desired as new developments and, owning property, have remained as these sites developed.[43]

And Weaver found while there were large FHA war housing programs for Negroes in seven southern and border cities (Washington, Baltimore, Norfolk-Portsmouth, New Orleans, Jacksonville, Atlanta), only nine of the priorities set up for one phase of the programs (H-1) went unused in these cities whereas 273 were not taken up in the North, presumably because the impediments associated with segregation were greater there.[44] Definitive comparisons of housing market operations as between different types of cities as well as between cities South and North are needed—for here is the machinery by which most segregation, racial and otherwise, is brought about.

Racial segregation, then, is a universally observed feature of urban ecological structures in the South, a feature which has also been adopted, of course, in northern cities especially since World War I. The literature to which we have referred describes its principal variations, though not without error as we have noted.[45] The gravest deficiency of these studies, however, is that no fundamental explanation, no sociological theory of segregation, has been

43. C. S. Johnson, *op. cit.*, p. 10.
44. R. C. Weaver, *op. cit.*, pp. 147-149.
45. Some minor forms of segregation, especially interesting because they are extremes, have not been mentioned. We refer to all-Negro towns like Mound Bayou and the Institute community at Tuskegee, and to all-white towns where Negroes are banned entirely.

developed which explicitly handles the ecological dimension. Although they begin in the right direction, it is not enough to say with Davis and Gardner, for example, that spatial separation is used to symbolize the separate and subordinate status of the Negro and let it go at that. We are not prepared to formulate an adequate sociological theory here. The data at hand do not permit it. Yet we believe the data do suggest the probable validity of a functional theory of segregation.

More specifically, we believe Hiller's approach offers a likely explanation of racial segregation in ecological context. The observations at hand would seem compatible with his idea. Working from a conception of community as a social group which employs locality as a datum in group composition, in addition to the generic elements of all social groups, Hiller observes:

> While residence in an area permits of a high degree of isolation from social actions, there is always the implicit conformity to norms and sharing in certain minimal rights and duties. . . .
>
> . . . location in a given area or within certain boundaries becomes a symbol of various rights and duties or is made an occasion for comparing statuses and judging the personal acceptability of people. In other words, area, locality, or space is taken as a datum in defining social relations. It is symbolic. When locality or space has such symbolic significance, admission thereto constitutes a test of access to corresponding social relations, whether these be prescribed politically or otherwise. As soon as admission into defined space is allowed, various norms, such as certain legal rights and duties, are expected to operate. . . . Thus, the so-called law of settlement is seen to rest on normatively given presuppositions which are built up with reference to ingress into a recognized social space and which have varied in form and content in different times and cultures.[46]

Here, it seems, is the cue to a sound theory of racial segregation which throws a psycho-social bridge between the more abstract value theory of a Myrdal, say, and the theoretically puerile local area data whose concrete particulars have been scarcely transcended in such ecological analysis as we have had to date.

46. E. T. Hiller, "The Community as a Social Group," *American Sociological Review*, 6 (April 1941), pp. 195, 197.

CONCLUSIONS

It is evident from this survey that our knowledge of urban ecology in the South is spotty and sparse. Nevertheless, a few broad generalizations appear relatively sound, though their principal value may well lie in their usefulness as hypotheses for further examination.

As census data have long revealed, the most prevalent kind of southern city is the small city, characteristically a retail trade and market center serving a limited agricultural area. The chief difference between small cities in the South and elsewhere in the United States is the bi-racial population in the South. Most of the labor jobs in small southern cities are culturally assigned to Negroes whereas white-collar jobs are reserved for whites. The principal social cleavage, correspondingly, is between Negro and white. This is mirrored ecologically in "white" residential areas occupying the better sites and in one or more back-of-the-tracks areas of Negro residence. Some Negroes may live on or near the premises of their present or sometime white employers. Segregated schools, churches, and (to a lesser extent) business and professional services are linked with this segregation of residence and also leave their imprint on the physical order of each community. The "center of town" remains, not unaffected however by the fact that the "edge of town" is no longer as distinct in these small cities as it used to be. Just as in the larger cities, the automobile continues to merge the small city and its countryside, with the attendant disadvantages and advantages of the "rurban fringe."

Many of the South's larger cities are such small cities grown up with the help of the automobile and expanded service areas. Many also began as break-of-bulk points at railroad intersections or along the sea coasts. As multiple economic activities developed, so there developed a greater variety of jobs and a more highly differentiated occupational structure. Especially significant in this connection were the increases in laboring jobs for whites and skilled professional and managerial positions for Negroes. Correspondingly, both races in southern cities, and particularly the larger cities, have become multi-class. And what the larger city compared with the small city lacks in informal contacts between Negroes and whites it probably makes up for by more formalized Negro-white relations in associations devoted to purposes of politics, health, welfare, education, religion, and to some extent economic interests.

The physical correlates of the South's changing social structure, relatively more advanced in the larger cities, are by no means clear. Apparently the two races live in separate social worlds no less in the large city than in the small. Though class-differentiated in greater degree for both whites and Negroes, residential and related ecological segregation seems at least as pronounced in the larger cities. To what extent the physical orders of cities lag behind their changing social orders we do not know. That there is such a lag, and that the physical correlates of by-gone social orders survive almost without function in the present, we may be fairly certain.

Southern cities have tended to disperse their residential areas over the countryside just as have other cities during the automobile age. Because southern cities have had their main growth during this period, however, the extent of this dispersion is probably greater in the South than elsewhere. In cities where the retail function is very important, the central business section remains a dominant core around which the residential areas are arranged. The pattern of this arrangement probably is a semblance of a zonal arrangement but is greatly distorted in most cities by topography and radial growth. Where a factory, college, or other important activity seeks a distant suburban location, it becomes the nucleus for a residential and business development and also produces "shoe-string" development along the thoroughfare connecting it with the city. Apparently in some newer industrial areas these nuclei shoestring patterns are dominant, with very little in the way of central cores and concentric zones.

The resort and retirement activity is an important and rapidly growing one for certain southern cities. The Atlantic and the Gulf coasts are well-known foci; the mountain resort areas and now many parts of the Tennessee Valley all have towns small and large in which this is an important source of revenue. Unfortunately, no study seems to have been made of the ecology of southern resort towns.

Many southerners and their fellow Americans, prompted perhaps by recent court actions, are asking: will Negro segregation in southern cities increase or decrease? Probably no conclusive answer to this question can be given. However, certain trends which may furnish a clue to the answer should be pointed out. As indicated above, one of the factors which restrained segregation historically seems to have been the desire of white employers to have Negroes live near their work. As more varied kinds of work open for the southern Negro, and as there are more places where Negroes may work, there may be less segregation of residence. On the other hand, there has been a trend in recent years to provide more and better public services for Negroes. In locating these facilities, administrative efficiency dictates that they be located where their clienteles are concentrated. Thus, schools, health centers, settlement houses, parks, playgrounds, and other public facilities for Negroes are apt to be established in existing areas of Negro concentration. The more the Negro becomes urbanized and the more his standard of living is raised, the more he may value these services and the more he may wish to live where he will have access to them. Unless, therefore, segregation in the use of such facilities disappears in the South, these trends would indicate even more segregation in the future.

Such are the broad generalizations that seem warranted on the basis of the ecological literature and the authors' random observations. Our present knowledge of urban ecology in the South as elsewhere is long on description of cities as they are, and short on explanations of their becoming, either past or future. Until we build a systematic theory of urban form and function on the basis of many more comparisons of the parts as well as wholes of cities, and do this according to functional complexes, stages of urban development, and influences of technology and natural setting, we cannot claim to understand our cities. Moreover, until we learn the relationships—symbolic and meaningful as well as "natural" and material—between the physical and social orders of our cities, we cannot act with maximum effectiveness to better adjust our urban mechanisms to human needs. No greater opportunity exists for students of southern cities than the study of ecology set in social and cultural perspective.

CHAPTER EIGHT

Social Class in the Urban South

HAROLD F. KAUFMAN

How is urbanization affecting the traditional class structure of the South? How extensive is stratification in the southern city? What social contacts are there between the classes? What opportunities are there for movement up (and down) the class ladder? These questions indicate some of the facts needed for an understanding of stratification in southern cities. They also indicate the contents of this chapter and suggest certain directions for much needed firsthand studies.

The dominant values of any society provide the basis for its stratification. The South, historically and contemporaneously, is no exception. Certain individuals are considered superior because their activities, attributes, and possessions are more highly valued than those of others. Similarly, the social positions of greater prestige are those which are considered the more important and those which are the more difficult to attain. Thus, the position of mayor has greater prestige than that of the average citizen, and the office of factory manager stands considerably above that of the unskilled employee.

Things of high value constitute the rewards and, correspondingly, the "life chances" of a class system. Economic rewards, such as the possession of consumption items and the holding of wealth with its concomitant power, are particularly important, especially in urban society. Other important rewards and life chances include good health, long life, and extensive formal education. One observer has aptly stated that "the influential are those who get most of what there is to get." [1] How the social rewards are distributed in a given population is a major concern in the economic and demographic approaches to the study of stratification.

The distribution of social rewards is an important component of many public problems. Questions which deal with income distribution among the several occupational groupings—whether through earnings, taxation, or welfare legislation—are of this type. Certainly slum clearance programs and special health, welfare, and educational services for disadvantaged groups result in some change in the distribution of rewards and the nature of the class structure.

I. URBANIZATION AND THE RURAL HERITAGE

A brief description of the class structure of the agrarian South is desirable background for analysis of the present-day urban scene. Agrarian social strata in the South before the Civil War consisted of the planters or slaveholding group, the commercial or yeomen farmers living in the valleys and on the prairies, the highlanders, the poor whites, the freed Negroes and the slaves.[2] In the agricultural and non-agricultural groupings, considered together, highest ranking was given to the large planters and members of the learned professions. Other groupings in the order of their prestige were (1) merchants, small planters, and lesser professionals, (2) artisans and yeoman farmers, (3) laborers and servants, and (4) slaves. The freed Negro occupied an ambiguous position on the periphery of the class-caste system and was a perennial threat to it.[3]

The large planters, whose way of life provided the basis for the stereotyped "southern gentlemen," are said to have comprised "a very thin upper crust" of the society. Recent study has shown that the yeoman farmer comprised a larger proportion of the population and the poor whites a smaller proportion than had been formerly assumed. Extensive evidence has been presented to show that ante-

1. H. D. Lasswell, *Politics: Who Gets What, When, How* (New York: McGraw-Hill Book Co., 1936), p. 3.
2. L. C. Gray, *History of Agriculture in the Southern United States to 1860* (Washington: Carnegie Institution of Washington, 1933), I, chap. 21; and H. Weaver, *Mississippi Farmers, 1850-1860* (Nashville: Vanderbilt University Press, 1945).
3. W. E. Moore and R. M. Williams, "Stratification in the Ante-bellum South," *American Sociological Review*, 7 (June 1942), pp. 343-351.

bellum society, contrary to popular notion, was largely middle class in character.[4]

Most of the distinguishing ideologies of the South, at least those conventionally so defined, are rural in nature and some bespeak European origin. The upper class southern male, as commonly portrayed, is noted for his hospitality and manners, his leisureliness, his chivalry toward women, and his acceptance of certain caste and class relationships.[5] On the other hand, the person who has been reared in the urban and industrial North is generally regarded as more distant in his social contacts, more aggressive, and more likely to believe that anyone regardless of his background should be able to "get ahead" as much as he desires. Social elements which have been distinctively emphasized in the South are family and family name, informality and cordiality among acquaintances, and rather well-defined white-Negro patterns.

Some evidence as to the effect of urbanization on southern society may be found in regional comparisons. Ogburn has found that differences between the South and non-South in demography and in welfare and educational services are appreciably diminished when comparisons are made only for cities of similar size.[6] This suggests that as the rurality of the South declines and urbanization increases the South will become more like the rest of the nation with respect to the measurable characteristics referred to above.

With the development of cities it seems that stratification has increased together with greater opportunities for movement up and down the class ladder. The occupational specialization, described by Thompson in Chapter 3 of this volume, has been associated with a widening of the extremes of wealth and power and, concomitantly, with increases in class distinctions and exclusiveness. Urbanization has facilitated social mobility by providing new channels

4. F. L. Owsley, *Plain Folk of the Old South* (Baton Rouge: Louisiana State University Press, 1949); Weaver, *op. cit.*

5. See W. F. Ogburn, "Ideologies of the South in Transition," in H. W. Odum and K. Jocher (eds.), *In Search of the Regional Balance of America* (Chapel Hill: University of North Carolina Press, 1945), pp. 92-100.

6. W. F. Ogburn, *Social Characteristics of Cities* (The International City Managers' Association, 1937), chap. 7; and O. D. Duncan, "Regional Comparisons Standardized for Urbanization," *Social Forces*, 26 (May 1948), pp. 430-433.

of inter-class movement as well as new opportunities for such movement. With an increase in the relative number of secondary social contacts, personal qualities have no doubt become less important criteria of social positions. At the same time the symbols of wealth have probably become more important.

II. CONTEMPORARY CLASS STRUCTURE

The idea of a continuum or ladder is probably a more accurate representation of class structure in American society and in the modern South than are concepts of distinct groups or castes.[7] This notion is especially useful when class rank is defined in terms of such measurable characteristics as income and years of schooling. Class structures in American communities have been graphically represented both as diamond-shaped figures and as pyramids.[8] The former indicate a predominantly middle class society while the latter show a relatively large proportion of lower rank.[9] Although the effects of urbanization on the relative size of the various classes in the South are not entirely clear, there is no doubt that the growth of cities makes for increased stratification. That is, the social and economic distance, however it may be measured, between persons of the lowest and the highest rank is decidedly greater in cities than in rural areas. In economic terms, at least, the extent of stratification ("height" of the class structure) appears to be greater in northern

7. Some of the best field studies of social class in the South have tended to blur the idea of class as a continuum by emphasizing that of caste. It should be noted, however, that the reality of multi-class distinctions and mobility of Negroes as well as whites has become more apparent in the decade or more since these studies were made. See John Dollard, *Caste and Class in A Southern Town* (New Haven: Yale University Press, 1937); Hortense Powdermaker, *After Freedom* (New York: Viking Press, 1939); and A. Davis, B. Gardner, and M. Gardner, *Deep South* (Chicago: University of Chicago Press, 1941).

8. W. L. Warner and P. S. Lunt, *The Social Life of a Modern Community* (New Haven: Yale University Press, 1941). The writer in a study of a village-centered rural community was able to delineate 11 class groupings without difficulty; see *Cornell Agricultural Experiment Station Memoir 260* (1944).

9. The method of definition appears to influence the resulting classification. For example, if people rate themselves, a diamond-shaped figure results; if classification is made in terms of income, the resulting figure more nearly approximates a pyramid.

than in southern cities because of the greater concentration of the ownership of property in the North and East.[10]

Relative Size of the Class Groupings

The relative number of persons of upper, middle, and lower rank[11] is determined by classifying populations in terms of one or more indices of class standing. Indices or items that are available and are most frequently employed for large populations are occupation, years of schooling, rentals, income, and possession of consumption items. Occupation is especially useful because it bears some relationship to functional groups and is fairly comparable from population to population.

The generally accepted classification of broad occupational groups gives executives in large businesses and other enterprises and a few top leaders in the professions and government the highest prestige rank. Next follow the free and salaried professionals, managers, and owners of small businesses. Of middle rank are the white-collar workers, clerks and kindred workers, and skilled craftsmen and industrial workers. Groups of lower rank include the semi-skilled workers, unskilled workers, and the unemployed who are indigent.

Because of its rural character, the South has a low proportion of persons in all of the occupational groupings listed above.[12] Urbanization, however, is bringing the occupational structure of the South more in line with that of the nation. When cities in the South are compared with those elsewhere, it is found that southern cities have decidedly smaller proportions of persons employed in manufacturing industries and in the professions.[13] As Thompson shows in Chapter 3, these proportions are increasing.[14] The rela-

10. See W. L. Crum, "Regional Diversity of Income Distribution," *American Journal of Sociology*, 42 (September 1936), pp. 215-225.

11. Because of the nature of the presentation, no rigorous definition of the upper, middle, etc., class is suggested here. Rather, major groupings along a continuum are delineated, such as upper, middle, and lower rank. In this discussion the cultural pattern rather than the associational aspect of stratification is emphasized.

12. K. Evans, "Some Occupational Trends in the South," *Social Forces*, 17 (December 1938), pp. 184-190.

13. W. F. Ogburn, *Social Characteristics of Cities*, chap. 7.

14. See especially Tables 3 and 4 in Chapter 3.

tively smaller numbers of teachers, engineers, and social workers in the South have helped to account for the differential. The percentages of persons in both law and medicine, however, is high for southern cities. Although the Southeast as a whole has a low ratio of physicians to population when compared to the Northeast, when cities alone are compared the former region has a decidedly higher rate.[15] This, together with the high proportion of tradespeople in southern cities, indicates that they are service centers for a sizeable rural hinterland. Historically, most southern cities developed as commercial centers rather than as industrial towns.

Occupational statistics support the observation that southern cities have a smaller proportion of persons of middle rank than have cities in the North. Data on rentals and income [16] point in the same direction,[17] for the modal (also the median) rental and income groupings in southern cities are generally at a lower level than elsewhere. In most southern cities the median person has not gone beyond grade school whereas the average individual in cities in other regions has attended high school. A complex of factors expressing social rank is involved here. For example, of the 48 states, those with highest percentage of persons in the professions also rank highest in education, industrialization, and other indices of social well-being.[18] The proportion of persons of middle social rank in southern cities can be expected to increase with the development of industry demanding skill and the growth of educational and related services.

A more detailed picture of stratification in the southern city is seen when the two major racial groups are studied separately. The class structure of the Negro group is well depicted by a pyramid with a broad base. The white population, on the other hand, has a rather substantial middle class with a smaller lower class than

15. O. D. Duncan, "Regional Comparisons Standardized for Urbanization," loc. cit.

16. Data are taken from Sixteenth Census of the United States, 1940: occupational information from Population, II, Part K, Tables 70-73; years of schooling from the same volume, Tables 58-61; income data from Population, III, Parts 2-5, Table 15; and rentals from Housing, II, Table 18.

17. It is well to point out here, however, that a house renting for $60 a month in a southern city may have as much prestige value as one renting for $90 in a northern city.

18. See A. L. Porterfield, "Rank of the States in Professional Leadership and Social Well-being," Social Forces, 25 (March 1947), pp. 303-309.

otherwise because of the occupational contribution of the Negro at this level.

Ecology of Stratification

Stratification may be observed not only in terms of social indices and cultural patterns but also in its spatial or geographic aspect as well. In this volume Chapter 7 by Demerath and Gilmore treats such ecological patterns. Here, therefore, it is sufficient to set forth a few of the more general characteristics. Segregation or the separation of the population geographically along class lines is a consequence of urbanization with its increasing differentiation.[19] Whereas in the small town the banker and the janitor may live next door to each other,[20] in the city persons of these two occupational levels are more likely to reside in separate neighborhoods with others of similar rank. In the typical southern town (and elsewhere as well) the socially prominent families lived adjacent to the business district. If the town grew and developed into a city, these families generally moved to the suburbs. Here they were likely to find families of lower rank, especially Negroes, which they displaced. The poorer families in turn moved to less desirable areas.[21]

Woofter found that each city had a comparatively distinct physical pattern of its own determined by the percentage of Negroes, the occupational structure, and the size of the area in which the population resided.[22] Industrialization in the South, taking place in the age of electricity and the automobile, has not resulted in the concentration of population in large cities as is found in other regions. Rather it is observed that the pattern is one of a small or medium-sized central city with a scattering of smaller centers around it. It is questionable whether this type of settlement results in as clear-cut and well-defined segregation as is found in urban

19. The existence of segregation has been utilized in classifying a population as to rank. See Warner and Lunt, *op. cit.*

20. Even in villages, however, an "incipient" form of segregation may exist. The writer found this to be true in a New York village of 600 people.

21. Several instances of this same pattern are cited by R. Heberle, "Social Consequences of the Industrialization of Southern Cities," *Social Forces*, 27 (October 1948), pp. 29-37.

22. Study by T. J. Woofter (ed.), *Negro Problems in Cities*, quoted in I. de A. Reid, "Methodological Notes for Studying the Southern City," *Social Forces*, 19 (December 1940), pp. 228-235.

areas of great population concentration. Firey observes that the extensive "rurban fringe" tends to remain a marginal residential area, not clearly differentiated as to use.[23]

III. CLASS AWARENESS AND INTERACTION

The dynamics of stratification shows how groups and individuals gain, maintain, or lose their power, prestige, and social rewards. Such questions as the following are relevant: How are class interests expressed? Who are the persons and groups of greatest influence? What is the role of the industrial worker and also that of the person of middle rank?

Class interests are expressed both formally and informally, the informal expressions being much more important probably. Choices bearing on status are continually expressed through the behavior of cliques and through such individual actions as "getting ahead," "making good on the job," and "going to school." Most people have little or no contact with organized groups which possess pronounced class interests. With urbanization, however, increased organization of economic and political interests occurs with such groups as trade associations, taxpayer leagues, and labor unions appearing. But these and other similar groups are never homogeneous in their memberships. As Cox points out, this is true especially of political groups,[24] which contain people who have similar views but who range a considerable distance up and down the class ladder. The "liberal" group, however, is likely to have a larger proportion of persons of lower rank than is the "conservative" one.[25]

Centers of Power and Influence

Floyd Hunter's study of a southern metropolis found a relatively small group of men to be the major policy-makers. These were

23. W. Firey, "Ecological Considerations in Planning for Rurban Fringes," *American Sociological Review*, 11 (August 1946), pp. 411-421.

24. O. C. Cox, *Caste, Class and Race* (Garden City: Doubleday and Co., 1948), Part Two, especially chap. 10. This writer has made a contribution to class theory by distinguishing between "social classes" and "political classes."

25. D. Anderson and P. E. Davidson, *Ballots and the Democratic Class Struggle* (Stanford: Stanford University Press, 1943).

for the most part persons "in the top bracket of one of the stable economic bureaucracies." Below the policy-makers were the "under-structure professionals" and the leaders in the many associations serving the community; these latter two groups were largely "executors of policy." The personnel of the "pyramid of power" varied from project to project. A similar power structure was noted by Hunter in a southern university town.[26]

The position of the upper class power groups in the South is probably stronger because of the comparatively weak organization of industrial workers and the one-party political system. The industrialists, land owners, and others providing this leadership cannot be called an aristocracy, however, since they are neither closely knit nor have they inherited their rank as a group.[27] The political field, for example, may be characterized by decentralized control and the existence of factions. Not only is the "ruling class" not hereditary, but its composition is also changing. As one observer has noted, the older group in the southern city—composed of the commodity merchants, bankers, small manufacturers, and businessmen—is being gradually superseded by the larger industrialists and executives of big corporations.[28]

There is some evidence that liberalism as well as the status quo receives strong support from persons of upper rank. Myrdal observed that the so-called liberal movement in the South is largely composed of persons of higher rather than lower rank.[29] It is also predominantly urban, as is the leadership of most institutions and movements.[30]

26. F. G. Hunter, *Community Power Structure* (Chapel Hill: University of North Carolina Press, 1953).
27. For distinction between an "autocratic" and "democratic" ruling class, see G. Mosca, *The Ruling Class*, trans. by Hannah D. Kahn (New York: McGraw-Hill Book Co., 1939), chap. 15.
28. R. Heberle, "Social Consequences of the Industrialization of Southern Cities," *loc. cit.*
29. G. Myrdal, *An American Dilemma* (New York: Harper and Brothers, 1944).
30. One might observe that because persons of upper rank are the more likely to be organized they are the more likely to be class conscious. Cf. T. Harrison, "Notes on Class Consciousness and Class Unconsciousness," *The Sociological Review*, 34 (July-October 1942), pp. 147-164.

Relative Position of the Industrial Worker

In the present urban world a certain degree of organization is essential to gain and maintain power. Industrial workers in southern cities, however, are still relatively unorganized compared with their northern counterparts. A brief survey of factors relevant to this situation is presented below.

Although today in southern cities many factory workers are city-born, this was not true a generation or more ago when textile and tobacco workers were recruited largely from a class of low-income farm people.[31] Low wages kept them from improving their economic position to any considerable extent. Their individualism, their personal relationship with paternalistic employers, and the mobility of their leadership prevented them from organizing and developing a group consciousness. The first evidence of organized action on their part came in the twenties and thirties. Within the last decade, union membership has grown at a more rapid rate until today in some communities certain industries are entirely unionized. What form employer-employee relationships will take in some industries where unionization has not advanced remains to be seen. The bi-racial pattern also complicates the picture.

With the growth of industry the class of manual workers has increased considerably in number. Likewise social distance between the workers and the employer and business groups has grown greater as urban areas have increased in population and segregation of residential areas has developed. With more formal education and experience in group organization, industrial workers will probably find their way gradually into political groups that will express to some extent their class interests and will aid them in improving their lot.[32] To date, however, there has been little mass political organization in America and especially in the South. The chief movements receiving support from persons of lower and middle rank were Populism, possibly the Ku Klux Klan, and the followings of certain political leaders who have had special appeal to the "little man." In some cases of conflict on issues involving labor

31. See H. L. Herring, "The Industrial Worker," in W. T. Couch (ed.), *Culture in the South* (Chapel Hill: University of North Carolina Press, 1934), chap. 17.
32. Anderson and Davidson, *op. cit.*

organization, groups of lower rank have been found to be pitted against each other.

The average man in the South, as elsewhere in America, appears to take little interest in day-by-day political activity. In the South he is less likely to be a voter; this is true not only of the Negro but also of the white. Shugg has noted that the Agrarian and Populist movement of the South was not to be explained by "the rise of the poor whites" aware of their common interests and how to attain them, but rather by their "uprising" against economic and social conditions which they would tolerate no longer.[33] Likewise it has been observed that the chief concern of the American worker is not to identify himself with his class but to get out of it. Factors which have prevented the development of an organized class consciousness among the "working people" are: the decided opportunities for individual and group mobility; the rise in status of the potential leadership for such a group; and the diverse backgrounds of its members—e.g., in the South, the two major racial groups.

Role of the Middle Groups

The middle classes in the South as in the non-South are highly heterogeneous, including professionals, white-collar workers, business people, and many manual workers. Their political, educational, and other interests are equally diverse. Meusel has described the "middle class" generally as "a mixture of heterogeneous elements, some in undisguised conflict."[34] This indicates a mobile society, one in which it is more nearly accurate to speak of "middle classes" than "a middle class"—since interests, as well as social rank, are important in differentiating a population into significant groups.

It is said that middle rank persons are politically impotent. Mills found the white-collar strata in a middle-sized American city largely unaware of "their economic and political interests." Distinctive occupational attitudes expressed, for the most part, non-economic values.[35] On the other hand, through independent voting, which is

33. R. W. Shugg, *Origins of Class Struggle in Louisiana* (Baton Rouge: Louisiana State University Press, 1939), chap. 9.

34. A. Meusel, "The Middle Class," *Encyclopedia of the Social Sciences* (New York: Macmillan, 1930-34), vol. 10, pp. 407-415.

35. C. W. Mills, "The Middle Classes in the Middle-Sized Cities," *American Sociological Review*, 11 (October 1946), pp. 520-529. Because of the

not uncommon among certain groups of middle rank, one sees an expression of choice in political matters. A study by Ogburn and Jaffe showed a positive correlation for the urban South between an index of economic well-being and independent voting.[36]

The civic contributions and community leadership provided by certain groups of middle and upper rank have frequently been observed. Mills and Ulmer found that the size of business operations reveals that cities with the larger "independent middle class" also have a higher level of civic welfare, better retail facilities, and less difference in income between the rich and the poor.[37] Civic-minded educational and religious groups, led by persons of middle rank, are inclined to employ a presentation of the facts and ethical teachings in promoting social change rather than a "class-interest" approach. Thus, it may be no accident that there is a lack of strong class identification in groups that stress the total community welfare. MacIver has observed that "class sentiment and community sentiment" work in opposition.[38]

IV. SOCIAL MOBILITY AND OPPORTUNITY

The dynamics of stratification can be observed in the interaction of groups who are attempting to gain for their members "the most of what there is to get" and in the movement of the individual from one rank to another. Perhaps the most striking feature of the class structure in America is the relative freedom of movement from one social rank to another—the opportunity to rise on the basis of merit. The relative opportunities in southern cities today compared with those in cities elsewhere or in southern society a century ago depend on the channels of and barriers to social movement.

"political impotency" of the middle classes, some see them as losing their present rank and gradually being absorbed into the lower groupings. See L. Corey, The Crisis of the Middle Class (New York: Covici, Friede, 1935).

36. W. F. Ogburn and A. J. Jaffe, "Independent Voting in Presidential Elections," American Journal of Sociology, 42 (September 1936), pp. 186-201.

37. C. W. Mills and M. J. Ulmer, Small Business and Civic Welfare, Report to Special Committee of United States Senate to Study Problems of American Small Business (Washington: U. S. Government Printing Office, 1946).

38. R. M. MacIver, Society (New York: Rinehart, 1937), chap. IX.

Improved employment opportunities in the South have accompanied urbanization. Industrialization has in general resulted not only in better-paying jobs for the rural migrant to the city but for many city dwellers as well. The rural South, because of the relatively high rate of natural increase and the very limited opportunities in agriculture, possesses a large reservoir of labor readily available to southern industry. Urbanization also means an increase in professional and white-collar jobs providing additional opportunity for the capable to rise occupationally.

Upward mobility not only of individuals but also of groups may be observed. Wage levels in southern industry have increased with the size of the plant, efficiency of workers, and unionization. The use of consumption items in the home has become more widespread; there has also been a rise in the educational level and a decrease of illiteracy.

Another force making for upward mobility in the urban population is the fact that professional, white-collar, and related groups are not producing enough children to replace themselves. Even though the total number of jobs for such groups did not increase, their low birth rate provides opportunities for the more capable of lower rank to rise.

The school is also a most important institutional channel of vertical mobility. It not only raises the level of the great majority of the population by providing them with knowledge and skills for better adjustment and a greater contribution to complex urban society, but it also selects the more able and gifted and allows them to rise to higher levels. Upward mobility can be facilitated in the southern city by improving the schooling of persons of lower class. Anderson finds that the educational level of persons of higher rank in the southern city compares very favorably with that of individuals of such standing in the rest of the country, but that educational attainment for persons of lower rank is decidedly less in the South than elsewhere.[39]

Another channel of vertical mobility, and one closely related to education, is the voluntary association or organization. Such groups

39. See C. A. Anderson, "Social Class Differentials in the Schooling of Youth Within the Regions and Community-Size Groups of the United States," *Social Forces*, 25 (May 1947), pp. 434-440. Rentals are used as the index of social rank.

have many functions, and educational attainment is highly associated with participation in them. The number of such organizations
increases with urbanization, so that at the same social level the
urbanite is likely to have a higher participation rate than the rural
dweller. Hunter's investigations in a southern metropolis found
that most of the people with the most power had at one time
earlier in their careers held leadership positions in important voluntary associations but had since "graduated" from these positions.[40]

Limitations on Vertical Mobility

The absence of factors facilitating upward movement may be
considered barriers to social mobility. Such barriers include lack
of education, poor health, and jobs with inadequate incomes. Porterfield points out that industrialization alone is not sufficient to raise
the level of living in the South. Alabama, for example, has as high
a proportion of workers in manufacturing as California, and Mississippi as high a proportion as Kansas, yet indices of social well-
being and educational attainment in the two southern states are
much lower than in the other two. Educational advancement in the
southern states does not appear to have kept up with industrialization.[41]

Lack of training for urban life may hinder the upward mobility
of rural migrants. Beers and Heflin in one southern city showed
that the rural migrant, as compared with the urban-born, had
decidedly less schooling and was not equal to the latter in "income,
job and status." [42]

By implication, at least, the view has been expressed that the
average person of lower or middle rank in the South has had less
drive and desire to climb the class ladder than has his northern
counterpart. Whether or not this is true, the relative number of
aggressive and socially mobile people in a population should be
seen in relation to the opportunities for rise in rank. If the channels

40. Hunter, *op. cit.*
41. Porterfield, "Rank of the States in Professional Leaderships and Social
Well-being," *loc. cit.*
42. H. W. Beers and C. Heflin, *Rural People in the City*, Kentucky Agricultural Experiment Station Bulletin 478 (1945). See also discussion in
Chapter 4 of this book.

for vertical mobility are absent and if a large number of people possess a strong desire for improved status, they either greatly modify their aims or they fall victims of tensions which threaten social order. The amount of stimulation that youth receives "to get ahead" should thus be seen in relation to the opportunities for social ascent. Havighurst and others have observed that a population's mobility drive may change greatly in a short time.[43]

A pertinent question here is how urbanization has affected opportunities for Negroes. In addition to the barriers listed above, this group also suffers discrimination because of color. A common observation is, of course, that the city with its increased employment and educational opportunities has allowed the Negro to rise more rapidly in social rank than was possible on the farm. That Negroes themselves feel this to be true is evidenced by the mass migration from farms to cities both within and without the South.

V. CONCLUSIONS

Southern cities like others are stratified on the basis of rank. Here the urban class system has been influenced by the South's rural heritage and unique historical forces. Industrialization and the massing of population in cities are increasing stratification and appear to be shaping the class structure of the South into a pattern similar to the rest of the nation.

Stratification of urban life in the South has been described in terms of the demographic and cultural aspects of the class structure, social mobility, class awareness and association. These ideas not only serve to organize the limited and sometimes indirect evidence bearing on stratification, but also provide orientation for much-needed field research. Given the paucity of field studies, the latter is probably the major contribution of this chapter.

43. R. J. Havighurst, "The Influence of Recent Social Changes on the Desire for Social Mobility in the United States," in L. Bryson et al. (eds.), *Conflicts in Modern Culture* (New York: Harper and Brothers, 1947), chap. 8.

CHAPTER NINE

Crime in Southern Cities

AUSTIN L. PORTERFIELD AND
ROBERT H. TALBERT

O UR PREVIOUS STUDIES of differences in trends and patterns of crime in time and space have led us to the conclusion that crime is hard to define and therefore difficult to measure. Yet there are some tentative approaches to its definition and measurement.[1] (1) Psychologically, crime is in the nature of destructive aggressiveness; it exists in the tendency to strike right and left to attain one's ends, regardless of what happens to others.[2] (2) Legally, it is the violation of statutes which may or may not be well crystallized in the local mores.[3] (3) From a sociological viewpoint, patterns of crime are best considered as cultural phenomena which vary from group to group and vary with the social context in time and space.[4] (4) As cultural phenomena, patterns of behavior may be in keeping with the local mores though in conflict with the legal requirements of society.

1. Austin L. Porterfield and Robert H. Talbert, *Crime, Suicide, and Social Well-being in Your State and City* (Fort Worth: Leo Potishman Foundation, 1948), pp. 17-20.
2. *Ibid.;* cf. Austin L. Porterfield, "Personality, Crime, and the Cultural Pattern," in *Current Approaches to Delinquency* (New York: The National Probation and Parole Association, 1949), pp. 214-230.
3. See Austin L. Porterfield, "Law and the Mores," *Sociology and Social Research,* 37 (March-April 1953), pp. 223-229.
4. Austin L. Porterfield and Robert H. Talbert, "A Decade of Differentials and Trends in Serious Crimes in 86 American Cities by Southern and Non-Southern Pairs," *Social Forces,* 31 (October 1952), pp. 60-68.

PATTERNS OF CRIME AS SOCIO-CULTURAL PRODUCTS

In brief, criminal patterns like other patterns of behavior are socio-cultural products. This hypothesis can be emphasized in the following ways: (1) In the processes by which they grow, patterns of crime as cultural phenomena develop in the interaction of persons and groups with one another as ways of behaving in conflict situations. (2) Conflict situations which contribute to crime vary with the presence or absence of class, caste, ethnic groups, and fragmentized social worlds in the community. However, if a minority ethnic group is large enough and protected enough from outside impacts to develop its life as an organized community, it may have lower rates of crime than the white native-born populations of some other areas. (3) The greater the number of lines of conflict in a society, the greater is the amount of crime. (4) In-groups are themselves bound together with cultural ties which may yet permit aggressive responses to in-group members on occasion; and aggressive responses to out-group members on many occasions may be motivated by cultural compulsion although legally these acts are crimes.[5] (5) The southern cities which are the objects of our concern in the present study have more of these conflict groups and more aggressive cultural definitions than most non-southern cities. The presence of large numbers of foreign-born and their descendants in many non-southern cities, we suspect, is accompanied by neither the sharp lines of conflict nor the cultural definition of aggressive responses that exists in the South.[6] The non-southern cities, by differences in social structure and by cultural differences, tend more to suicide than to crimes against persons.[7] (6) Therefore, the southern cities will have more crime than the non-southern cities with which they are compared. (7) Yet there may be a gradual process of equalization in crime rates

5. *Ibid.*, pp. 67-68. See also Porterfield, "Personality, Crime and the Cultural Pattern," *loc. cit.*, pp. 225-230; cf. H. C. Brearley, *Homicide in the United States* (Chapel Hill: University of North Carolina Press, 1932).

6. Observed percentages of the foreign-born in the population of our cities in 1950 as compared with crime rates support our position.

7. Austin L. Porterfield, "Suicide and Crime in Folk and in Secular Society," *American Journal of Sociology*, 57 (January 1952), pp. 331-338.

between the southern cities and the non-southern cities with which we have compared them, with a possible trend toward greater similarity in social structure and in cultural patterns.[8]

The present study selects out of these areas of interest for emphasis: (1) the striking contrasts in southern and non-southern rates of crime; (2) the importance of (a) variations in *class structure* or *socio-economic status* and (b) certain *barriers* to social participation, unity, and achievement as apparent factors in the contrasts; and (3) the manner in which patterns and rates of crimes fit into the whole complex of *anomie, group conflict, interpersonal and intrapersonal turmoil,* and *depressed populations* from community to community, as conditions indicative of the lack of integration in society.

I. METHOD OF STUDY

We have emphasized comparison of what is criminal in the urban South with criminal behavior elsewhere, for without comparison there is no measurement and without adequate data there can be no significant comparison. Urban crime in the South cannot be studied in a vacuum. We have therefore chosen two groups of cities, 43 southern and 43 non-southern, which we have placed together in pairs.[9] The former group includes all the urban places in the South of more than 50,000 population in 1940. The latter, without regard to location, are chosen to match the former in population for the same year. The period 1940-1949 is the first time span studied; the second period covers 1950 and 1951.

Six crime patterns are compared. None of them represents white-collar criminality which, if data were available, we should like to include. Those chosen are *murder, robbery, aggravated assault,*

8. Porterfield and Talbert, "A Decade of Differentials and Trends in Serious Crimes in 86 American Cities by Southern and Non-Southern Pairs," *loc. cit.,* pp. 63-66.

9. The original study in which this comparison appeared was published in the *American Sociological Review,* 14 (August 1949), pp. 481-490, under the title, "Indices of Suicide and Homicide by States and Cities: Some Southern—Non-Southern Contrasts with Implications for Research," and in Porterfield and Talbert, *Crime, Suicide, and Social Well-being in Your State and City.*

burglary, *larceny*, and *auto-theft*. These are included in *Uniform Crime Reports* as "crimes known to the police." [10]

Space Variations.—Comparison of these patterns of crime *in space* (city to city) is made by using the mean annual rate for each pattern in all 86 cities (in the period 1940-1949) as a common divisor for the mean annual rate in each city to obtain an index. All rates per 100,000 in each city (and for all cities) in this period are based on the mean of the population for 1940 and 1950. For example, the mean murder rate for all 86 cities here indicated was 9.6 per 100,000 people, as shown in Table 1. This rate is assigned

TABLE 1. Average 10-Year Rate for Six Part 1 Offenses in 43 Southern and 43 Non-Southern Cities, 1940-1949 *

Group of Cities	Murder	Robbery	Aggra-vated Assault	Burglary	Larceny	Auto-theft
All 86 cities	9.6	59.2	91.3	432.9	1068.0	226.7
Southern cities	15.5	68.0	143.9	484.9	1162.2	242.3
Non-southern cities	3.2	49.6	34.4	391.6	966.5	207.8

* Part 1 offenses in *Uniform Crime Reports* include also the offense of rape, but the reports on rape are too inadequate to include here.

an index score of 100, and the individual index scores of the cities range above and below 100 as percentages of this mean rate. Scores for all six offenses are then combined, as a mean of the six, into a composite index by which cities are compared in the tendency of their populations to commit serious crimes. The same method is

10. In Porterfield and Talbert, *Crime, Suicide, and Social Well-being in Your State and City*, chap. 3, we have pointed out the difficulties of employing these data. Though the Department of Justice, operating through the Federal Bureau of Investigation, has furnished all the police departments of the nation definitions of these offenses and has asked them to report quarterly and annually all crimes of these six types known to the police, whether arrests are made or not, we may well believe that the reporting is not "uniform" as the name implies. Some police departments may be reluctant to report all crimes known over and above arrests made, fearing that failure to make arrests will reflect discredit upon the department. Moreover, police departments are not aware of all crimes committed. Problems of boundary lines, the relations of cities to hinterlands, to cross-country lines of communication, and the high mobility of the criminal population also present difficulties. As the data appear, however, they suggest certain important trends and hypotheses.

used in determining the indices of crime for the second period, 1950 and 1951.

Time Variations.—The comparisons of these patterns *in time* are based on trends over the 10-year period from 1940 to 1949 for all 86 cities, or southern-non-southern combinations of cities. In the indices which here constitute the foundation of trend lines (contained in Figures 1, 2, 3, and 4), 100 as an index score represents the 10-year average for each offense, or the composite score for all offenses for the same period. Rates for successive years per 100,000 population have been estimated as though the cities grew (or declined) each year of the decade by 10 percent of the total change from the Sixteenth to the Seventeeth Census. Index scores for successive years for the southern and non-southern groups of cities move up and down with the trend lines in our figures as percentages of the mean 10-year rate of any given offense, or as the composite score for all offenses.

Comparisons with Other Series.—If, however, variations in patterns of criminal behavior are to be compared with variations in other social characteristics of urban areas for the purpose of determining how criminal behavior is related to the social context, it is necessary to develop other continua, or indices, with which various continua representing gradations in patterns of crime can be compared. To see how variations in patterns of crime are related to variations in socio-economic status, we must develop indices for the latter. To observe the relationship of crime to the presence of higher or lower barriers to participation in the benefits and achievements of a society requires some yardstick to measure these barriers. To know how crime patterns fit into the complex of anomie, group conflict, conflict in intrapersonal and interpersonal areas, and depressed populations requires a complex index or continuum for social integration-nonintegration into which they can be fitted.

These indices of social status, social barriers, and integration-nonintegration are explained in the three sections following.

Index of Socio-Economic Status.—The index of socio-economic status contains index numbers which are the mean of like numbers for the cities studied in degrees of (a) *health*, (b) *education*, (c) *adequacy of housing*, and (d) *amount of income*. These sub-series are, in turn, composed of means of scores representing specific conditions. The index of *health* is based on (a) comparative rates for stillbirths and infant mortality combined, (b) percentage of children born outside hospitals, and (c) combined deaths from such diseases as syphilis, tuberculosis, pneumonia, diarrhea, and enteritis (for 1948-1949).

The index of *education* is a composite of the mean of the scores for (a) per pupil appropriations for the schools in 1952-1953, (b) percentage of children in school aged 16-17 years as compared with the number aged 7-13 years in 1950, and (c) median school year completed by persons who were over 25 years old in 1950.

The *housing series* is a composite of the index numbers for each of the 86 cities in their relative standings in (a) presence or absence of overcrowding, (b) units with private baths, (c) average monthly rent, and (d) average total value (as of 1950).

The *income* index is based on (a) median income of "families and unrelated individuals," and (b) the percentage of those who received incomes under $2,000.

The mean scores for the sub-factors which make up the *socio-economic* index number for Asheville, North Carolina, for example, are *health* 73, *education* 91, *housing* 97, and *income* 83. The mean of these four sub-scores is 86, which indicates that Asheville is 14 points (or percent) below the average in socio-economic status in the configuration of 86 cities. The corresponding scores for Hamilton, Ohio, which is paired with Asheville, are *health* 94, *education* 100, *housing* 98, and *income* 128, with a mean score of 105. Thus Hamilton is represented as standing 5 percent above the average socio-economic rating for all cities.

When the series for socio-economic status is reversed, it may be taken as an index of depressed classes or of socio-economic inadequacy.

Index of Social Barriers.—Since crime from a psychological standpoint may hypothetically be viewed as the behavior of people who go out of the field of "normal striving" when frustrated by barriers which stand between them and their goals,[11] it becomes important

---

11. Austin L. Porterfield, "The Problem of Response to Personality Frustration: A Concrete Example," *Social Forces*, 21 (October 1942), pp. 75-81; cf. John Dollard and others, *Frustration and Aggression* (New Haven: Yale University Press, 1939); Neal E. Miller and others, "The Frustration Aggression Hypothesis," *The Psychological Review*, 48 (1941), pp. 337-

to compare communities with respect to the presence or absence of such barriers. Hypothetically, we have chosen the index of *depressed classes*, referred to above as the reverse of the *socio-economic* series, as one of these indices. As another, we have selected an index of *individuation*, based on the percentage relation of the number of "unrelated individuals" over 14 years old to the total number of "families and unrelated individuals" as reported in the Seventeenth Census. It is assumed that *individuation* so defined is a barrier to social participation of the more intimate sort. And, finally, in the light of the class-caste tendencies which prevail in our culture, the factor of *race*, the percentage of the population in the "nonwhite" category, was chosen as an index of barriers to social achievement (Table 4).

The mean of these three scores is taken as representing for each city its index number for social barriers, for conditions contributing to frustration of persons, which in turn may become a factor in crime.

The Integration-Nonintegration Continuum.—Our most inclusive index hypothetically places cities along a continuum of *integration-nonintegration*. It constitutes our ACID test of the relative effectiveness of a community's group life and institutions; the letters stand for *anomie, conflict between groups, interpersonal and intrapersonal disaffection*, and *depressed populations*. The last named series enters the complex without modification (Table 3).

Anomie, defined as lack of social belongingness accompanied by loneliness and perhaps loss of direction and hope, takes in as subindices: *individuation* (described above), and a series representative of low degree of church membership near the beginning of the 10-year period (1936).[12]

Conflict between rival groups, it is assumed, may be indicated by two community characteristics: *religious schism* and the *color line*. Therefore the first, an index of religious schism, is constructed on the mean rates of the approximate number of congregations per 100,000 population over 13 years of age and the number of con-

---

342; Karl Menninger, *Man Against Himself* (New York: Harcourt, Brace, 1938), Parts II, III, and IV.

12. It is unfortunate that a nation-wide census of religious bodies has not been conducted since 1936. But even so, the church scores seem to be significantly related to other series, even the latest ones.

gregations per 100,000 population at the beginning of the period.[13]

Though the rates for suicide and crime as a rule vary in opposite directions (see Table 4), as Porterfield and others have shown, it is in the I score that these apparently opposite types of response enter the index of integration-nonintegration as representing *interpersonal and intrapersonal disaffection*. It seems logical to combine them into one score here, since divergent crime and suicide rates among cities indicate merely varying degrees of disaffection from one source or another. Robert C. Angell ignored suicide in his studies of the "moral integration of cities." [14]

When the A, C, I, and D scores are combined as a composite mean (Table 3), this complex index summarizes the results of our attempts to "measure" the over-all effectiveness of our communities to provide for the normal development of all their members as "good citizens" and as persons who may happily share in the "fruits of the American democratic ideal." Such citizens are surely the opposite of criminals.

II. FINDINGS FROM DATA ANALYSIS

Contrary to some commonly advanced hypotheses, the data show that: (1) Age and sex differences in the population of the cities account for none of the observed contrasts in indices of crime;[15] the non-southern cities in 1950 had more males (the "criminal sex") per 100 females, and also more males over 14 years old (the "criminal age") than urban places in the South. (2) Southern cities do not have higher rates of crime known to the

13. See the high correlation of the number of congregations per 1,000 people with crime rates by census tracts in Fort Worth, Texas, in Porterfield, "Suicide and Crime in the Social Structure of an Urban Setting: Fort Worth, 1930-1950," *American Sociological Review*, 17 (June 1952), pp. 341-349; cf. Porterfield, "The Church and Social Well-being: A Statistical Analysis," *Sociology and Social Research*, 31 (January-February 1947), pp. 213-219; and Porterfield, "Suicide and Crime in Folk and in Secular Society," *loc. cit.*

14. Robert C. Angell, "The Moral Integration of American Cities," *American Journal of Sociology*, 57 (July 1952), Part 2.

15. An examination of the Seventeenth Census will show that sex and age differences do not account for the contrasts. In fact, in 36 out of the 43 pairs of cities, on the basis of age and sex differences alone, it would be expected that the non-southern cities would have higher rates of crime.

police because their central cities constitute smaller percentages of their metropolitan areas than their non-southern mates.[16] (3) Though the classification "nonwhite" is accepted as a good index to disjunctive processes, it is not because of an alleged predisposition to "crime" in the heredity of colored people. Because of widespread misunderstanding on this point, special attention is given below to the relation of Negroes to rates of crime.

Crime and the Negro.—Although it is generally true that gross crime rates among Negroes are higher than rates among whites for similar crimes, it is not valid to attribute the higher crime rates of urban places in the South to genetic characteristics of the Negro or to the size of the Negro population as such. The incidence of crime varies greatly among southern cities; these variations are not always in positive relation to the proportion of Negroes in the total population. This can be seen in the similarities and contrasts shown in Table 2, which indicate that the number or percentage of Negroes in a city's population is not an adequate explanation of its crime rates. Certainly the evidence given in Table 2 is sufficient to warrant looking to other conditions for an explanation.

If we could determine carefully the relative opportunities of Negroes in different cities for achieving social status, economic security, and personality growth, we could have a more adequate explanation of the criminal behavior of Negroes—which is true for the criminal behavior of the whites also. It could be true that the white man "misbehaves" in the same kinds of situations in which the colored man "misbehaves" and that the circumstances under which the white man "behaves himself" are also the same for the Negro.

Crime and the Size of Cities.—Another common error is the belief that larger cities are more "criminal" than smaller ones. Porterfield and Talbert have clearly shown the fallacy of this theory.[17] Furthermore, on the basis of Zipf's $\frac{P_1 P_2}{D}$ hypothesis on

16. In spite of the fact that from 1940 to 1950 the southern cities outgained the non-southern cities 21.8 percent compared with 10.8 percent, the non-southern cities still exceeded the southern cities in total metropolitan population by 780,000 people in the latter year.

17. See Porterfield and Talbert, "A Decade of Differentials and Trends in Serious Crimes in 86 American Cities by Southern and Non-Southern Pairs," *loc. cit.*

TABLE 2. Contrasts Between Crime Scores in Selected Southern Cities and Proportions of Negroes in the Population, 1950

City	Ratio or Percentage of Negro Population	Crime Scores: Six Offenses 1950-1951	Crime Scores: Six Offenses 1940-1949	Crime Scores: M + B * 1950-1951	Crime Scores: M + B * 1940-1949
I. SIMILAR CRIME SCORES, VARYING PERCENTAGES OF NEGROES					
Atlanta	36.6	169	172	215	212
Louisville	15.7	160	170	149	153
Jacksonville	35.5	135	165	161	195
Miami	16.3	143	168	164	177
II. SIMILAR PERCENTAGES OF NEGROES, VARYING CRIME SCORES					
Beaumont	29.4	83	80	103	100
Greensboro	24.7	223	195	138	132
Roanoke	15.9	53	60	47	56
Dallas	13.2	172	148	167	171
III. CONTRASTS IN INDICES FOR COLOR AND FOR CRIME					
Dallas	83 **	172	148	167	171
St. Petersburg	91	58	71	82	103
Knoxville	96	161	142	141	170
Louisville	98	160	170	149	153
Roanoke	100	53	60	47	56
Miami	102	143	168	164	177
Greensboro	161	223	195	138	132
Charlotte	175	161	160	144	165
Beaumont	184	83	80	103	100
Norfolk	186	261	204	160	202
Chattanooga	188	121	131	180	195
Columbus	195	55	107	80	130
Nashville	197	144	144	141	187
New Orleans	200	103	82	96	83
Shreveport	208	63	66	97	87

* The mean of murder and burglary.

** The numbers in this column are index scores of the Negro population based on the percentage of Negroes in each city divided by the percentage of Negroes in the total population of the entire configuration of cities.

the "intercity movement of persons," [18] the larger cities ought to draw more heavily on their hinterlands for incoming criminals. Thus approximately one-fourth of all jail commitments in Houston, Fort Worth, Dallas, and Beaumont are from outside the central cities.[19]

18. George Kingsley Zipf, "The $\frac{P_1 P_2}{D}$ Hypothesis: On the Intercity Movement of Persons," *American Sociological Review*, 11 (December 1946), pp. 677-686.

19. See Porterfield and Talbert, *Crime, Suicide, and Social Well-being in Your State and City*, pp. 56-58, and Table 45, pp. 115-118.

A Further Note of Caution.—The writers are aware that they have developed only tentative measures. The formula $\dfrac{ACID}{4}$, as constituting the index of nonintegration, expresses the mean of four hypothetical conditions. It does not symbolize the belief that our "quantities" are critically "noncorrosive" or suggest that the inhabitants of Dallas ought to move to Fort Worth. We cannot place any city at exactly the point or in the exact order in which it belongs along any continuum. But we can do what we started out to do—locate some of the problems that are related to urban crime in the South and see the way in which these problems fit into other social problems. To this objective, at this point, we may turn.

III. SOME SHARP CONTRASTS

The data, as suggested above, present some sharp contrasts between rates of crime in urban places in the South and in other areas. Only two non-southern cities exceeded their southern mates in the crime index based on six offenses for the period 1940-1949 (Table 4); only two did so in 1950-1951 (Table 3). In each case, the difference was slight. Similar results appear in comparing the cities by scores based only on the rates for murder and burglary (Tables 3 and 4), except that in 1950-1951, the lone southern city of St. Petersburg, Florida, fell two points below Springfield, Missouri, on the latter index.

Among the 22 cities in the configuration of 86 with index scores of 125 or more (1950-1951), only two are non-southern. Among the 20 highest scores during the previous decade, 18 were southern. Not one of the 20 cities with scores of 50 or below (in 1950-1951) was southern; not one of the 22 with crime scores as low as 50 for the previous decade was southern. Only one of the 23 cities that fell to 50 or below on the murder-burglary score (1950-1951) was southern; during 1940-1949, none of the 25 such cities was southern.

In the main, however, the tendency is for the gap between scores for the southern and the non-southern pairs to grow narrower. In this connection, Figures 1, 2, 3, and 4 tell an interesting story. Figure 1 presents an over-all contrast for 1940-1949. Figure 2 is

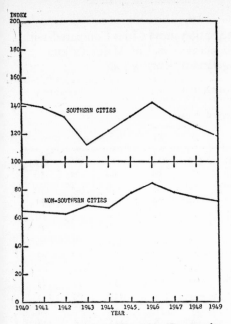

Figure 1. Crime Trends: Composite Index Score Variations for Southern and Non-Southern Cities, 1940-49 (Ten-Year Average Composite Score for All Cities Equals 100)

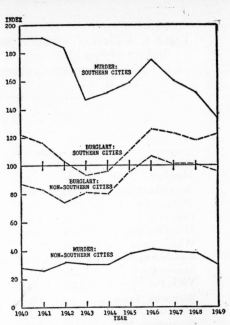

Figure 2. Crime Trends: Murder and Burglary Index Score Variations for Southern and Non-Southern Cities, 1940-49 (Ten-Year Average Score for All Cities Equals 100)

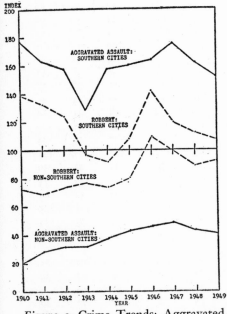

Figure 3. Crime Trends: Aggravated Assault and Robbery Index Score Variations for Southern and Non-Southern Cities, 1940-49 (Ten-Year Average Score for All Cities Equals 100)

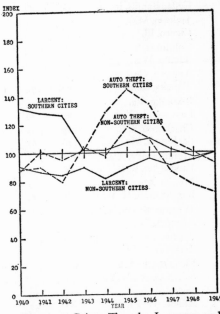

Figure 4. Crime Trends: Larceny and Auto Theft Index Score Variations for Southern and Non-Southern Cities, 1940-49 (Ten-Year Average Score for All Cities Equals 100)

TABLE 3. Indices of Social Nonintegration in 86 Cities Compared with Indices of Spatial Mobility (1949-1950) and of Major Crimes (1950-1951). Average Index Score is 100

City	Indices of Nonintegration (NI) based on indices of (A) anomie, (C) conflict-group, (I) interpersonal disaffection, and (D) depressed classes					Mobility Index	Index Major Crimes	
	A	C	I	D	NI		Six Offenses	Murder and Burglary
Asheville, N. C.	101	136	142	116	124	111	166	132
Hamilton, Ohio	90	66	68	95	80	84	69	56
Amarillo, Texas	144	66	80	81	93	156	147	130
Waterloo, Iowa	100	67	78	84	84	93	36	31
Columbus, Ga.	92	200	91	133	129	124	55	80
Holyoke, Mass.	68	26	65	72	57	36	21	10
Waco, Texas	98	122	79	118	104	134	75	76
Kalamazoo, Mich.	127	69	108	78	96	91	58	42
Macon, Ga.	89	259	135	141	156	102	125	180
York, Pa.	83	84	110	99	97	59	55	45
Beaumont, Texas	90	184	84	104	111	113	83	103
Malden, Mass.	62	25	55	69	50	54	27	34
Greensboro, N. C.	122	158	141	94	128	113	223	138
Decatur, Ill.	98	66	73	79	79	91	44	58
Durham, N. C.	130	186	141	108	140	85	217	114
Fresno, Calif.	86	81	161	84	103	102	157	115
St. Petersburg, Fla.	158	115	119	96	122	122	58	82
Springfield, Mo.	115	77	81	94	91	115	63	84
Covington, Ky.	80	61	91	100	83	76	93	78
Cedar Rapids, Iowa	109	58	79	72	79	88	41	23
Jackson, Miss.	109	205	73	141	132	33	59	92
Cicero, Ill.	83	18	87	55	61	52	70	41
Columbia, S. C.	93	204	120	125	136	100	118	103
Racine, Wis.	79	63	83	67	75	64	41	41
Augusta, Ga.	89	206	96	125	129	102	153	113
Topeka, Kans.	105	79	92	91	98	103	96	72
Roanoke, Va.	89	119	72	93	93	87	53	47
Lakewood, Ohio	86	26	66	39	54	64	41	24
Charleston, S. C.	108	214	126	122	143	92	96	124
St. Joseph, Mo.	110	61	94	122	97	97	55	44
Montgomery, Ala.	182	211	84	152	134	128	112	144
Pawtucket, R. I.	68	30	50	68	54	46	33	30
Mobile, Ala.	89	171	112	137	127	101	124	153
Binghamton, N. Y.	84	43	68	76	69	63	33	35
Winston-Salem, N. C.	104	200	85	122	128	83	123	160
Altoona, Pa.	70	59	60	82	68	54	33	34
Austin, Texas	146	105	76	100	107	93	86	82
Berkeley, Calif.	120	82	93	68	91	114	62	57
Little Rock, Ark.	108	142	100	112	116	116	81	85
Schenectady, N. Y.	88	50	71	65	67	66	42	39
Savannah, Ga.	84	230	106	137	139	94	96	109
Allentown, Pa.	86	47	78	85	74	57	27	20

TABLE 3 (continued)

| City | Indices of Nonintegration (NI) based on indices of (A) anomie, (C) conflict-group, (I) interpersonal disaffection, and (D) depressed classes | | | | | Mobility Index | Index Major Crimes | |
	A	C	I	D	NI		Six Offenses	Murder and Burglary
El Paso, Texas	77	36	90	120	81	121	124	104
Evansville, Ind.	97	70	110	105	98	98	79	60
Shreveport, La.	102	149	79	114	111	116	63	97
Waterbury, Conn.	68	35	72	79	63	46	29	23
Charlotte, N. C.	107	152	114	97	118	111	161	144
Lowell, Mass.	72	29	40	92	56	43	31	41
Tampa, Fla.	101	134	131	111	119	109	142	133
Tacoma, Wash.	135	90	130	78	109	117	94	94
Knoxville, Tenn.	105	122	109	119	114	108	161	141
Wichita, Kans.	109	79	75	82	88	123	72	82
Chattanooga, Tenn.	109	166	114	137	128	101	125	180
Albany, N. Y.	104	52	63	90	74	57	33	30
Tulsa, Okla.	120	86	103	93	101	120	96	92
Scranton, Pa.	61	39	53	93	63	40	35	37
Norfolk, Va.	154	147	161	127	147	160	261	160
Yonkers, N. Y.	84	45	57	70	64	53	31	27
Nashville, Tenn.	113	171	123	116	131	107	144	141
Des Moines, Iowa	115	62	67	85	82	98	64	66
Miami, Fla.	144	101	149	95	122	142	143	164
Grand Rapids, Mich.	94	62	70	74	75	74	62	56
Jacksonville, Fla.	128	178	134	116	139	124	135	161
Hartford, Conn.	92	61	98	80	80	66	61	55
Fort Worth, Texas	108	93	94	89	96	133	114	145
Youngstown, Ohio	75	84	89	84	81	60	50	52
Richmond, Va.	98	151	131	105	121	101	143	145
Syracuse, N. Y.	102	38	69	80	72	82	40	32
Oklahoma City, Okla.	120	74	83	88	94	144	128	115
Dayton, Ohio	97	90	112	87	96	87	92	82
San Antonio, Texas	88	58	99	133	94	101	100	98
Providence, R. I.	83	38	56	88	65	73	54	57
Birmingham, Ala.	98	189	97	125	127	104	128	154
Toledo, Ohio	89	65	108	80	85	75	90	72
Memphis, Tenn.	98	172	90	130	121	112	83	100
St. Paul, Minn.	99	45	62	79	71	74	58	41
Dallas, Texas	106	100	138	88	104	110	172	167
Oakland, Calif.	130	82	110	77	110	138	138	96
Atlanta, Ga.	105	179	130	114	134	101	169	215
Portland, Ore.	136	72	156	74	109	110	95	72
Louisville, Ky.	81	97	139	108	108	90	160	149
Denver, Colo.	121	58	127	88	98	115	121	102
Houston, Texas	106	120	106	96	107	127	121	180
Indianapolis, Ind.	99	98	110	99	101	93	97	101
New Orleans, La.	94	131	76	119	105	83	103	96
Minneapolis, Minn.	119	44	75	76	79	89	50	32

TABLE 4. Indices of Social Integration in 86 Cities Compared with Indices of Social Barriers, Crime, Individuation, and Suicide for Designated Years

City	Index Integration: NI in reverse	Index Social Barriers 3 factors *	Indices of Crime 1940-1949 Six Offenses **	Indices of Crime 1940-1949 M + B **	Index Individuation	Index Suicide ***
Asheville, N. C.	80	124	190	122	108	93
Hamilton, Ohio	125	65	53	46	68	83
Amarillo, Texas	108	65	83	62	84	77
Waterloo, Iowa	119	68	49	37	95	96
Columbus, Ga.	77	131	107	130	66	74
Holyoke, Mass.	175	52	35	35	81	69
Waco, Texas	96	111	83	75	109	75
Kalamazoo, Mich.	104	80	69	60	134	147
Macon, Ga.	64	168	164	216	99	106
York, Pa.	104	76	53	40	95	167
Beaumont, Texas	90	124	80	100	79	87
Malden, Mass.	200	47	37	34	65	72
Greensboro, N. C.	78	134	195	132	148	87
Decatur, Ill.	127	68	51	51	93	94
Durham, N. C.	72	162	203	132	149	79
Fresno, Calif.	97	79	151	103	104	171
St. Petersburg, Fla.	82	104	71	103	126	166
Springfield, Mo.	110	71	58	64	100	103
Covington, Ky.	120	70	63	71	75	119
Cedar Rapids, Iowa	127	59	32	16	97	125
Jackson, Miss.	76	170	86	104	113	59
Cicero, Ill.	164	36	60	34	53	113
Columbia, S. C.	73	159	139	147	93	101
Racine, Wis.	133	50	39	29	71	126
Augusta, Ga.	77	159	128	147	93	63
Topeka, Kans.	102	86	83	87	114	101
Roanoke, Va.	108	92	60	56	84	84
Lakewood, Ohio	185	38	22	22	75	109
Charleston, S. C.	70	178	164	148	135	88
St. Joseph, Mo.	103	77	67	73	105	121
Montgomery, Ala.	74	169	110	172	105	57
Pawtucket, R. I.	185	44	46	34	62	54
Mobile, Ala.	79	151	163	142	94	60
Binghamton, N. Y.	145	59	34	28	96	112
Winston-Salem, N. C.	78	163	111	113	104	58
Altoona, Pa.	147	53	38	46	72	82
Austin, Texas	93	92†	89	95	139	62
Berkeley, Calif.	127	82†	61	61	169	125
Little Rock, Ark.	86	121	104	109	106	96
Schenectady, N. Y.	149	56	34	32	98	108
Savannah, Ga.	72	158	120	125	84	91
Allentown, Pa.	135	58	29	27	86	127
El Paso, Texas	123	76	89	68	93	91
Evansville, Ind.	102	76	106	86	83	117

TABLE 4 (continued)

City	Index Integration: NI in reverse	Index Social Barriers 3 factors *	Indices of Crime 1940-1949 Six Offenses **	Indices of Crime 1940-1949 M + B **	Index Individuation	Index Suicide ***
Shreveport, La.	90	140	66	87	98	92
Waterbury, Conn.	159	59	35	35	75	108
Charlotte, N. C.	85	124	166	165	99	62
Lowell, Mass.	179	60	28	32	86	52
Tampa, Fla.	84	116	121	133	98	141
Tacoma, Wash.	93	66	96	85	102	164
Knoxville, Tenn.	88	105	142	170	100	76
Wichita, Kans.	114	71	50	53	99	99
Chattanooga, Tenn.	78	138	131	195	89	87
Albany, N. Y.	135	81	39	34	126	87
Tulsa, Okla.	99	83	117	122	93	89
Scranton, Pa.	159	56	35	34	72	70
Norfolk, Va.	68	167	204	202	188	117
Yonkers, N. Y.	156	52	27	28	66	87
Nashville, Tenn.	76	146	144	187	125	102
Des Moines, Iowa	122	74	50	48	109	84
Miami, Fla.	82	108	168	177	126	129
Grand Rapids, Mich.	133	64	59	47	95	80
Jacksonville, Fla.	72	150	165	195	112	102
Hartford, Conn.	125	80	88	85	116	107
Fort Worth, Texas	104	88	99	119	93	89
Youngstown, Ohio	123	80	92	78	75	85
Richmond, Va.	83	139	149	143	115	112
Syracuse, N. Y.	139	74	40	32	127	98
Oklahoma City, Okla.	106	80	96	83	93	70
Dayton, Ohio	104	86	110	98	84	114
San Antonio, Texas	106	86	109	95	79	89
Providence, R. I.	154	72	50	48	106	62
Birmingham, Ala.	79	152	130	167	81	63
Toledo, Ohio	118	74	87	76	90	128
Memphis, Tenn.	83	153	124	102	95	56
St. Paul, Minn.	141	65	47	44	104	76
Dallas, Texas	96	88	148	171	94	87
Oakland, Calif.	91	96	137	96	121	162
Atlanta, Ga.	74	152	172	212	113	98
Portland, Ore.	92	73	129	103	124	182
Louisville, Ky.	93	99	170	153	90	107
Denver, Colo.	102	77	97	98	116	157
Houston, Texas	94	107	122	161	93	90
Indianapolis, Ind.	99	95	108	96	93	111
New Orleans, La.	95	140	82	93	100	72
Minneapolis, Minn.	127	71	43	36	126	106

* Mean of individuation, depressed classes, and nonwhite scores; ** mean of six offenses; M + B—mean of murder and burglary scores; *** years 1939-1948; † factor of individuation omitted because of the size of university student body in city.

a study in contrasts as well as trends in murder and burglary in the southern and non-southern cities.

Opportunities for committing murder or burglary are probably more nearly the same everywhere than for any other offenses. Yet the trend lines for murder (as shown in Figure 2) move out from the first year of the decade 163 points apart (191-28) for the southern and non-southern cities and remain 104 points apart (134-30) at its close, with the southern cities remaining four times as "murderous" as their non-southern mates in 1949. The trend lines for burglary, however, follow very different patterns. These depart from 1940 with a distance of 35 points between them (122-87) and end the decade 26 points apart (122-96), with the score for the southern cities exactly what it was at the beginning.

A similar picture prevails in the comparison of rates for aggravated assault and robbery (Figure 3), with the southern-non-southern trend lines being much farther apart for the former than for the latter offense. Observe, however, the similarities and dissimilarities between the two groups of cities in trends for larceny and auto-theft, as shown in Figure 4. It is true that murder and aggravated assault trends are similar, and that burglary and robbery trends are more similar than trends for auto-theft and larceny. The main difference in the latter pair of offenses is that the trend lines for larceny move out from 1940 with the two groups of cities 41 points apart (137-96), the southern cities predominating, and reach 1949 with an identical score of 100, while in auto-theft the non-southern group starts out leading the southern group by 1 point (88-87) and ends 22 points behind in 1949 (93-71).

IV. CORRELATION OF SERIES FOR CRIME WITH OTHER SERIES

The relationship of various crime series with each of the series outlined above is as striking as the contrasts we have observed in patterns and trends of crime. There is a high correlation between the index for depressed classes (the index of socio-economic status reversed) and various indices for crime (Tables 3 and 4). The Pearsonian coefficient is +.51 between the former and the crime series based on the mean of six offenses in 1950-1951. Between the depressed classes index and murder-burglary series, it is +.62. If the murder index only is compared with the index for depressed classes, the coefficient is +.70 for the decade preceding 1950.[20]

If the series hypothetically representing social barriers to achievement and social participation is compared with series for crime (Table 4), the comparison with the six-offense series (1950-1951) yields a coefficient of +.66, and with the murder-burglary series (for the same period), +.75.

Possible explanations of these relationships include the hypothesis that southern cities, because of differences in social structure and psycho-cultural differences as previously indicated, tend more to crime than most urban places in other areas. Crime may be in considerable part a manifestation of resentments against unfavorable roles and statuses and other social misfortunes. These resentments, which it is not wise to express overtly against the more powerful who ascribe these positions, can be displaced toward friendless persons of one's own class.[21] Again, members of depressed classes may not have opportunity to become adequate persons; also, they are in a position to commit none but the crimes which conventionally attract most of the public's attention and therefore most of the attention of the police and of the courts. Upper class criminals, who seem to be numerous,[22] turn more to crimes which the depressed classes have little opportunity to commit and which are less fully reported. Finally, since the proportion of depressed classes is larger in the South than elsewhere and the middle classes correspondingly smaller, the proportion of the population which commits what is conventionally thought of as crime is larger. Therefore, the rates of crime in the South seem larger than elsewhere. We might assume, however, that members of the middle and upper classes in urban places in the South are no more given to crime than corresponding classes elsewhere.

The high correlation of indices of crime with the social barrier

20. See other significant related comparisons in Porterfield, "Suicide and Crime in Folk and in Secular Society," *loc. cit.;* "Suicide and Crime in the Social Structure of an Urban Setting: Fort Worth, 1930-1950," *loc. cit.;* and "The Church and Social Well-being: A Statistical Analysis," *loc. cit.*

21. *Ibid.*

22. Edwin H. Sutherland, *White Collar Crime* (New York: Dryden Press, 1949). Sutherland proves thoroughly that upper class people commit much crime in business operations.

series—as a composite of the mean for depressed classes, individuation, and nonwhite social status—shows that the conditions of not being part of a more favored class, of not being a member of a family group, and of not belonging to the majority group, when combined, are highly conducive to high rates of crimes known to the police.

V. CRIME AS A COMPONENT OF THE INTEGRATION-NONINTEGRATION SERIES

We have said that the ACID test of the relative effectiveness of a community's group life and institutions lies in our integration-nonintegration continuum (Tables 3 and 4), which has as its components the factors of *anomie, conflict between groups, interpersonal and intrapersonal disaffection,* and *depressed populations.* That greater numbers of persons are displaced from satisfying roles and statuses in southern urban places than in some other areas is also clear from the observation of the relationships of these series with one another and with crime. It may be significant that *individuation* (as a component of *anomie*) comes nearer being positively related with indices of both suicide and crime than does any other index (Table 4). It would be extremely difficult, however, to construct an index to show this.

Apparently there are more lines of conflict in southern urban places in close association with crime-as-conflict-within-itself. This is indicated not only by the presence of minority group members in great numbers but by the greater number of congregations per 100,000 church members over 13 years old [23] and by the greater number of congregations per 100,000 total population. Crime rates are significantly associated with the latter (+.67 in Fort Worth census tract comparisons,[24] +.49 with the six-offense series by states for 1939-1948, and +.60 for the same period with homicide; with these two series in the 86 cities, it was +.40 and +.57 re-

23. Data from U. S. Bureau of the Census, *Religious Bodies: 1936* (Washington: Government Printing Office, 1941).
24. The higher positive relationship of congregations (per 1,000 people) by census tracts in Fort Worth in 1948 with crime rates may indicate that more recent data on congregations would lift, not lower, the coefficients observed between these series in the 86 cities.

spectively).[25] Those who are convinced that the characteristics of the Negro are productive of crime would probably not agree that the fractionation of church members into many congregations *causes* crime. Is not the presence of group conflict rather than either of these factors productive of criminal behavior?

Crime is not only related to *anomie;* it is also related to residential mobility which in turn varies significantly with the integration-nonintegration series. In comparison with the integration series, mobility (as percentage of movement from one residence to another) between 1949 and 1950 presents a coefficient of −.72 (see Table 4); with the six-offense series (1950-1951), +.65; with the murder-burglary series, +.67.

All in all, then, crime seems logically to be one of the components of the integration-nonintegration continuum. When the composite for six offenses (1940-1949) is included with the index for suicide for the same period as the I component of the ACID test (in spite of the fact that suicide and crime rates vary in opposite directions), the nonintegration series which it helps to form is very highly associated with the murder-burglary series for 1950-1951, the coefficient being +.81. Crime is in itself a real index of nonintegration (Table 3).

VI. SUMMARY AND CONCLUSION

It has been our objective to outline some correlates of crime in the urban South. This we have tried to do by contrast and comparison of 43 southern with 43 non-southern cities which had more than 50,000 population in 1940 and which we have placed side by side in equal population pairs. We have shown that urban crime rates are greater in the southern than in the non-southern cities. We have shown that barriers to social participation and achievement are more in evidence in some cities than in others. We have also shown that conditions of *anomie, group conflict, interpersonal and intrapersonal disaffection,* and *depressed socioeconomic standing* are more prevalent in the urban South than in

25. See Porterfield, "Suicide and Crime in the Social Structure of an Urban Setting: Fort Worth, 1930-1950," *loc. cit.;* "The Church and Social Well-being: A Statistical Analysis," *loc. cit.;* and "Suicide and Crime in Folk and in Secular Society," *loc. cit.*

other urban areas. Also we have seen that these conditions are correlates of various series representative of crime. Crime itself thus appears logically to be a component of the continuum for integration-nonintegration.

Our data show that there may exist a trend toward equalization in rates of crime for southern-non-southern areas; if so, the process will take a long time to bring about results. It proceeds only as the two groups compared become more alike in their social structure and patterns of culture.

We are keenly aware that our measures are not adequate and that much more research remains to be done; but we believe we have made a beginning toward a better understanding of the sources of crime in the urban South.[26]

26. *Uniform Crime Reports* for 1952 were not available when we compiled our rates and indices of crime. But in 1952 the rates in the southern and non-southern cities respectively were: murder, 14.3 and 3.2; robbery, 64.2 and 58.0; aggravated assault, 145.6 and 42.3; burglary, 584.7 and 423.7; larceny, 1212.6 and 1136.1; auto-theft, 309.9 and 189.6. If the trend lines in Figures 1, 2, 3, and 4 were projected to these rates, the distance would appear to widen again slightly between them. This change heightens the probability that it will take a long time for the rates between the two groups of cities to become equalized.

Part Three

URBANISM, CHANGE, AND TRADITION

Introduction

H AVING CONSIDERED the forces responsible for city growth in Part One, and having viewed four especially important aspects of contemporary urban life in Part Two, we turn now to the question: "How will the South's new urbanism affect the region's future?"

Urban and metropolitan life now involve more southerners more variously than ever before. The old class system geared to the predominantly rural society of an earlier period has gone. The housing and neighborhood arrangements of the "Old South" are fast disappearing. People believe differently and behave differently, their behavior—both criminal and law-abiding—reflecting the stimuli and strains of a greatly altered social organization. These and other changes already wrought by urbanization and industrialization are indeed great, but more are yet to come. Never-ending change is a certainty in all life, of course. In the South, however, it is a certainty which perhaps is less easily overlooked. Here one sees much and feels more; change and process, matters unfinished and to come, are "in the air." The South is moving in new directions.

For some problems the social sciences can even now make quite accurate predictions. Such is not the case, however, with the question of the South's future. The question is too complex and the relevant research has been insufficiently rigorous. However, certain rather specific forces and mechanisms of change present in the contemporary urban South can be identified. This we have done in the five chapters which follow. These chapters suggests *how* and *why*, in part, the South will continue to change, but it is left to the reader to draw his own inferences as to *what* the outcomes will be and *when*.

The partial nature of the account to follow should be noted. In the first place, almost no pointed attention has been given the important lines of mutual influence between the South, the nation, and the world. Secondly, even within the southern context, only incidental attention has been given the labor movement, industrial development programs, and such prospects as Alexander Heard recently dealt with in his book, *A Two-Party South?* Nor have we dealt with movements in religious belief and the importance of a continuing shift from religious fundamentalism to liberalism, or other changes in matters of belief and value such as Morton Rubin and Hylan Lewis treat in their studies of southern culture, *Plantation County* and *Blackways of Kent.*

The authors of this final part of the book, however, have dealt with five significant forces and mechanisms in the South's ongoing reorganization. These center, respectively, in race relations, politics, rationalized community organization, city planning, and the social hegemony of the big city over its hinterland.

Bullock's analysis of the changing patterns of race relations associated with urbanism suggests the locus and dynamic of a force which will continue to reshape southern institutions and southern behavior generally. That change in the Negro's way of life involves reciprocal change in white patterns is abundantly clear. It is also clear that Bullock welcomes such change as prerequisite to an improved level of living for the southern Negro. And the very features of urban life which Porterfield and Talbert in an earlier chapter find associated with higher southern crime rates (impersonality, anonymity, mobility of job and residence, individualization of behavior), Bullock finds at work in the break-up of southern traditionalism and the improvement of the Negro's lot. These authors remind us in their way that urbanism, like every mode of life, entails both gains and losses.

In the case of southern politics, Ewing and Titus find the legislatures still dominated by their rural members. At the same time they find clear evidence of two breaks with the past which have occurred under urban conditions and which, with continuing urbanization, may well do much to alter the traditional political pattern. These differences associated with urbanization are (1) greater voter participation in the cities, not surprisingly, and (2) a greater liberalism of urban Congressmen on issues of modern industrial and urban life.

Ewing and Titus might also have noted the important activities and expert government services of the several state Leagues of Municipalities in the South, as well as the numerous municipalities with manager-council forms of government, quite in contrast with "wool hat" and machine types.

In his chapter, Hunter defines "community organization" as a purposive device which involves social study and social action in an effort to better serve human needs on a community basis. No occupant of an ivory tower, Hunter realistically notes that what community organizers say is often quite different from what they can do, given the power structures in which they must necessarily act, and given the common assumption that to develop agriculture and industry is to "put first things first." As to whether the now numerous community chests, united funds, and councils of social agencies have been a "lever" for broad social change in the South, Hunter thinks not. The forces of inertia continue so great that new social devices are needed to offset them. One suspects that a re-modeled community organization may serve to effect considerable change in the future.

In Chapter 13, Chapin views another kind of social prevision in urban reorganization: namely, city planning. This device for guiding community development by rational and purposive means resembles the community organization agencies described by Hunter. Chapin sees city planning as an instrument for deriving, organizing, and presenting broad and continuing programs of physical improvement for the social, economic, and physical well-being of communities. He reports a considerable increase of planning agencies with full-time resident staffs over the past forty years in the South. Like Hunter, Chapin is concerned with problems of action and execution, with doing as well as talking and drawing. While he is mindful of the South's rather singular chance to protect and continue the dispersed type of urban development which has already occurred, he also calls attention to the problems of citizen interest, financing, and the creation of planning techniques suitable for small cities.

H. C. Nixon in the final chapter says a somewhat reluctant good-bye to "Possum Trot," one of the many once autonomous and closely knit rural communities of the South whose social identities have been lost in the extension of urban influence. Recognizing the inevitability—barring H-bomb disaster—of urban centralization and dominance, Nixon argues for a degree of civic participation and responsibility along democratic lines so that ". . . Possum Trot and its county may not find it natural to echo and re-echo the voice from the big capital city with no additional sense of civic duty." With the county as a revitalized political and social unit, he believes it would be possible to save the life of Possum Trot, a life which he values highly. His argument is a modified and reasoned expression of the great Jeffersonian tradition that is at once southern and American. It is also reminiscent of Lilienthal's "grass roots" theme in *Democracy on the March*.

With such changes underway in the South's traditional culture, it is small wonder that the importance of cities in the region has often been misunderstood and, not infrequently, deliberately misinterpreted by certain politicians and romantics. Surely the idea of city versus country is a myth, given the fact that urban and rural southerners are partners in the life of the region who depend on one another for an ever-increasing variety of goods and services. All of us, it seems, are joined inseparably in a common destiny, and what happens in cities to city people inevitably affects the rest of us. If such an objective account as this book may be said to have a moral, that is perhaps the moral.

CHAPTER TEN

Urbanism and Race .Relations

HENRY ALLEN BULLOCK

T HE DRASTIC IMPACT on race relations of the Negro's movement
to northern cities is generally accepted. It is the contention of this
chapter that similar trends are present in the urbanization of the
South. As Negroes concentrate in the growing cities of the South,
race relations change from the pattern prevalent in the small towns
and rural areas from which these Negroes come. Urbanization
appears to be changing the traditional relationships between the
two races (1) indirectly through the natural processes of city
growth and (2) more directly through conscious movement of
urban Negroes in the field of social action.

Recent research supports these conclusions. For example, Davis
and Dollard in their study of "Old City" and its plantation background found caste taboos more numerous and related punishments
more severe in the rural areas than in the city. The severity of controls upon Negroes increased in direct proportion to the distance
of rural areas from a large town or city.[1] Johnson has observed
that the homogeneity of the Negro group has been broken down
by rapid urbanization and that contact with impersonal agencies
within the city has compelled Negroes to develop new patterns
of personality and behavior in place of the economic and personal dependency characteristic of an earlier day.[2] Before examin-
ing such developments in some detail, it will be useful to note

1. Allison Davis and John Dollard, *Children of Bondage* (Washington:
American Council on Education, 1940), p. 247.
2. Charles S. Johnson, "Race Relations and Social Change," in E. T.
Thompson (ed.), *Race Relations and the Race Problem* (Durham: Duke
University Press, 1939), p. 295.

some of the traditional patterns of southern race relations. To realize the extent to which southern urbanization has altered race relations, one must remember the depth and force of the traditional patterns in southern rural society.

I. SOUTHERN TRADITIONALISM AND RACE RELATIONS

The southern mind has made strong in-group and out-group delineations. Its tradition of opposition to northern regions is of long standing, and southern people have been slow to change their conception of the Negro. Given these attitudes, southern sectionalism is changing to regionalism only by a slow process.[3] Over the years the South developed a system of required conformities and neatly shaped norms designed to regulate the attitudes and behavior of whites and Negroes toward each other—"the etiquette of race relations."[4] The system is personal in nature, with the concepts of right and privilege drawn neatly along racial lines.

Crop-lien laws, passed in 1865, legalized the dependency of the sharecropper upon the planter. As sharecropping became the basic labor pattern of southern agriculture, many Negroes and poor whites were pressed into this service.[5] It was at this time that the element of paternalism was placed in the traditional pattern of southern race relations, for the plantation had set the cultural norm.[6] Born of sharecropping, this dependence of servant upon master continued in many other occupations. Southern tradition has defined the master-servant pattern as the only stable condition in which the white community feels secure.[7] In this type of atmosphere, the Negro gets his desires not according to well-defined rights, but rather as protection and as favors resulting from temporary indulgences on the part of a master class. Likewise, a show

3. For the types of socio-economic conditions that encourage sectionalism in the southern region, see Rupert B. Vance, *All These People* (Chapel Hill: University of North Carolina Press, 1945), p. 479.
4. Bertram Wilbur Doyle, *The Etiquette of Race Relations in the South* (Chicago: University of Chicago Press, 1937).
5. Gunnar Myrdal, *An American Dilemma* (New York: Harper and Brothers, 1944), I, 224.
6. E. T. Thompson (ed.), *op. cit.*, p. 183.
7. R. A. Schermerhorn, *These Our People* (Boston: D. C. Heath, 1949), p. 111.

of proper deference and humility on the part of Negroes of these areas not only preserves the equilibrium of the society but also gives the whites an agreeable sense of status.[8]

The social organization of small southern towns is usually of such nature that this pattern of race relations is easily enforced. Here racial anonymity is very difficult from both the physical and sociopsychological point of view. Negroes who can pass for white seldom attempt it, for parentage is almost certain to be known in a small town. Since everyone knows everyone, there is little occasion for whites to treat Negroes outside the framework set by the cultural norm of southern tradition.

The Negro's drift urbanward represents a movement to areas where enforcement of the traditional pattern of race relations is more difficult. The city is more rational; relations are impersonal and contractual; its people tend to reflect more. Reflection undermines tradition; "Conscious reflection," writes Sumner, "is the worst enemy of the mores." [9] The city is a place of change: norms are not always firmly established, and thus new social structures and norms can come into existence.[10] The increasing anonymity of urban existence makes it easier to escape the personal scrutiny that serves so well as a mechanism of social control in the small town. We may say, then, that the Negro's urbanward drift is also a shift in his way of life. What he means to himself and what he means to others both undergo a change. The traditional system of mutual expectation between the races is impaired, and the traditional pattern of southern race relations is changing to this extent.

II. URBANISM AND INDIRECT CHANGES IN SOUTHERN RACE RELATIONS

How do the processes of city growth contribute to the erosion of southern traditionalism in matters of race? The expansion aspect of urbanization has played a considerable part. Cities grow outward from their centers by the process of incorporating new lands and

8. *Ibid.*, p. 112.
9. William Graham Sumner, *Folkways* (New York: Ginn and Company, 1940 printing), p. 60.
10. Muzafer Sherif, *An Outline of Social Psychology* (New York: Harper and Brothers, 1948), p. 160.

populations into a single organization. They also grow inward by developing a center sufficient to maintain integration and coordination over the expanding complex of relationships. These two ways of urban expansion have been referred to as centrifugal and centripetal movements.[11] It is the latter movement that is so meaningful for southern race relations, for it indirectly affects this aspect of southern life in two ways. It lures Negroes to the southern city in numbers greater than the traditional land areas formerly set aside for them can accommodate, and it provides them with economic opportunities on a broader base than is found in rural areas and small towns. Population pressure generated by expansion usually gives Negroes a new spatial position in the southern city. Urban economic opportunities, in turn, give them a new position in the southern economy and a different conception of themselves.

Population Shift and Urban Expansion

As is well known, southern cities get their population growth mostly through favorable net migration, reflecting the "pull" of city life and the "push" of rural life with associated changes in agricultural practice. The proportion of southern Negroes living in cities indicates how great has been the urban pull of the cities on this group. Although the proportion of Negroes living in cities has been lower in the South than in other parts of the United States, the rate of urbanization has been greater. The percent increased from 15.3 in 1890 to 36.5 in 1940. This represents a percentage change of 138.6 as against the respective changes of 44.7 and 53.9 for cities of the North and West.

State by state evidence of this urban pull is found in the proportion of each state's Negro population living in its leading cities.[12] Nine of the 13 states composing the South held over one-half of their urban Negro population in their five leading cities in 1940. Some of these cities obviously had a greater pulling and holding power than others. New Orleans held approximately 47.4 percent of all urban Negroes in Louisiana; Memphis, Louisville, Birmingham, Atlanta, and Richmond possessed over one-fourth of all urban

11. Amos Hawley, *Human Ecology* (New York: Ronald Press, 1950), p. 178.
12. Where leading city is defined in terms of population size.

Negroes living in their respective states. Also, the growth of the Negro population in these cities has been steadily upward.

There is another condition to be considered. It is well known that tradition has given Negroes a relatively fixed spatial position in the cities of the South. Documents show that the first Negroes to settle in southern cities secured a foothold under very rigid codes of interracial relations. The free Negroes of Virginia who moved to cities occupied huts along the docks and around the market places because their presence was tolerated only in such areas.[13] Summerhill, one of the first areas of Atlanta to be occupied by Negroes, was once used as the city dumping ground.[14] Where a highly diffused pattern of Negro settlement was found, as in Charleston, it resulted from the historic practice of having Negro servants live in the backyards of their wealthy employers.[15] Beginning under the effective control of a rigid code, these Negro communities developed into some of the most characteristic natural areas known to the urban South. The areas have been marked by main stems or streets which are by tradition identified with Negro urban communities and their ghetto-like quality—for example, Beale Street in Memphis, Rampart in New Orleans, Second and Leigh in Richmond, Dowling and Lyons in Houston. This tendency for southern cities to have designated places where Negroes can live limits the group's space while population goes unlimited. Here is the first major source of population pressure upon traditional Negro areas.

A second source is more directly dependent upon the expansion of the city itself. The location of Negro areas in southern cities renders these areas susceptible to the force and power of urban expansion. Since the city's growth is outward from the central business district, areas adjacent to this district feel the impact of the city's industrial and commercial expansion first. Rendered unstable by this force, such areas decrease in value for residential purposes but gain in value as places for industrial and commercial

13. Works Progress Administration, *The Negro in Virginia* (New York: Hastings House, 1940), p. 335.
14. Dorothy Slade, Evolution of Negro Areas in Atlanta (unpublished master's thesis, Department of Sociology, Atlanta University, 1946), p. 19.
15. Charles S. Johnson, *Patterns of Segregation* (New York: Harper and Brothers, 1943), p. 9.

function.[16] The rational policy of "good business" dictates neglect of houses engulfed by the tide of expansion. Rents drop, and people of lower income move in on the heels of more fortunate ones who move out. Because the greater proportion of Negroes is in the lower income group, most Negro urban areas are located almost within walking distance of the city's central business district.[17] Therefore, the forces of city growth, pulling more people and more institutions into the Negro areas, place people and institutions in competition for living space. The resulting inadequacy of housing for Negroes sets in motion a process of community reorganization that alters considerably the features of traditional Negro areas and the spatial pattern according to which this population group is usually distributed in the southern city.

Changing Spatial Position

The first effect of population pressure in these areas is that it brings housing inadequacy into glaring focus, and the public tends to define the condition as a problem of general community concern. Atlanta, for example, has four local low-cost housing projects. Although these projects can accommodate 2,965 families, the 8,000 applications on the waiting lists have shown that Atlanta's Negro housing needs are still unmet. Numerous southern cities, with a growing awareness of housing inadequacy in their Negro areas, have initiated ameliorative action programs. These programs have facilitated housing through government sponsorship and encouraged the release of private capital to the Negro housing market. Both have had significant effects upon the traditional pattern of race relations in the southern city.

Substantial construction programs to relieve the Negro housing shortage have been developed in Atlanta, Macon, Nashville, New Orleans, Lubbock, and various other cities.[18] More significant changes in the traditional spatial pattern of Negro urban settlement

16. Ernest W. Burgess, "Residential Segregation in American Cities," *The Annals of the American Academy of Political and Social Science,* 140 (November 1928), pp. 105-106.

17. Charles S. Johnson, *The Negro in American Civilization* (New York: Henry Holt and Company, 1930), p. 199.

18. Nelson C. Jackson, "Candlelights in the Darkness," *Survey Graphic,* 36 (December 1947), p. 693.

are being made through private enterprise. Stimulated by the in-sured loan system of the Federal Housing Administration, capital has found its way into the Negro housing market, and loans are becoming more available to those who seek to buy or build. Negro leaders throughout the South report this form of housing improve-ment.

This increased availability of capital for housing sounds a new note in race relations in the South. It means, on the one hand, that white and Negro investors have recognized new opportunities in the Negro market and, on the other, that a new type of spatial distribution of the Negro population is coming into vogue in the southern city. As capital flows more freely toward the Negro housing market, new residential subdivisions for Negroes appear at non-traditional points in the southern city. Large-scale real estate developments of this type have appeared in such cities as Memphis, Nashville, Atlanta, Orlando, Houston, and Louisville.

Private capital is also facilitating the invasion process. This is hap-pening in several large cities of the South. In Richmond, approxi-mately 24,000 dwelling units formerly owned by whites have been bought by Negroes during the past five years. Cities like Atlanta, Birmingham, Chattanooga, Dallas, Houston, Knoxville, and Okla-homa City have been experiencing invasion also, but not on so large a scale as that reported for Richmond. It is well known that invasion is an initial step in the process by which Negroes displace whites in an area. The process usually starts in a marginal zone between the more traditional white and Negro areas. As the forces of city growth render the traditional Negro areas unstable and undesirable, they have the same effect upon the white areas. Both groups seek to improve themselves by moving. The homes occupied by whites are much better than those Negroes have previously occupied; therefore, the houses are worth more on the Negro than on the white market. This makes a tempting situation for white owners of such houses, and their homes become available for Negro pur-chase. With capital made more readily available, together with some form of secure employment, Negroes are able to enter into long-time mortgage agreements for home purchasing.

The initial stage of these invasions is usually accompanied by some reaction on the part of whites. There was widespread resent-ment when Negroes moved into white areas in Knoxville; many

"For Sale" signs appeared in the invaded area. Bombings of Negro homes have been reported for several cities, and in Birmingham and Dallas reactions reached serious proportions. However, alert interracial and civic cooperation has gone a long way toward making the problem of Negro invasion less destructive than it would be otherwise. These invasions are not always accompanied by intense violence: the movement of Negroes into the Washington Terrace and Riverside areas of Houston is a good case in point. The invasion occurred in a series of leaps, whereby a few Negroes moved into a block and consolidated to the extent of dominating the area. This move was followed by another wave which went deeper into the territory, so that an area covering an entire census tract northwest of a traditional Negro community was dotted with Negro residents. Only during the last leap taken by Negroes into the area was there reaction sufficient to claim public attention; however, this little disturbance died with the same suddenness that marked its birth.

The story of Negro housing in the South shows the impact that urban growth is making on the traditional pattern of southern race relations. Although the expansion of southern cities creates a Negro housing problem, it also lays the foundation for its solution. City growth renders traditional Negro areas inadequate. The pressure of population shows up; it captures public interest; and it offers a fertile market for urban capital. Capital becomes available to Negroes who seek to buy or build, and the members of this group become somewhat relieved of the residential chains which tradition has forged about them.

Increasing Economic Opportunities

The expansion process of city growth is also changing the traditional pattern of southern race relations by giving Negroes a new functional position in the urban economy. We now have an understanding of how the second change is taking place.

Limitations have been placed upon the Negro's employment opportunities throughout the nation, and the South has enforced these limitations more than other regions. Consequently, there have developed in the nation generally and the South particularly what have come to be known as "Negro jobs." This means that a division of labor, ordinarily based upon talents and abilities of individuals, has been based upon cultural traditions inherited from slavery.

The movement of Negroes to the cities of the South has given this group greater opportunity for self-expression because the pattern of participation exacted by tradition cannot be easily enforced there. The tendency for southern cities to expand by multiplying and specializing their functions occasions a diversification of roles within the population. Although meeting resistance to change, southern Negroes are experiencing this diversification through advantages they derive from increased job opportunities. The modern industrial system, guided more by reason than by sentiment, requires a relatively free movement of workers both in physical and social space. This peculiarity accounts for the fact that industrialization has tended to break down barriers of nationality, caste, and status in industrial employment wherever it has appeared in the world.[19]

The mechanization of agriculture pushed a redundant Negro population off the farms, but increased industrialization of the southern region drew Negroes to the cities and absorbed a large proportion of them into the industries and secondary enterprises of the urban economy. The economy of cities is naturally broader than that of rural areas or small towns; consequently, Negroes who move to cities find a greater variety of jobs available to them.

Urban residence thus broadens employment opportunities for the Negro worker. Although Negroes are still employed in agriculture and personal services, there is less concentration in these fields in the urban areas of southern states. South Carolina, Tennessee, and Texas may be used to illustrate this fact (Table 1). More than 80 percent of all nonwhite workers in the rural areas of these states were employed in agriculture and personal services in 1940, but barely 50 percent of those in the urban areas were so employed during this same year. Obviously, urban nonwhite workers tend to spread more over such industry groups as manufacturing, various forms of trade, professional services, and construction. Some southern cities have far more of their share of the state's

19. Rudolf Heberle, "Social Consequences of the Industrialization of Southern Cities," *Social Forces*, 27 (October 1948), p. 36.

TABLE 1. Percent Distribution of Nonwhite Workers in Selected Southern States, by Industry Groups, Urban and Rural, 1940

	South Carolina		Tennessee		Texas	
	Urban	Rural	Urban	Rural	Urban	Rural
Total	100.0	100.0	100.0	100.0	100.0	100.0
Agriculture	2.0	75.9	1.4	68.2	1.9	67.4
Mining	0.2	0.3	0.3	0.8	0.2	0.4
Construction	6.4	1.7	5.3	1.6	4.3	1.3
Manufacturing	13.0	4.0	16.5	3.9	7.6	6.5
Transportation	5.4	1.3	6.9	1.9	7.7	1.9
Wholesale and Retail	11.9	1.8	14.3	2.5	14.5	3.1
Finance	0.8	0.1	2.1	0.3	2.1	0.2
Business	1.0	0.3	1.3	0.4	1.7	0.5
Personal Service	50.2	12.3	43.6	17.7	52.3	15.5
Amusements	0.6	0.2	0.9	0.2	1.1	0.2
Professional	7.7	2.0	6.3	2.3	5.7	2.8
Government	0.8	0.1	1.1	0.2	0.9	0.2

Source: Compiled from U. S. Bureau of Census, *The Labor Force*, III, Part 6 (Washington: U. S. Government Printing Office, 1943).

nonwhite workers in these industry groups than chance would allow.

The advantages of urban residence show themselves not only in the larger number of industries in which Negroes can work, but also in the larger number of occupations they can follow. Although there is little opportunity for them to work as electricians, machinists, musicians, carpenters, plumbers, and the like in rural areas and small towns, the big cities offer them a chance to try their talents at these kinds of occupations. This process of differentiation results in increased opportunities for Negro workers to move higher up the occupational scale. We can see this advantage when we compare rural and urban Negro workers according to major occupational classes (Table 2).

This comparison, using three strategically located southern states for illustrative purposes, shows generally that the urban areas have from two to four times more Negro workers employed at the skilled level and above than do the rural areas. An examination of other southern states shows a similar pattern.

More specifically, it is the cities that offer these workers their best chances for employment on the higher levels. Atlanta accounts for more than one-fifth of all Negroes employed on the skilled

TABLE 2. Percent Distribution of Nonwhite Workers in Selected Southern States, by Major Occupations, Rural and Urban, 1940

Major Occupations	South Carolina		Tennessee		Texas	
	Rural	Urban	Rural	Urban	Rural	Urban
Total	100.0	100.0	100.0	100.0	100.0	100.0
Professional	1.4	4.8	1.5	3.2	2.2	3.5
Semi-professional	0.1	0.3	0.1	0.3	0.1	0.3
Farmers	26.4	0.3	36.1	0.2	31.7	0.3
Proprietors, Managers, etc.	0.2	1.2	0.2	1.4	0.5	2.0
Clericals	0.2	1.3	0.2	2.2	0.3	1.7
Craftsmen	1.4	6.2	1.3	5.1	1.0	3.0
Operatives	3.3	14.7	3.6	16.0	2.9	10.6
Domestics	10.5	40.4	15.9	32.7	13.8	40.7
Service	1.7	12.0	3.3	19.0	3.2	20.7
Laborers, all	54.8	18.8	37.8	19.9	44.3	17.2

Source: Compiled from U. S. Bureau of Census, *Population*, II (Washington: U. S. Government Printing Office, 1943).

level and above in Georgia. New Orleans and Memphis account for more than one-third in their respective states. Memphis and Houston have almost one-third of all Negro electricians in their states, and New Orleans, again, has over one-half of all Negro social workers, mail carriers, stenographers, bookkeepers, and typesetters in Louisiana. Negro employment in other leading southern cities enjoys an equally greater advantage.[20]

Reports received from a large number of southern cities show that the Negro's chances to work on higher occupational levels are on the increase. The Jacksonville Urban League reports that calls for Negroes to fill non-traditional jobs come so much more rapidly than Negroes are being trained for them that only 60 percent of the requests can be filled.[21] The Dallas branch of the National Association for the Advancement of Colored People reports that significant professional opportunities in the field of government employment are being opened to Negroes in the city.[22]

20. Shown by reports received from Executive Secretaries of Urban League branches and Presidents of colleges located in large southern cities.
21. Report from L. M. Armwood, Executive Secretary, Jacksonville Urban League, Jacksonville, Florida.
22. Report from A. Maceo Smith, Executive Secretary, Dallas branch of the N.A.A.C.P., Dallas, Texas.

Several white enterprises in Houston have begun to use Negro girls as clerical workers. The girls have replaced white workers at the same salaries. A random file sample of 736 manufacturing firms in Texas showed eight such firms to be employing Negro chemists and nine to be employing engineers of all types.[23] It is significant that all except one of these establishments are located in the leading cities of Texas.

Negroes are gaining a significant foothold in municipal employment in the South. Sixteen leading cities of the region employ 6,487 Negroes for public work. Approximately 10 percent of these are at the skilled level or above, with 7.2 percent employed on the managerial or professional level.[24] The Negro is regaining his position as a firefighter in the southern city, and his opportunities for such employment are increasing. Six southern cities were employing Negro firemen in 1951,[25] and Oklahoma City has begun the practice since that time.

Greater purchasing power inevitably follows the Negro's newfound economic opportunities, and this power serves to stimulate additional opportunities. One instance of this relationship is found in the larger number of Negroes who are being employed as salesmen in southern cities. Negro urban consumers offer an attractive market to those who have something to sell. The lure of this market has caused sellers to use Negro salesmen as a means of reaching it. Negro salesmen have been used with particular success in the lines of household appliances, alcoholic and soft beverages, automobiles, tobacco, and food products.

We have some evidence also that the increased purchasing power of Negroes has helped to open opportunities in the field of professional sports. Major league baseball teams have found little difficulty in using their Negro players against minor league teams in southern cities. When Negro athletes appear on mixed teams in southern cities, gate receipts increase considerably. Negroes attend the events in large numbers, mainly because of racial loyalty and the oppor-

23. Henry Allen Bullock, "Racial Attitudes and the Employment of Negroes," *American Journal of Sociology*, LVI (March 1951), 450.
24. Harold O. DeWitt, "Negro Municipal Workers in the South," *New South*, 6 (May-June 1951), p. 1.
25. Harold O. DeWitt, Negro Firefighters in Selected and Border Cities (unpublished manuscript, Industrial Relations Department, National Urban League, 1951), pp. 3-4.

tunity to identify themselves with achievements that claim national interest. Whites attend likewise, but probably more because of curiosity.

Changing Self-Conception

Out of the new spatial and functional position which they have gained incidental to urbanization, southern Negroes are slowly developing a new conception of themselves. The very nature of urban life is contributing heavily to this fundamental racial change. Urban life offers a specialized kind of existence for human beings. Its heterogeneity offers each individual an opportunity to develop highly individualized behavior patterns that would not be tolerated by the mores of rural areas.[26] Urban anonymity means close physical proximity coupled with vast social distances between men. It alters profoundly the bases of human association, and it subjects to severe strain the traits of human nature molded by simpler social organizations.[27] Opportunities for individualized behavior and anonymity of person make their impact upon the urban Negro personality especially through the pattern of employment and the types of social contacts that urban living forces upon him.

The shift of many southern Negroes from rural to urban employment has meant a shift from a personal to an impersonal form of employer-employee alliance. Southern urban Negroes are finding themselves in increasing contact with our fundamental industrial characteristic of wide social distance between employer and employee, which requires that loyalty be given on an organizational rather than on a personal level. There is evidence that the southern urban Negro worker is rapidly learning this new pattern.

The Negro is becoming an integral part of American organized labor; his greatest progress toward this goal has been made in the last half-century. Dubois estimates that Negro membership in labor unions increased from about 30,000 in 1900 to 1,000,000 at the height of the war employment period.[28] Much of this progress in

26. John F. Cuber, *Sociology: A Synopsis of Principles*, rev. ed. (New York: Appleton-Century-Crofts, Inc., 1951), p. 393.

27. Louis Wirth, "The Urban Society and Civilization," *American Journal of Sociology*, XLV (March 1940), 752.

28. W. E. B. Dubois, "The Negro Since 1900: A Progress Report," *New York Times Magazine Section*, August 8, 1948.

unionization has been made among southern Negro workers through the CIO, which has constitutional provisions against discrimination.

Ranking next to changed employment patterns as a force helping southern urban Negroes to gain a new conception of themselves is the phenomenon of impersonal social contact. Both the speed and magnitude with which urban contacts are made have heightened the difficulty of enforcing traditional policies; the result is that the formalized and routinized methods of modern businesses are being increasingly extended to include all persons impartially.

Whether as a result of an earnest attempt to exploit the Negro market or of the sheer bigness and speed of urban life, policies of segregation in business relations are being relaxed in southern cities, and Negroes are being given a greater opportunity for self-respect. With the emergence of a new conception of himself as a worker and a greater respect for himself as a person, the southern urban Negro is becoming a new social type.

III. COLLECTIVE-ACTION MOVEMENTS AND CHANGES IN SOUTHERN RACE RELATIONS

Facts presented so far in this chapter show that significant changes have occurred in the traditional pattern of southern race relations incidental to the urbanization process. Were we to stop here, however, we would perhaps leave the impression that southern people have been relying completely upon natural processes to rid themselves of the discontents involved in Negro-white relations. But if natural processes have not solved the problem, neither have southern people been entirely passive about it. This section undertakes to examine conditions in southern cities favorable to racial discontent, and to view the various types of collective-action movements designed to stimulate changes in race relations.

Urbanization and Collective-Action Movements

Several conditions of urban life favor the collective action of southern people against racial discrimination. One is the tendency for cities to aggregate protesting personalities and tolerate their protests. The city is a breeding ground for discontent. Changes occur there more rapidly, and resulting disorganization is more certain. A sizeable minority of the urban population, composed of protesting individuals, is more often critical of the status quo.[29] Southern liberals have grown out of this dynamic quality of urban life, and they have become the main support of the "public suasion" type of collective-action movements.

Southern Negroes express their discontent through an aggressive corps of Negro leaders found in every southern city. The city gathers Negroes who are not only quick to express their dissatisfaction with the status quo, but are also quick to initiate action against it.

Crowning the class structure of every Negro urban community are its artists, businessmen, clergymen, dentists, editors, lawyers, physicians, social workers, and many others who constitute an elite that is rapidly growing toward some degree of economic power. As Woodson showed several years ago, southern cities attract more than their share of Negroes of the professional class.[30] Even the segregation which they so bitterly dislike has given them opportunities to grow economically while in the service of their own people. Warner believes that the emotional instability of this group as compared with Negroes of lower positions may be due to the instability and skewness of the social position in which they live. This lack of balance keeps them struggling to achieve an equilibrium not provided for them.[31] It is our contention that this struggle organizes itself into collective-action movements against the racial status quo.

The Negro's urban settlement pattern is another condition favorable to collective-action movements. A study of tracts in which Negroes composed 70 percent or more of the population gives a picture of how sharply Negroes are separated from the rest of the city's population.

29. Noel P. Gist and L. A. Halbert, *Urban Sociology*, 3rd ed. (New York: Thomas Y. Crowell Company, 1948), p. 318.

30. Carter G. Woodson, *The Negro Professional Man and the Community* (Washington: The Association for the Study of Negro Life and History, 1934), p. 13.

31. See Lloyd Warner's "Introduction" in Allison Davis, Burleigh B. Gardner, and Mary R. Gardner, *Deep South* (Chicago: University of Chicago Press, 1941), p. 13.

With few exceptions, large areas having a high percentage of whites are separated from large areas having a high percentage of Negroes by smaller areas of Negro-white mixture. We can see the intensity of Negro population concentration within the city when we observe the number of "Negro areas" necessary to account for 50 percent or more of the city's Negro population. Such analysis shows that racial separation and racial concentration may be two different things. It implies that a group may be sharply separated but not necessarily concentrated within the city itself. As we know, the concentration pattern is present in varying degrees. In fact, there are four specific patterns of racial concentration within the more general practice of racial separation. (1) There are cities in which one-half or more of the Negro population is concentrated within one "Negro area." Birmingham and Oklahoma City are of this type. (2) Some of the cities concentrate this proportion of their Negro population in two areas, separated by clusters of tracts having a lighter Negro-white mixture. Atlanta, Houston, and Savannah illustrate this type. (3) Memphis spreads more than half of its Negro population over three areas, although these areas are not so far apart. (4) Finally, certain cities as Louisville, Nashville, New Orleans, and Richmond have no "Negro areas" with so much as one-half of all Negroes living in them. (See Chapter 7, by N. J. Demerath and H. W. Gilmore, for further discussion of residential segregation.)

These facts show that residential segregation has given Negroes the spatial proximity necessary for collective expression. This proximity serves as a basis for the development of a common cultural heritage and a common institutional structure. As Arnold Rose has so clearly stated, every Negro community institution promotes group morale and group identification through the practice of bringing Negroes together regularly and frequently.[32]

From the point of view of collective mentality as well as collective action, the Negro press is one of the most powerful institutions of the Negro urban community. It is the main channel through which racial discontent is expressed and stimulus to collective action against discrimination is communicated. It is difficult to keep track

32. Arnold M. Rose, *The Negro's Morale* (Minneapolis: University of Minnesota Press, 1949), p. 97.

of all the different newspapers and magazines that go to make this important institution of Negro life. However, it is known that 155 Negro newspapers had an aggregate circulation of 1,276,000 in 1940. It has been reported that 84 of these papers in the South had a combined circulation of 474,500 per issue during this same year. Every southern state and practically every large city in these states can lay claim to some type of Negro newspaper.[33] All except one are weeklies; five of them circulate to all regions of the United States.

Negro newspapers play the general role of supplying direction for collective-action movements. Wherever they circulate, one can be sure that they appeal to the Negro masses and classes. Their policies are permeated with intense militancy, for they attribute much of the instability and disorganization of Negro life to segregation and discrimination. An examination of a variety of Negro newspapers, using an outline similar to that given by Rollin Chambliss,[34] shows that scarcely any discriminatory aspect of race relations goes without attack from them. The interests that keep them alive make them different in character from American newspapers in general. Bits of news which they report are punctuated with propaganda and highly dramatized facts in order for them to comply with their cultural mission of stimulating discontent. The press's great power of suggestion and control over the minds and behavior of Negroes gives the group a certain amount of unanimity.[35]

The massing of Negroes within urban communities places each individual within seeing distance of the effects of segregation upon the other. Negro newspapers, most of whose readers are found in southern cities, keep them irritated by constant mention of the discrimination Negroes suffer in all sections of the country. With the diffusion of knowledge about what is happening to Negroes in other areas, collective action is more easily stimulated.

33. Florence Murray (ed.), *The Negro Handbook, 1944* (New York: Current Reference Publications, 1944), pp. 264-268.
34. Rollin Chambliss, What Negro Newspapers of Georgia Say About Some Social Problems (unpublished master's thesis, University of Georgia, 1934).
35. Gunnar Myrdal, *op. cit.*, II, 911.

Public Suasion Type of Collective-Action Movements

White liberals of the urban South are also counted among the basic sources of change in the race relations picture. Usually they have been willing to give aid to the Negro's cause short of war with segregation practices. Consequently, they join hands with those organizations that seek to reduce racial discrimination by educating southern white people to be more tolerant toward Negroes.

The Commission on Interracial Cooperation, the Southern Regional Council, and the National Urban League are examples of the public suasion types of collective action, for their effectiveness as forces of social change has rested upon liberal whites and the educational process of persuasion.

The Commission (now dissolved) began as a joint effort of whites and Negroes to bring representatives of the two groups together as a means of improving race relations in the South. It was mainly a white people's organization, dominated by southern liberals. Although it surrendered its identity and merged with the newly-formed Southern Regional Council in 1944, its basic ideas and program are still carried on by the Council. These interracial groups have sought to change interracial attitudes by sponsoring educational programs of personal contact and public suasion, and by encouraging fair economic opportunities for Negroes, equal participation in public welfare programs, equal justice under the law, equal rights of suffrage, and other forms of civil liberties.[36] They have not attacked segregation *per se*, but instead waged a war against discrimination.

Nevertheless, both the Interracial Commission and the Southern Regional Council have had significant impact upon the traditional pattern of southern race relations. Many southern leaders think the Commission was effective in decreasing the South's lynching rate, and its opposition to the Ku Klux movement in the 1930's was a significant contribution to interracial harmony. It also supported the work of the Farm Security Administration. Both organizations have waged war against police brutality by conferences with police authorities, publicizing instances of brutality, and by

36. *Ibid.*, pp. 844-845.

distributing information concerning ways by which the menace can be curbed.[37] Outstanding Negro leaders have been brought before white audiences in the South as a result of various types of interracial activities sponsored by these units. The Southern Regional Council has worked for racial harmony without effecting fundamental changes in the social order.

The National Urban League is much more highly specialized in its aim than the Commission or the Southern Regional Council, but the absence of pressure behind it leads us to classify it as a movement of the public suasion type. Its effectiveness rests more upon its force as an educational agency than on its power as a pressure group. It originated as a social service institution, designed to adjust Negroes to industrial employment and urban living, but its objectives have been considerably widened since that time. Its program centers on the general problem of Negro urban welfare.

The League's most significant achievement is its work in behalf of Negro labor. It has made decided progress in "selling" Negro labor to white employers by breaking down the attitude that Negro workers are inferior to white workers. Through Career Conferences sponsored by Negro colleges, the National Urban League launches a dynamic program aimed at informing young Negroes of job opportunities available to them and the types of training they must undergo in order to take advantage of these opportunities.

Legal-Action Movement

The fundamental attack against segregation and discrimination has been carried by the National Association for the Advancement of Colored People. Significant changes have resulted from this organization's program. The bulk of the N.A.A.C.P.'s southern membership has been supplied by cities; each southern city supports a branch unit of this organization, and the major activities of each unit are coordinated with the operation of the national office in New York.

The organization operates on the theory that segregation and discrimination are twin-born, and that the elimination of the former is necessary to the destruction of the latter. By defining discrimina-

37. See Southern Regional Council, *Race and Law Enforcement* (Atlanta: Southern Regional Council, 1951).

tion in terms of those racial inequalities that violate provisions of the Constitution of the United States, the N.A.A.C.P. has become the champion of the Negro's civil liberties in the federal courts. The program has been very effective in realizing its aims. Its achievements involve changes in public education, transportation, residential segregation, and political participation. Its attacks on discrimination in public education in the South are well known. In all these changes the urban Negro group has been the vanguard.

Suits were brought against those public school systems that paid their Negro teachers salaries unequal to those paid white teachers with similar qualifications. During the early stages of the program, Negro teachers in Little Rock, Dallas, Norfolk, and other cities risked their jobs in behalf of all Negro teachers in the South. On the strength of its legal accomplishments in these cases, the N.A.A.C.P. has forced practically every southern state to introduce salary equalization policies for its teachers.

Legal success in the Morgan case, where the constitutionality of segregation in interstate travel was tested, resulted in travel relief for southern Negroes. Pullman reservations have become more readily available, and some railroad companies have introduced mixed coaches in intrastate travel. A court victory in the restrictive covenant case made it possible for Negroes to buy and use property in areas previously closed to them. The Supreme Court, in the Sweatt and McLaurin decisions, opened the majority of southern publicly-supported graduate and professional schools to Negroes; its more recent decisions gave promise of the virtual elimination of segregation in southern public education.

Political-Action Movement

Several changes suggest the significance of the Negro's rise to political power in the South. Especially prominent is the rapid growth of qualified Negro voters following the Supreme Court decision in the "Texas Primary" case. Moon estimates that the number of Negro voters in the South more than doubled two years after the Supreme Court decision.[38] Heard reports that the number

38. Henry Lee Moon, "The Negro Vote in the South: 1952," *The Nation*, September 27, 1952, p. 246.

of qualified Negro voters in southern states rose from approximately 151,000 in 1940 to 595,000 in 1947, and to 900,000 in 1950.[39] Although these estimates may be a bit optimistic, it is certain that the Negro vote has become strong enough for present-day southern politicians to solicit it.

Whatever its size, there is abundant evidence that the southern Negro vote is being organized and harnessed for political action. Practically every southern city has a Negro voter's league as a part of the institutional complex of the Negro community. Many of these leagues are city-wide only; some extend to incorporate cities and towns on a state-wide basis.[40] They have become the main force through which Negro voters are organized and made vocal in expressing their political demands. The Greater Fifth Ward Citizen's League of Houston is an example. Organized in 1947, the League has grown to include more than 1,500 voters in its present membership. An examination of the League's activities shows that it is one of the most active pressure groups in Houston. It uses the lobby method to get what it wants for Negro citizens. Its members appear as a body before the City Council, and they present evidence to justify the improvements they seek for Negroes of their area. Bus lines have been changed, streets have been paved, and areas have been better drained through the League's influence.[41]

Through this organizational technique, Negro voters of southern cities have not only been able to influence the election of white candidates, but they have also been able to nominate candidates from their own group and get some of them elected. Negroes have offered as candidates in cities of most southern states since 1940. Oliver Hill of Richmond lost the Democratic nomination to the Virginia State House of Delegates by only 200 votes in 1947, but became the first Negro to be elected to a Richmond office when he won a seat on the City Council in 1948. Also, in 1951 two Negroes were elected to the City Council in Nashville. In this same year, Kermit Parker qualified as a Democratic candidate for Governor of Louisiana.

39. Alexander Heard, *A Two-Party South?* (Chapel Hill: University of North Carolina Press, 1952), p. 181.
40. See *ibid.*, pp. 188-199.
41. Tandy Tollerson, The Negro in Houston Politics (unpublished master's thesis, Texas Southern University, 1952), pp. 44-45.

Not all of the success of Negro candidates in political races has been due to the Negro vote. Some victories have come as a result of a coalition with other minorities in southern cities. Negroes and Spanish-Americans joined their political strength in an election at San Antonio, and Negro G. J. Sutton succeeded in getting elected to the board of the Negro Junior College of that city. Although the coalition was the result of a trade, the incident shows the possibility of a trend toward a voting strength involving Negroes and other urban minorities in the South.

It is this type of strategy—the internal organization of Negro voting strength and the multiplication of this strength by coalitions—that foreshadows a new political and social order for the South. Ever since the New Deal raised more than 20,000,000 white and Negro tenant farmers of the South from the legal and economic prostration they had suffered over years past, the Negro voter has remained alien to the Republican Party with which he had for so long been traditionally associated. The fact that he broke tradition shows the opportunism inherent in his vote. As long as the southern Negro remains a minority group, irritated by the discriminations that inevitably grow out of segregation, we can expect him to be an active force in the political camp of the liberal South. His political weight will be thrown toward reform tickets, and we can expect his growing political strength to stimulate more social welfare, reforms, and security in the South.

IV. SUMMARY

Urbanization is introducing a new form of social organization in the South. It influences changes in many societal relations from personal and non-contractual to impersonal and contractual patterns. Since the traditional pattern of race relations has been an inseparable part of the South's social organization, this tradition too has felt the impact of rapid urbanization. This chapter has shown that there are two basic ways in which the urbanization of the South is changing the traditional pattern of race relations in the region. One is indirect and results from the natural processes of city growth; the other is more direct and grows out of the conscious collective-action movements of Negroes.

Indirectly changes in traditional patterns have grown out of the expansion inherent in the urbanization process. Cities grow outward from their centers by incorporating new lands and populations; they also develop more economic complexity at their centers. This latter aspect of urban growth lures to urban centers more Negroes than can be accommodated by the traditional areas provided them. It sets up for them new economic opportunities on a broader base than that found in rural areas and small towns. These changes set into motion a chain of social and economic reactions which gives Negroes a new and non-traditional spatial position in the southern city. The latter, growing out of more diversified economic demands and functions, has helped to open the doors of non-traditional occupations to Negroes. Because job relations grow more impersonal and contractual in urban employment, Negro workers change their loyalty from employer to fellow worker. They become conscious of the power of organization, they develop new conceptions of themselves, and they come to play a greater part in the labor movement.

It is mainly from this new self-conception that conscious collective action among Negroes has stemmed. The tendency for cities to tolerate personality differences not only gives to Negroes an opportunity to speak and act against the traditional pattern of southern race relations, but it also makes possible the concentration of a sizeable proportion of white liberals. Protests of Negroes and white liberals have furnished public suasion, legal pressure, and political action against the southern race relations pattern. One type has been mild—tolerant of segregation, but seeking to reduce racial discrimination. A second type has been aggressive—mindful of discrimination, and endeavoring to destroy segregation by encouraging the federal courts to declare it unconstitutional. Each movement has made its dents in the armor of southern tradition, and both are fully identified with the rising tide of urbanization in the South.

CHAPTER ELEVEN

Urbanism and Southern Politics

CORTEZ A. M. EWING AND
JAMES E. TITUS

I. RURAL CHARACTER OF THE SOUTH

T HE PREVAILING pattern of southern politics is essentially rural. Of the South's more than 34 million residents, 67 percent are rural dwellers.[1] The rural pattern is further revealed in respect to southern counties. Fewer than one in 10 counties in 11 southern states contains urban majorities. Omitting Virginia on account of her unique local government organization,[2] the other 11 states have 1,085 counties, of which only 104, or 9.5 percent, contain majorities of urban residents.

As a guide to the understanding of political behavior, the urban-rural census classification is questionable in certain respects. Many communities designated as urban are in fact rural in character. They are only collections of rural people who happen, for convenience, to be living together. This is true especially of urban counties in southern and western Texas. On the other hand, there are unorganized communities, such as those adjacent to coal mines or lumber camps, which reveal more of the urban spirit and are more concerned with urban problems than the larger centers in

1. Based on Sixteenth Census (1940) figures. The 1940 Census data are used in this study because of the greater political experience under 1940 apportionments than under more recent apportionments based on the 1950 Census.

2. Virginia is organized into 101 counties, all of which are rural except Arlington. The municipalities (24) are organized separately from the counties. They range in size from Williamsburg with 3,942 to Richmond with 193,042 people. However, the state is 64.7 percent rural, which makes it the most representative state of the section on the urban-rural classification.

which retired farmers and ranchers build their permanent domiciles and from which they go into the countryside to direct their agricultural operations.

The impact of increasing urbanization upon a traditional ruralism is revealed in many channels of political action. An increase in population density produces an increase in personal irritations; the urban community must invoke many legal controls upon human behavior. Laws are no more than standards for human behavior and are formulated for the plain purpose of reducing personal conflicts in society. But if the city must increase the number of rules for human behavior, it nevertheless frees the individual from many of the shackles imposed by rules of customary morality in rural communities. Since the dissolution of European feudalism, the city has appeared to rural peoples as a free community; the moral norms of city and country have always been in conflict, it seems.

The aim of this brief study is to identify and evaluate the principal impacts of urbanization on the traditionally rural political practices of the South. Many matters which tend to be distinctively southern will be disregarded, for uniqueness is by no means synonymous with urban modification of rural patterns. For instance, the South's reliance upon the city-manager system of municipal administration is unique but apparently has little effect on rural public administration. Likewise, the South's practical disfranchisement of the Negro is unique, but it would come into this study only if the Negro were to find fewer or more impediments to political participation in cities than in rural areas. The same would apply to the peculiar brand of political leadership, to the utilization of the run-off primary, and to the existence of uni-party political systems in the South.

The modern American political scene features the interplay of rural and urban forces at every level of government. Though each of the great major parties seeks to reconcile the conflict, their efforts are never completely successful. Even short memories can recall the virtual disappearance of party discipline when agricultural, labor, and other such vital questions come before Congress or state legislatures. While this struggle is not peculiar to the South, it is found there in a very pronounced form. One of the principal evidences of it lies in the state constitutional provision relating to representation in state legislative chambers.

II. RURAL DOMINATION OF STATE LEGISLATURES

Rural-urban struggles for control of state legislatures have been sharpened by the growth of cities and the continued refusal of rural elements to relinquish their control. The legislative power of cities has been curbed through inadequate representation. This, in turn, has been made possible by provisions of state constitutions. Rurally dominated legislatures adopt convention acts which assure a preponderance of rural delegates in constitutional conventions; the conventions submit proposed constitutions in which rural dominance is perpetuated.[3] It is not a tendency restricted to the South; it is present in all regions of the country. Moreover, if a state does not provide a system of popular initiative and referendum, there is no opportunity short of revolution for urban populations to achieve equality of representation in their state legislatures. Indeed, some of the drive for municipal home rule has derived from the realization by urban leaders that this rural domination promises to remain in American state politics.

Each of 12 southern states [4] has constitutional provisions limiting the number of seats in the lower house of its legislature. The top figure is that of 150 for the lower house in Texas if the ratio does "not exceed one member for every 15,000 population." [5] The smallest lower house is that of Florida with 68 members. Alabama is limited to 105 house members, except that new counties are each allowed one representative. Arkansas, Louisiana, and Virginia are limited to 100 members, while Mississippi has 133, South Carolina 124, North Carolina 120, and Tennessee 99. Georgia's constitution

---

3. Concerning this problem in the South, see: Hallie Farmer, *Legislative Apportionment* (University, Alabama: Bureau of Public Administration, University of Alabama, 1944); Cullen B. Gosnell, "Rotten Boroughs in Georgia," *National Municipal Review*, 20 (July 1931), pp. 393-397, and "The Gerrymander System in Georgia," *Social Forces*, 11 (May 1933), pp. 570-573; L. V. Murphy, "Legislative Apportionment in Oklahoma," *Southwestern Social Science Quarterly*, 13 (September 1932), pp. 161-168; Stuart A. MacCorkle, "Texas Apportionment Problem," *Southwestern Social Science Quarterly*, 34 (December 1945), pp. 540-543; and H. V. Thornton, "Oklahoma Cities Weakened," *National Municipal Review*, 35 (June 1946), pp. 295-298.

4. The 11 secession states and Oklahoma.

5. See Elizabeth Durfee, "Apportionment: Study of State Constitutions," *Michigan Law Review*, 43 (June 1945), p. 1112.

provides "three members to each of the eight most populous counties; two each to the next 30; one each to the remaining counties";
with 159 counties, its lower house automatically has 205 members.
In Oklahoma the house is limited to 120 members, but a curious
flotorial system is used whereby counties with major fractions over
their quotas are awarded additional members in one or more of the
legislatures of a decennial period.[6]

Upper chambers of southern legislatures are limited numerically
by either an absolute upper limit or by ratio in relation to the size
of the lower house. For example, Alabama sets a maximum of 35
and further provides that the senate shall never be less than one-
fourth nor greater than one-third the size of the lower house. The
Tennessee constitution specifies that the membership of its upper
house shall not exceed one-third the number of representatives.
Arkansas limits its senate to 35 members, Florida to 38, Georgia
to 52, Louisiana to 39, North Carolina to 50, and Texas to 31.
Oklahoma provided for an original senate of 44 members; but,
if in future reapportionments, any county was entitled to more
than three senators, the number above three should be in excess of
the 44.[7] Virginia has no limit on the size of the upper house, while
South Carolina provides that a county may elect no more than
one senator. And Mississippi permits a statutory discretion of from
30 to 45 seats.

The results of these constitutional limitations are immediately
apparent. The rural areas are in no mood to surrender their preponderant power to the urban districts. In North Carolina, Camden
County receives one representative for its 5,440 inhabitants, while
Guilford County with 153,916 people receives but three members.
By the Camden yardstick, Guilford County should have 28 representatives and the lower house should boast of a membership of
657, greater even than that of the British House of Commons. In
Georgia, Fulton County with its 392,886 residents is granted, ironi-

6. H. V. Thornton, "Oklahoma Cities Weakened," *loc. cit.,* p. 296.

7. However, the provision has remained a dead letter, for the upper
chamber, due to recalcitrance of the rural members, has not been re-
apportioned since statehood (1906). Oklahoma County, with a population
equal to four quotas, elects one senator and shares another with an adjoining
county, while Tulsa County, with a three-quota population, elects only one
senator. This means that the upper house is firmly in the grip of the rural
senators.

cally enough, a total of three assemblymen. Echols County, Georgia, however, has one member for its 2,964 people. By the Echols standard, Fulton County would receive 133 members, and the state would have to provide quarters for an assembly of 1,054 members. At the house level, one resident of Echols exercises as much political power as 44 citizens of Atlanta. Examples of this gross violation of the principles of representative government could be multiplied without end in other southern states and in states above the Mason-Dixon line.

Strict limitation in size and unethical gerrymandering by rural leaders render impossible any flexibility of representation, which is necessary to progress in this age of expanding industrialization and urbanization. Population shifts incident to industrializaton, similar to the one in Alabama so graphically described by Miss Farmer,[8] result in control of the state legislature by rural majorities which are far too often indifferent or even downright unsympathetic toward the fundamental problems of urban communities.

In all but two of the southern states,[9] the reapportioning agency is the legislature, a situation that offers opportunity for the conscious rural majorities to perpetuate their control in subsequent legislatures in direct contradiction to the basic principle of representative democracy. Rationalization of the rural position is generally that urban centers are breeding grounds of dangerous radicalism. On this point, P. Orman Ray has written:

It should be remembered that the radicalism of yesterday is apt to become the conservatism of tomorrow, and that to check unduly what is regarded by some people as radical today may prove a serious bar to the progress of the state in years to come.[10]

This determination to preserve rural dominance does not stop with the composition of state legislatures; it is reflected in the lower

8. *Op. cit.*

9. Virginia has no constitutional provision for reapportionment. Arkansas has an ex officio constitutional board adopted in 1936, composed of the governor, secretary of state, and attorney general. Non-legislative apportioning agencies are also found in Ohio, Maryland, California, and South Dakota.

10. Frederic A. Ogg and P. Orman Ray, *Introduction to American Government,* 7th ed., rev. (New York: D. Appleton-Century Company, 1942), p. 734.

house of the United States Congress, for the legislatures are the districting agencies in their states.

A customary constitutional provision denies to the reapportioning agency the right to divide counties unless they are entitled to two or more legislative seats, as is the case in North Carolina, Louisiana, and Texas. Virginia and Georgia constitutions make no provision for dividing counties. This formula tends to "preserve the supremacy of the rural areas. It should be possible to join parts of counties when necessary to avoid undue inequalities of population among districts." [11] Nor does this provision improve the representative system to create a joint-legislative district in order to reduce, in theory, discrimination in representation.[12]

Political literature on the subject is in unanimous agreement that legislatures are extremely hesitant to reapportion their membership, even though most state constitutions provide for such reapportionment after each decennial census. These provisions are not self-executing, and the courts will not issue mandamus orders—on the ground that reapportionment is a "political question." [13] In regard to Alabama, Miss Farmer writes:

11. Elizabeth Durfee, "Apportionment: Study of State Constitutions," *loc. cit.*, p. 1096.

12. This practice is followed in Oklahoma. Oklahoma County with 244,159 people (four senatorial quotas) is given one senator; but to take care of the remaining three quotas, it is joined with Canadian County with a population of 27,329, which is only 51.5 percent of a quota. However, the law provides that Canadian County should be the nominating district for the joint-senatorial constituency. Thus Canadian County always gets the senator and the people of Oklahoma County merely have the right to choose between two Canadian County citizens.

13. "The Legislature, being a co-ordinate branch of the government, may not be compelled by the courts to perform a legislative duty even though the performance of that duty is required by the constitution." *Jones* v. *Freeman* et al., 193 Okla. 554 (1943), 146 P (2d) 564. See also *Fergus* v. *Marks*, 152 N.E. 557 (1926); and *American Political Science Review*, 21 (August 1927), pp. 573-576; *People* ex. rel. *Barrett* v. *Hitchcock*, 241 Mo. 433 (1912), 146 S.W. 40; *People* v. *Clardy*, 334 Ill. 160 (1929), 165 N.E. 638; *Fergus* v. *Kinney*, 333 Ill. 437 (1928), 164 N.E. 665; *Fergus* v. *Blackwell*, 342 Ill. 223 (1930), 173 N.E. 750; *Keogh* v. *Neely* (CCA 7th, 1931) 50 F. (2d) 685, 52 S. Ct. 39 (1931); *People* ex. rel. *Carter* v. *Rice*, 135 N.Y. 473 (1892), 31 N.E. 921; *Bowman* v. *Dammann*, 209 Wis. 21 (1932), 243 N.W. 481; *People* ex. rel. *Woodyatt* v. *Thompson*, 155 Ill. 451 (1895), 40 N.E. 307; *Prouty* v. *Stover*, 11 Kans. 183 (1873).

Serious discrepancies in representation exist because the legislature of Alabama, in respect of legislative reapportionment, has for forty years ignored or defied the constitution it is sworn to uphold.[14]

In Oklahoma, the same reticence is displayed by the rural legislature in regard to the senate but, even where the apportionment bills have been regularly passed in regard to the house, the rural legislators have "found extra-legal means of enhancing rural representation to the disadvantage of urban areas." [15]

The natural result of the reapportionment struggle is violation of principles of flexibility, of equality, and even of ethics, to assure continuance of rural dominance. The result is that legislative power continues to be held by those who are unfamiliar with urban problems and disinclined to governmental action in such fields as public housing, sanitation, education, delinquency control, and labor relations.

III. REPRESENTATION IN CONGRESS

The rural-tempered state legislatures are empowered, under American political institutions, to create the districts from which members of the lower house of the national Congress are elected. This power gives to rural sections opportunity for retaining control in the face of growing urban and industrial problems. Gerrymandering is generally employed to give advantage to one party over another; in the South, it is employed to the disadvantage of urban areas. Extremes in population size of the 113 congressional districts are 177,476 for the Third of Alabama to 528,961 for the Eighth of Texas.[16] The vagaries of the redistricting process are such as to make sizeable differences in district populations almost inevitable. Single counties cannot be divided except to create two or more congressional districts. Thus, large urban counties—such as Bexar, Dallas, and Harris counties in Texas—are condemned to under-representation by procedural specifications.

As Table 1 shows, the average quota for each of the 113 southern congressional districts is 302,366. The average quota for the 21

14. *Op. cit.*, p. 29.
15. H. V. Thornton, "Oklahoma Cities Weakened," *loc. cit.*, p. 295.
16. The Eighth Congressional district of Texas includes only Harris County, in which Houston is located.

urban districts is 353,008; for the 92 rural ones, it is only 290,807. Thus in the average urban district, there are five persons for the four in the average rural constituency.[17] That some of this excess is not the result of rural conspiracy is proved by the fact that six of the urban districts comprise but a single county each.[18] And of these six, only the Sixth of Tennessee is smaller than the average congressional quota. Another might have been created in Louisiana. New Orleans had a population of just under a half-million; [19] but the legislature of Louisiana, in violation of the prevailing rule, divided Orleans Parish into two districts, and added six rural parishes to the two districts.[20] A similar combination was also made in Georgia. Though it had a population of 392,886—more than 25 percent above the average quota for the state—Fulton County was not designated as a single district; De Kalb and Rockdale counties were attached to it, making a total district population of 487,522, which was 56 percent above the state average.[21] This large district was 107 percent larger than the smallest district, a district more than 87 percent rural.[22]

State legislatures, however, usually hesitate to add to large municipal areas adjoining counties that are principally rural. This is because of objections of the rural dwellers who believe themselves

17. An urban district is defined as one with a majority of its inhabitants residing in organized urban areas.

18. The single-county districts are: Alabama, Ninth, Jefferson County, Birmingham; Tennessee, Sixth, Davidson County, Nashville, and Tenth, Shelby County, Memphis; and Texas, Fifth, Dallas County, Dallas, Eighth, Harris County, Houston, and Twentieth, Bexar County, San Antonio.

19. This is far less than the figure for the Eighth of Texas.

20. Plaquemine and St. Bernard were added to the First, and Jefferson, St. Charles, St. James, and St. John the Baptist to the Second.

21. This is only another instance of the bitter urban-rural controversy in Georgia. The squabble over the gubernatorial office (1947) illustrated the attempt of rural areas to retain control. The inequitable unit system is another rural tactic in the struggle for power.

22. In Oklahoma, both Oklahoma and Tulsa counties were larger than the smallest rural district. Despite the fact that Oklahoma County was larger than four rural districts, six counties were attached to it to create the Fifth district, making this district 110 percent larger than the smallest rural constituency. The First district (Tulsa and nine adjacent counties) was 120 percent larger than the smallest district, but this large size was the result of a rural Democratic legislature's partisan tactics in handling the sizeable Republican strength in the Tulsa area.

TABLE 1. Southern Popular Quotas, National

State	Population	Number of Representatives	Average Quota	Population of Urban Districts
TOTALS	34,167,460	113	302,366	7,413,180
Alabama	2,832,961	9	314,773	459,930
Arkansas	1,949,387	7	278,484	
Florida	1,897,414	6	316,235	1,301,698
Georgia	3,123,723	10	312,372	487,552
Louisiana	2,363,880	8	295,785	608,245
Mississippi	2,183,796	7	311,971	
North Carolina	3,571,623	12	297,635	314,659
Oklahoma	2,336,434	8	292,054	814,248
South Carolina	1,899,804	6	316,634	
Tennessee	2,915,841	10	291,584	1,001,695
Texas	6,414,824	21	305,467	1,782,533
Virginia	2,677,773	9	297,530	642,620

practically disfranchised and swamped by the numerous and strange political problems of their urban neighbors.

The population figures reveal the discrimination against urban centers. In none of the nine states having urban districts is the urban quota smaller than the rural one.[23] From Table 1 it seems that the Louisiana averages are fairest, and those of Georgia the most inequitable.

IV. VOTER PARTICIPATION

A reasonable measurement of the impact of urbanization is a comparison of voting participation records of rural and urban districts. Do cities stimulate citizens to meet their civic responsibilities? Do rural dwellers, particularly Negroes and low income earners, move to cities to escape the traditional impediments to voting in rural areas? [24] It is axiomatic that the poll tax in southern states

23. Arkansas, Mississippi, and South Carolina have no urban congressional districts.
24. A wealth of material on the Negro's political position in the South may be found in Gunnar Myrdal, *An American Dilemma* (New York: Harper and Brothers, 1944), especially chap. 22. See also Howard W. Odum, *Southern Regions of the United States* (Chapel Hill: University of North Carolina Press, 1936), pp. 125-153.

House of Representatives, Urban-Rural, 1940

Number of Urban Representatives	Average Urban Quota	Population of Rural Districts	Number of Rural Representatives	Average Rural Quota
21	353,008	26,754,280	92	290,807
1	459,930	2,373,031	8	296,628
0		1,949,387	7	278,484
4	325,424	595,716	2	297,858
1	487,552	2,636,171	9	292,907
2	304,122	1,755,635	6	292,605
0		2,183,796	7	311,971
1	314,659	3,256,964	11	296,087
2	407,124	1,522,186	6	253,697
0		1,899,804	6	316,634
3	333,897	1,914,146	7	273,449
5	356,506	4,632,291	16	289,518
2	321,310	2,035,153	7	290,736

disfranchises more whites than Negroes. The threat of the tenant-farmer groups to come to power under the Populist banner in the early 1890's spurred the "economically respectable" to strategic action.

The poll tax as a restrictive political device was adopted with the help of the Populists whose support was enlisted on the issue of white supremacy. Many northern observers have never understood the real basis of the poll tax. Leaders of the great plantation black belts did not fear the Negro vote because they controlled the Negro, both economically and politically. A mere Negro vote was not dangerous; it was a threat only if it were an independent vote. The real leadership in the drive for Negro disfranchisement derived, therefore, from those white agrarian economic groups in which the Negro was a potential competitor. The Tillmans and Watsons, otherwise quite radical in political programs, served as a vanguard of the white supremacy legions. The net result generally was that millions of white supremacy whites were deprived of their political privileges in their campaign to escape the threat of Negro political action. And the South, from 1900 to the New Deal era, came to be dominated by the upper economic groups. The South's voter participation rate of 1896, despite the doubling of the electorate through woman suffrage, was not equalled again until 1928, when a fear prevailed throughout the section that political Catholicism was a threat to the liberties of free men.[25]

That new forces are in operation in the section is proved by the fact that five of the 12 states do not now require poll tax payment as a qualification for franchise.[26] In a sixth (Tennessee), legislative repeal was nullified by court decision. Also, the Supreme Court of the United States declared unconstitutional the white primary law of Texas.[27] After 1946, Negroes voted in varying numbers in both primary and general elections.[28]

In the general elections of 1944, total votes and participation ratios in the 12 states were as shown in Table 2. The average participation ratio in the non-poll tax states was 82.4 percent higher than in those states imposing the tax as a voting qualification. There are, however, several factors which should be evaluated before any sweeping generalization is attempted. The figures are for congressional contests, in most of which there was not even the semblance of a race; there was therefore no incentive for the average voter to go to the polls. On the other hand, it was a presidential election year, which always boosts the total congressional vote. The non-poll tax states are those in which there exists some Republican strength.

The control of southern politics by the "economically respectable" citizens has led in recent years to the increasing number of unopposed congressional candidates at both the primary and general election levels. The figures for 14 congressional elections are shown in Table 3. In Louisiana, 88.4 percent of all Democratic congressional candidates have drawn no opposition at all in the general election; Mississippi (75 percent), Georgia (65 percent), and

25. See Cortez A. M. Ewing, *Presidential Elections from Abraham Lincoln to Franklin D. Roosevelt* (Norman: University of Oklahoma Press, 1940), chap. 5.

26. The states and dates of repeal are North Carolina (1920), Georgia (1945), Florida (1937), Louisiana (1934), and Oklahoma. The latter has never used the poll tax for that purpose.

27. *Smith* v. *Allwright*, 321 U.S. 649 (1944). Prior decisions of that court on the same subject include: *Nixon* v. *Herndon*, 273 U.S. 536 (1927); *Nixon* v. *Condon*, 286 U.S. 73 (1932); and *Grovey* v. *Townsend*, 295 U.S. 45 (1935).

28. In both Mississippi and Georgia, the issue was bitter in 1946. In his bid for re-election, Senator Bilbo went so far as to advocate the use of violence in preventing Negroes from voting.

TABLE 2. Voter Participation in Southern States With and Without
Poll Tax, General Elections of 1944

	Vote	Participation Ratio *
Poll Tax States		
Total	2,767,534	115.3
Alabama	222,338	78.5
Arkansas	217,207	112.8
Georgia	274,374	87.8
Mississippi	152,712	69.9
South Carolina	100,862	53.1
Tennessee	398,622	136.7
Texas	1,058,439	165.9
Virginia	342,980	128.1
Non-Poll Tax States		
Total	2,138,140	210.3
Florida	416,353	219.4
Louisiana	282,569	119.5
North Carolina	754,658	211.3
Oklahoma	684,560	290.3
Total, The South	4,905,674	143.6

* These modified ratios are the number of voters per 1,000 population, without
regard to age distribution.

Arkansas (63.3 percent) are not far behind. At the other extreme,
Oklahoma has none in the category, while Virginia (9.1 percent)
and North Carolina (10.6 percent) usually witness the formality
of a contest at the November election.

When the 1944 general election data are analyzed from the
urban-rural viewpoint, some interesting facts are revealed. Of the
21 urban districts, only the Ninth of Alabama (with a ratio of
84.6) showed a participation ratio of less than 100. The average for
the 21 was 182.4, which was 27 percent above the average of the
113 districts. Moreover, 12 of the 21 urban constituencies are in
poll tax states with their lower participation ratios. In the upper
urban quartile (from 43.5 to 93 percent urban), the ratio was
183.1, which contrasts spectacularly with the ratio of 112.8 for
the 28 most rural districts, 23 of which were in poll tax states. Thus,
the most urban had a participation ratio of 62.3 percent above the
most rural districts.

The participation ratios range from 369.3 for the Eighth of

TABLE 3. General Election, Unopposed

State	1920	1922	1924	1926	1928	1930
Total, Poll Tax States	11	23	26	27	28	41
Alabama	1	10	2	2	7	6
Arkansas		7		4	1	7
Mississippi	2		7	8	8	8
South Carolina	5	4	6	7	7	6
Tennessee	1	2	5	6		5
Texas	2		4		5	9
Virginia			2			
Total, Non-Poll Tax States	14	20	18	21	19	16
Florida		2				1
Georgia	6	9	10	12	12	8
Louisiana	8	8	8	7	7	6
North Carolina		1		2		1
Oklahoma						
Total, The South	25	43	44	48	47	57

Oklahoma to 38.6 for the Third of Mississippi.[29] 17 of the 28 upper quartile districts on urbanization are above the average participation ratio for the 113 elections, while only seven of the lower quartile exceed that average. This shows again higher participation figures for urban areas. The cities are potential "freedom areas"; they may yet become real centers of political freedom for both whites and Negroes who are denied or otherwise deterred from voting in rural areas. The existing differentials are sufficiently striking to warrant prediction of increased migration to cities if the economic aspects of urban life can be maintained or improved.

It is often said that the real contests in southern politics occur at primary rather than general elections. Therefore, it is pertinent to compare election totals for 1946 primaries with certain general election data, southern as well as selected non-southern. In Table 4,

29. This Mississippi district with 38.6 percent is not in the upper quartile of Negro population, as that quartile runs from 38.8 to 73.9 percent. The First of North Carolina, with 44.6 percent Negro population, had a participation ratio of 139.3, which is 260.9 percent greater than the ratio for the Third of Mississippi. Even a glance at the data reveals the difference that poll tax repeal makes in the exercise of suffrage.

Congressmen in South, 1920-1946

1932	1934	1936	1938	1940	1942	1944	1946	Total
21	42	9	25	36	54	26	27	396
3	4	3	4	5	8	6	6	67
5	5	3	7	6	7	5	5	62
7	7	1	7	7	7	2	7	78
					6		1	42
	5	1	1	2	4	2		34
6	21	1	6	13	17	9	8	101
				3	5	2		12
14	17	14	17	12	22	20	15	239
3		2	4	2	4	3	3	24
3	9	6	3	3	5	9	5	100
8	6	6	7	6	8	8	6	99
	2		3	1	5		1	16
35	59	23	42	48	76	46	42	635

data on voter participation in 1946 primaries are presented with urban and rural as well as poll tax and non-poll tax comparisons.[30] The participation ratio for the entire South was 136.3 For the poll tax states this ratio was 129.7, and for the non-poll tax states it was 169.4, a difference of 30.6 percent. Thus, approximately four citizens cast primary ballots in non-poll tax states for every three who did so in the seven poll tax states. This marks a very considerable increase in political participation. The voiding of the white primary law in Texas led to considerable voting by Negroes. This was also true in Georgia where in 1945 Governor Arnall's administration rescinded the 37-year-old poll tax law.

In urban counties, disparity between poll tax and non-poll tax states was even more pronounced, amounting to 39.1 percent; in rural counties, the non-poll tax rate was but 28.5 percent greater. Thus, the effect of poll tax repeal is to increase urban voting more

30. Of course, not every state has in the off-years a statewide contest. In the selection of data, gubernatorial contests were given precedence, United States senatorial nominations second, and individual national House of Representatives races third. Seven of the 12 states elected governors; for three, senatorial nomination votes were selected; and the data for Louisiana and North Carolina came from the Congressional races.

TABLE 4. Voter Participation in Primary

State	Total Primary Vote	Total Population	Participation Ratio *	Urban Counties, Vote
Total, Poll				
Tax States	2,707,283	20,874,386	129.7	820,402
Virginia (B)	223,528	2,677,773	83.5	89,332
Tennessee (A)	312,805	2,915,841	107.3	86,029
South Carolina (A)	253,589	1,899,804	133.5	29,417
Alabama (A)	365,513	2,832,961	129.1	92,066
Mississippi (B)	191,806	2,183,796	87.8	36,815
Arkansas (A)	196,858	1,949,387	102.3	29,886
Texas (A)	1,163,184	6,414,824	181.3	456,857
Total, Non-Poll				
Tax States	1,951,296	13,293,074	169.4	777,852
North Carolina (C)	286,828 **	3,571,623 **	120.2	64,731
Georgia (A)	691,881	3,123,723	221.5	252,177
Florida (B)	336,545	1,897,414	177.4	249,812
Louisiana (C)	251,090 †	2,363,880 †	141.4	120,137
Oklahoma (A)	385,952 ‡	2,336,434	165.2	90,995 ‡
Total, The South	4,658,579	34,167,460	136.3	1,598,254

than rural voting. Traditional informal rural controls appear to remain even after the statutory bar is removed.

In the poll tax states, there is less difference between country and city in the matter of political participation. The average increase in participation of cities over rural areas was but 6.8 percent, while in the non-poll tax states the cities posted an increase of 15.6 percent. Here, two general conclusions may be drawn. First, states which feature newer industrial development, like Virginia and Florida, have larger numbers of middle class and organized labor groups in their cities; these groups, regardless of poll tax requirement, vote in larger numbers than do farm tenants and agricultural laborers. Second, those states in which large-scale agriculture is prevalent have larger numbers of farm owners and operators living in cities. Alabama and Mississippi are illustrative of this type. North Carolina, Tennessee, Oklahoma, and Texas are more complex in their organization. They have larger numbers of small farm owners and operators and also considerable industrial activity of a decentralized character. Citizens engaged in these activities vote in increasing numbers.

Elections, Urban and Rural Counties, 1946

Urban Counties, Population	Urban Participation Ratio *	Rural Counties, Vote	Rural Counties, Population	Rural Participation Ratio *	Percentage Urban Increase or Decrease Over Rural
6,077,378	135.9	1,886,881	14,797,008	127.2	+ 6.8
832,157	107.3	134,196	1,845,616	72.7	+47.6
795,995	108.1	226,776	2,119,846	107.0	+ 1.0
225,948	130.2	224,172	1,673,856	133.9	− 2.8
852,223	108.0	273,447	1,980,738	138.1	−21.8
318,053	115.8	154,991	1,865,743	83.1	+39.3
260,558	114.7	166,972	1,688,829	98.9	+15.8
2,792,444	163.6	706,327	3,622,380	195.0	−16.1
4,114,864	189.0	1,210,337	7,404,000	163.5	+15.6
580,964	111.4	222,097	1,804,724 **	123.0	− 9.4
1,029,216	245.1	439,704	2,094,507	209.9	+16.8
1,335,795	187.0	86,733	561,619	154.4	+21.8
608,240	197.5	130,953 †	1,167,365 †	112.2	+76.0
560,649	162.3	330,850 ‡	1,775,785	186.3	−12.9
10,192,242	156.8	3,097,218	22,201,008	139.5	+12.4

* These modified ratios are the number of voters per 1,000 population, without regard to age distribution.

** No contests in Districts 3, 4, 9 and 11, with population of 1,185,935.

† Districts 3 and 4 unopposed, with population of 588,275.

‡ Includes both Republican and Democratic totals.

A=Governor, B=Senator, C=Congressmen.

Five states show greater participation in rural than in urban counties, but the margins are smaller than in states which have a higher rate in urban areas. This reveals the promise of increased political participation as urbanization continues to impinge upon the southern rural scene.[31]

31. In his *Southern Politics in State and Nation* (New York: A. A. Knopf, 1949), V. O. Key does not cover the exact point at issue here. But he does (pp. 609-617) make very careful comparisons among Texas counties in relation to poll tax payments and finds properly that the rural counties generally post higher percentages. This finding supports our figures on voter participation. However, four of the seven poll tax states (Arkansas, Mississippi, Tennessee, and Virginia) show the opposite to be true in regard to voter participation. There is reason to believe, therefore, that Texas is not a proper sample for the entire South for this facet of southern

VI. SOUTHERN CONGRESSMEN: THEIR PERSONAL
CHARACTERISTICS

What kind of Congressmen does the South send to Washington? Some idea is provided by a study of the 113 southern members in the House of Representatives of the 79th Congress on eight personal and background characteristics: education, occupation, Masonic membership, religion, military service, age, years of prior public service, and years of prior service in Congress.

81 percent (92) of the representatives are college graduates. When the total number of members is divided into urban and rural classifications, there is a difference of only 10 percent in college graduates; 90 percent (18) of the urban members are graduates compared to 80 percent (74) of the rural members. Only 21 of the 113 representatives have not attended college.

77 percent (87) list the law as their profession. Urban and rural members are rather evenly divided here, the former with 70 percent (14) and the latter with 78 percent (73) lawyers. Professional businessmen rank second with 9 percent (10). 15 percent (3) of the businessmen come from urban areas while only 7 percent (7) come from rural districts. In third place are newspapermen with 3 percent (5), two of whom come from urban and three from rural districts. Farmers rate fourth with 2 percent (2), both of whom are rural representatives. The remaining two Congressmen are an educator and a professional politician. Only 6 percent (7) list no profession.

62 percent of the 113 southern representatives are members of the Masonic Order; 10 urban members and 60 rural representatives belong. 14 of Texas' 21 representatives and five of Oklahoma's do not claim membership. On the other hand, every representative from both Mississippi and South Carolina is a member.

The religious complexion of the southern group is predominantly Protestant. The largest single denomination represented is Meth-

---

politics. Even with the very large population of Texas, with its tremendous influence upon the section's poll tax averages, the urban counties of the seven states cast nine votes more per 1,000 inhabitants than did the rural counties. However, the difference was not nearly so pronounced as that in the non-poll tax states, where the urban counties led by more than 25 votes per 1,000 inhabitants.

odist with 29 percent (33) of the total. Second is Baptist with 22 percent (25). These two sects make up more than half of the religious preferences. Three denominations—Methodist, Baptist, and Presbyterian—compose more than 75 percent. The remainder of the group is made up of those who belong to the Christian, Roman Catholic, Episcopalian, Lutheran, or Unitarian denominations, or who express no religious preference. There is no particular distinction to be noted between urban and rural members in religious preference.

Military service is limited to 41 percent (47) of the southern representatives. There is very little difference in military participation between rural and urban members; 40 percent of the urban and 42 percent of the rural representatives have had military experience.

The average age is 51 years; this figure holds for rural. members, while urban representatives average one year older. In the upper quartile, the average age is 66 years while in the lower it is 42 years. The age range in the group is from 31 to 83 years.

Neither urban nor rural members show a great difference in average number of years of public service prior to serving in Congress. The average for urban members is seven and for rural members eight. In the lower quartile, the average length of service is one-half year; the maximum is two years. In the upper quartile, the average is 17 years, with a minimum of 12 and a maximum of 27 years.

Prior service in Congress ranges from none to a maximum of 32 years. The over-all average is nine years. Rural representatives average nine and one-half years and urban members eight years. In the lower quartile, the average is one year; in the upper, 21 years.

The foregoing analysis of selected personal characteristics of southern Congressmen reveals no major difference between urban and rural representatives. Possibly the most significant difference is the extra year of public service of rural members. On the basis of average figures, this indicates that rural constituencies do not "turn the rascals out" as often as urban centers, where political issues tend to grow more complex. Also the year advantage is a considerable amount of time in view of the 2-year term in the lower house. The high percentage of lawyers is not only typical of the South but of the nation as a whole. Yet one unusual feature, in light of the South's rural complexion and traditional political agrarianism, is the insignificant number of farmers chosen as national representatives. It is also interesting to note the high percentage of college graduates representing southern interests, both urban and rural.

VII. SOUTHERN CONGRESSMEN: THEIR VOTING RECORDS

Politicians may vote their personal convictions on some issues, but more often they reflect the political convictions of their constituents, lest they find themselves in that most impossible political situation—secure in the anonymity of private life! Consequently, one may expect to find that voting records differ according to whether the constituency is urban or rural. Congressmen must toe

TABLE 5. Liberal-Conservative Test Issues in the 79th Congress, as Selected by the *New Republic* Editors

Number	Liberal Vote	Issue	Date
1.	Yes	The British Loan	13 July 1946
2.	Yes	Extension of the Reciprocal Trade Agreements	26 May 1945
3.	No	UNRRA Participation Act (Free Press Amendment)	1 Nov. 1945
4.	No	Wolcott Amendment to Kill Price Control	15 April 1946
5.	No	Flannagan Amendment to Discontinue Livestock Subsidies	30 June 1946
6.	No	Bill to Eliminate Ceiling Prices on Existing Houses	6 March 1946
7.	No	Vote to Override Veto on the Case Anti-labor Bill	11 June 1946
8.	No	The May-Arends "Gag" Rule	11 Dec. 1945
9.	No	The Hobbs Anti-racketeering Bill	11 Dec. 1945
10.	No	Motion to Recommit the Atomic Energy Bill	20 July 1946
11.	No	Motion to Override the Veto on Tidelands Oil Resolutions	2 Aug. 1946
12.	No	Vote to Recommit the School Lunch Bill	21 Feb. 1946
13.	No	Dirksen Amendment to U. S. Employment Service	29 Jan. 1946
14.	Yes	Anti-poll Tax Bill	12 June 1945
15.	No	Wood-Rankin Bill for Permanent Committee on Un-American Activities	3 Jan. 1945

Source: *New Republic*, September 23, 1946, pp. 368-372.

the line on certain crucial issues or expect to be retired. Bills involving white supremacy and poll tax repeal are such issues for southern Congressmen.

There are no universal definitions of liberalism or conservatism: these ideological positions are perforce relative. In every Congress, however, there are bills whose support or opposition, many will agree, may be classed as liberal or conservative. In judging the voting records of the members of the 79th Congress, the *New Republic* editors selected 15 issues which in their opinion elicited unquestionably liberal or conservative decisions by the Congress.[32] Liberalism was defined as support of the New Deal program on labor, price control, and world politics. The issues in relation to liberal and, indirectly, conservative votes are shown in Table 5. Table 6 presents the corresponding voting record of southern Congressmen by urban and rural electorates or districts.

TABLE 6. Voting Record of Southern Congressmen, 79th Congress, on Selected Issues Noted in Table 5

Number of Issue	Urban Congressmen			Rural Congressmen		
	L	C	O	L	C	O
	(Percent)			(Percent)		
Average for all issues	41	45	14	30	53	17
1.	80	5	15	58	16	26
2.	75	5	20	84	7	9
3.	65	25	10	58	29	13
4.	30	60	10	21	68	11
5.	40	50	10	30	57	13
6.	30	60	10	16	68	16
7.	20	70	10	7	81	12
8.	30	55	15	9	82	9
9.	5	70	20	1	89	10
10.	60	10	30	48	16	36
11.	15	45	40	26	26	48
12.	60	30	10	33	52	15
13.	30	65	5	18	68	14
14.	30	65	5	5	88	7
15.	40	55	5	31	56	13

L = Liberal Vote
C = Conservative Vote
O = Absent or not voting

32. *New Republic*, September 23, 1946, pp. 368-372.

The issue upon which the sharpest separation of urban and rural representation occurred was repeal of the poll tax suffrage qualifications in national elections. 30 per cent of the urban Congressmen supported repeal, while only 5 percent of the rural representatives did so. It must be remembered that 12 of the urban districts are in poll tax states. Rural Congressmen were voting to retain traditional controls; urban members were presumably reflecting political demands of their constituents.

On the four labor bills [33] urban members were more than twice as favorable as their rural colleagues. 21 percent of the urban votes were cast for the liberal side as against only 9 percent of the rural votes. However, the general anti-labor convictions of the South are revealed in the fact that 65 percent of the urban and 80 percent of the rural votes were in the conservative category in these four divisions. Increased unionization of workers would no doubt tend to dissipate some of the traditional agrarian views on labor which have gripped the South throughout its history and which make so very difficult the formulation of a national program for the Democratic Party.

Four bills were in the field of world politics.[34] They received general support from southern members, with urban members being ahead 70 to 62 percent. This shows especially that southern conservatism is essentially in the field of domestic politics. Fear of Russian expansion with its threat to American institutions may well have influenced the votes. This issue came also in the bill to make the committee on un-American activities permanent. 55 percent of the urban and 56 percent of the rural members voted in favor.

There were three bills on price control. Here urban members were more liberal, 27 to 15 percent, indicative of the fear of city dwellers that a rise in the cost of living would work undue hardship upon them. Farmers are generally favorable to the sellers' market and visualized opportunity for increased prosperity.

The composite picture is fairly intelligible. The section has convictions and it tends to stand behind them. However, governmental action on the issues of modern industrial and urban life enlist much

33. Case anti-labor, May-Arends "gag-rule," Hobbs anti-racketeering, and the Dirksen amendment to the labor unemployment exchange bills.
34. British loan, reciprocal trade, free press amendment to UNRRA, and the atomic energy bills.

more support from urban Congressmen than from conservative rural members. The average of 41 percent liberal for urban Congressmen contrasts distinctly with the 30 percent for rural Congressmen.

VIII. CONCLUSIONS

The impact of urbanization on southern politics is difficult to appraise. By no means should all change in this realm be ascribed to urbanization. Improved public education, propaganda for civil liberties, blunting of ante-bellum memories, growing identification of the South with American national ideals, the effect of the war and its tendency to mitigate the harshness of racial antagonisms, the maturing realization that no section can be really economically prosperous unless the fruits of that prosperity are fairly generally distributed among the section's inhabitants—these factors also produce political change in the South. In two respects, however, we have found clear evidence of political differences associated with urbanization.

First, voter participation is higher in urban than in rural districts. Citizens are freer in cities. They may join labor unions and other citizen groups which place greater stress upon the political instrument. The 12.4 percent increase of urban over rural participation is important in a section in which the participation ratio is, by democratic standards, almost indecently low.

Second, the marked difference in voting records of urban and rural Congressmen points the way to further change in the politics of the section. The "Solid South" is less solid on labor and social legislation than it was in the days before the invasion of industry. And as industrial expansion produces increased urbanization, there is strong reason to believe that the South, with its tremendous stock of raw materials, will experience steady industrial expansion and, correspondingly, further mutation in her politics.

CHAPTER TWELVE

Community Organization: Lever for Institutional Change?

FLOYD HUNTER

SOUTHERN LEADERS, particularly those in the institutions of business and politics, are convinced that organized efforts on a large scale are necessary (1) to improve agricultural methods, and (2) to expand old and build new commercial and industrial enterprises. The principles embodied in these two ideas are a part of putting "first things first" in the South, and there is general agreement from the top down that nothing must stand in the way of these laudable aims. Other institutions, such as those of religion, education, and welfare, are caught up in the exhilarating idea of progress embodied in these building principles, and activities of the institutional members become functional to the scheme as a whole.

While the principles of agricultural and industrial expansion are key value orientations in current thought in the South, they are not particularly new. The "value" of industrial and commercial development has never been seriously questioned since the agrarian South was defeated in civil conflict by the industrialized North, but it took two major international wars and high post-war national productivity to make the value operative. Today all major southern institutions are busily engaged in defining and redefining their value systems in terms of progress and development. They all have the "forward look" and optimism is abroad in the land. To look backward or to dwell long on the social ills that have traditionally beset the region constitutes an almost unpardonable heresy.

Within this ferment of development, community organization has a place, but a place that is not too well defined or sharply delineated. Community organizers are prone to make a case for their activities by stating that they too are interested in progress, development, and bolstering of general productive morale; but they are prone to say also, in effect, that in order to facilitate achievement of the goals implied, considerable attention must be paid to what is happening in relation to the welfare of people in the process. They are likely to hint, if not openly say, that along with soil building and factory construction there must be time, money, and energy allotted to development of health and welfare services, school buildings, park facilities, hospitals, clinics, and the like. They are dedicated, often, to the idea that race prejudice, restricted social opportunities, and squalid environmental conditions can be greatly improved—at a price. They sound, in short, like "social workers." And very often they are. What they may correctly say and what they are able to do about these things may be two entirely different matters.

Community organization, as a disciplined set of activities, is largely concerned with social planning. It is a social process involving measurement of community social needs in terms of available resources and services, and upon such measurement, developing, extending, modifying, joining, and curtailing agency and associational services for an adequate meeting of the continuing needs of people. Community organization thus encompasses two major types of activity—namely, social study and social action. Both sets of activity are aimed at constructive social change, and both are competitive with all other types of community activities insofar as they require time, money, and energy from local citizens. The mandate of community organization may sound broad enough that its accomplishments would seem phenomenal, but viewed from the perspective of the sum total of all activities occurring daily in communities, the impact of social planning in most places may appear infinitesimal. Narrowed to a role of health-welfare planning, as many community organization agencies are, there is a real question as to whether or not they can be "levers of institutional change."

The question here arises from the fact that community organization, as patterned behavior of local citizenry, operates within the framework of many community institutions and its "lever" effect is modified by the inertia of some of them as well as by the dynamic force of others. Action patterns regulated by the factors of status, prestige, and power tend to nullify the broader purposes of those who would organize the community for the "good life" of all. Community organization as an action process has become institutionalized of itself, and thus we have the phenomenon of one institution, as a part of the total configuration of institutional arrangements, attempting to change integrally related institutions. Consequently there is much bootstrap activity in the whole situation.

To present more concretely what we are saying, let us look at a few problems that confront the institutional structure of the South, and measure the possibilities of action upon them by the traditional social planning agency. And perhaps before doing this, we should say more specifically what we mean by a "traditional social planning agency."

Social planning agencies in most communities have come to mean "councils of social agencies." Following World War I there was a great upsurge of the idea that health and welfare agencies in communities should find some means of coordinating their activities to prevent overlapping and duplication of services. This idea was abroad all over the nation, and the larger cities of the South joined the movement. Particular stress was laid upon joint charitable fund appeals and the community chest was a partial outgrowth of local social planning. From the beginning, the community chest movement made good headway in most of the larger cities, that is, cities of 20,000 and upward in population.

According to the records of the national organization of community chests, Community Chests and Councils of America, only four southern cities, out of 52 cities in the nation, had established chests before 1920.[1] Table 1 shows the trend of chest development prior to 1920. The southern cities by year of development are: San Antonio, 1912; New Orleans, 1914; Dallas, 1916; and Louisville, 1917. For the nation as a whole and by regions, the development before 1920 gives the largest number of chests to the Middle West, 28; the next largest number to the Central Atlantic states, 14; and the remainder to the South, New England, the Far West, including Hawaii.

1. Data obtained by correspondence with Lyman Ford, Associate Executive Director, Community Chests and Councils of America, New York.

TABLE 1. Organization of Community Chests in American Cities
Before 1920, by Dates

City	Date Chest Organized	City	Date Chest Organized
Denver, Colorado	1888	Portsmouth, Ohio	1917
Elmira, New York	1910	Bay City, Michigan	1918
Cedar Rapids, Iowa	1912	Gloversville, New York	1918
Cleveland, Ohio	1912	Hilo, Hawaii	1918
San Antonio, Texas	1912	Kalamazoo, Michigan	1918
Dayton, Ohio	1914	Rochester, New York	1918
New Orleans, Louisiana	1914	Springfield, Massachusetts	1918
Richmond, Indiana	1914	Tarrytown, New York	1918
Salt Lake City, Utah	1914	Wabash, Indiana	1918
South Bend, Indiana	1914	Akron, Ohio	1919
Baltimore, Maryland	1915	Bethlehem, Pennsylvania	1919
Cincinnati, Ohio	1915	Bronxville, New York	1919
Erie, Pennsylvania	1915	Honolulu, Hawaii	1919
Oshkosh, Wisconsin	1915	Kansas City, Missouri	1919
Dallas, Texas	1916	Lansing, Michigan	1919
Milwaukee, Wisconsin	1916	Mansfield, Ohio	1919
St. Joseph, Missouri	1916	Minneapolis, Minnesota	1919
Buffalo, New York	1917	New Bedford, Massachusetts	1919
Des Moines, Iowa	1917	New Britain, Connecticut	1919
Detroit, Michigan	1917	Orange, New Jersey	1919
Elyria, Ohio	1917	Plainfield, New Jersey	1919
Geneva, New York	1917	Rome, New York	1919
Grand Rapids, Michigan	1917	Saginaw, Michigan	1919
Louisville, Kentucky	1917	St. Paul, Minnesota	1919
Mt. Vernon, New York	1917	Terre Haute, Indiana	1919
Oberlin, Ohio	1917	Youngstown, Ohio	1919

The chest movement is a rough index of urbanization in the South. Since the 1920's, growth of cities has brought an increase in the number of community chests organized to handle the growing complexity of problems presented by people who look to a multiplicity of social agencies for help in urban communities. In the early stages of social agency development each agency raised its own funds in individual drives. From the 1920's on more and more southern cities, as they grew, federated their fund drives. Thus today most communities in the South with populations above 20,000 have chests. Such agencies as Boy Scouts, Girl Scouts, Children and Family Service Societies, Travelers Aid Societies, Y.M.C.A.'s, Y.W.C.A.'s, along with many others, federated themselves into local chest organizations for the purpose of financing their operations.

Along with federated fund raising, councils of social agencies were developed to help in coordinated social planning to insure that money raised in joint fund appeals was being spent in the most economical way, that needs of the individual community were being measured in some fashion, and that certain central services would be provided for all charitable agencies. These latter services usually consisted of research facilities, volunteer bureaus, and a social service index that listed clients of the relief-giving agencies to insure that there was no duplication of effort. To provide these council services, professional staffs of social workers were hired as "community organizers," and their salaries and supporting clerical salaries were paid out of funds raised by the community chest. Most councils of social agencies were housed in the same office space as the community chest, and often the director of the chest acted as professional secretary to the council. Most communities called the total operation the "Community Chest and Council," and the national organization of this movement bears the same title.

The two organizations (the chest and council) differed in function, however; the chest had as its primary function money raising, while the council became the planning body for social services. Most councils included within their membership public agencies as well as private ones, and most included agencies within the community that got support from private sources other than the community chest. The basic organization pattern has changed but little since the beginning.

The first councils were located in Milwaukee and Pittsburgh and came into being in 1909. We have no record of the first southern council, but we do know that Atlanta had a council as early as 1923, a council that antedated that city's Community Chest.

In some of the larger southern cities the council of social agencies may have a fairly large membership. In Atlanta, for example, there are more than ninety health and welfare agencies represented in the council. Most of these agencies can be classified as related to the fields of family and children's services, group work and recreation, public and private health agencies, and various civic organizations, such as the League of Women Voters, church federations, art groups, and some of the luncheon clubs that have no direct connection with welfare programs but that indirectly support some charitable enterprise.

Representation on a community council usually consists of two delegates from each agency, the president of the board, and the paid executive secretary, who gather periodically to discuss matters of policy for the council. Such meetings are known as delegate meetings. Reports are heard from subcommittees of the organization, including the executive board; speakers may discourse on timely topics; and a general exchange of information may take place from time to time as agency personnel explain the function of their particular organization and give expression to community needs as viewed by them. The council may have representatives, sometimes a majority of members, on the community chest budget committee. Problems related to distribution of chest funds are threshed out in this important committee and many council studies are projected here.

The council in these ways and in many other ways becomes a co-ordinating body, a clearing house for information, and a central service organization for community health and welfare agencies. In highly organized communities its work is vital and necessary. Some of its work may incur the displeasure of agencies or groups in the community—particularly those who feel disadvantaged in studies that may point to weaknesses in their particular agency programs. But in the main the council acts as a standard-setting agency for community welfare improvement, and there is general agreement as to its worth. It is a highly specialized type of organization, however, and most of its work is devoted to internal problems of organization within the limited fields of health and welfare rather than to external institutional adjustments.

Larger issues that are of current and deep concern to most of the major institutional groupings in the South very often escape the processes of study, discussion, and compromise that characterize the best efforts of community councils. If one selects five of the major institutions in southern communities and a major problem confronting each of them and asks the question, "Can a council of social agencies bring about change within the institutional structures?" the answer may bring a qualified "No." Let us illustrate this by taking the institutions of the family, economic, church, education, and political groups.

Can a council of social agencies directly attack questions of social status and prestige that may present restrictions on participation of individual families in the ideal framework of community culture insuring equal opportunities of development for individual members? Probably not on any fundamental level. Certainly not among Negro families.

Can a council be a vital force in changing the patterns of low incomes for substantial portions of the population operating within the economic institution? The answer here seems to be "No."

Could councils of social agencies suggest that churches coordinate their building programs so that materials and supplies used in new church construction be diverted to recreational purposes, for example, rather than be used to increase the number of physical structures that may be half-filled with people one or two days in the week? Such a suggestion might be made, but carrying out the program would require more ingenuity than most council personnel possess.

What stand have most councils taken upon the matter of improving the level of education open to all the people? Or upon the question of federal aid to education—pro or con? It is doubtful that many have considered these and related matters.

How strongly have councils of social agencies made a case for or against such political matters as non-voting? We may leave the question open.

Of course, all of these questions in some degree confront all cities in the nation—Boston, New York, San Francisco, Detroit, and Peoria included—but we are speaking of southern cities and smaller communities. The questions posed certainly confront southern institutional groupings today.

That councils of social agencies can make no frontal attack upon the larger issues confronting the major institutions does not prove that councils do not serve as social instruments—instruments mitigating the effects of poverty and social conditions related to the disadvantaged in a given community. It merely means that such councils do not have social sanctions to function as mediators of the questions put. In spite of the urgency of many human problems in communities, the problems loom larger than the scope of the social planning agencies that might be presumed to deal with them. Most political matters and other matters of public controversy are generally deemed to be "beyond the area of competence" of social planning councils. Few within council organizations would quarrel with this definition and limitation of function, and most would be startled to hear that more might reasonably be expected of them.

If councils of social agencies are the principal vehicles for the practice of the discipline known as community organization and if they are restricted in scope and function, what factors, we may ask, make this so? And we may further ask: is there any possibility that another type of community organization agency might deal more successfully with basic institutional problems? The answers may lie, partially at least, in some analysis of community social structures.

Community social structures reflect patterns of action. That is, when something needs to be done, when some need has to be met, people organize themselves to get the job at hand done. Business organizations, political parties, church sewing circles, bee-keeping societies, and an infinite range of organizations offer means by which citizens communicate with each other. Committees for special purposes abound to facilitate the organizational task. The pattern of organization is more often than not pyramidal. There is agreement by an organized group on the general aims and purposes of collective effort, and upon such agreement an authority structure is created. Officers are chosen and tasks are delegated through a vertical chain of command to carry out designated responsibilities. Such social structures may be loosely federated groups, such as councils of women's organizations, or they may be tightly controlled, in a command sense, as are many business and corporate establishments. But regardless of the degree of authority in a given organization, some authority exists, if for no other purpose than to maintain order. Thus within communities pyramids of power are formed—some more powerful and comprehensive than others.

Within community authority-structure, positions, roles, and offices are defined for all members; and within the community as a whole, organizations themselves are assigned relative positions in vaguely defined terms of status. Organizations as well as individuals find themselves measured in terms of social stratification. The status of an organization is likely to be a reflection of the composite status of its individual members. Thus the Chamber of Commerce in most communities "pulls more weight" than a Council of Social

Agencies, the Rotary Club may be considered a more important club than the local YMCA luncheon group, or the Rabbit Breeders Club may be outranked by any of these. In many communities, on a rough scale, the activities of a Council of Social Agencies may be considered "fourth-rate activities," while the Chamber of Commerce would be rated "first." These are the "facts of life" known by most community leaders; consequently, if one wants to "get something done on a community-wide scale," he would approach leaders within the first-rate groups and hope that they would "go along," and in turn "carry along" others. This principle of community organization is put into practice daily in most communities. The role of leadership in community affairs provides a link between the various associations and institutional groups as well as between community and community in the network of national life. The pattern of leadership offers a clue to the dynamics of community organization and action.

Working around and within the framework of principles of "putting first things first"—that is, developing agriculture and industry—the South's new developers pattern their own actions in conformity to hierarchical requirements of order in relation to individual community requirements and to productive demands of the nation. The traditional pattern of southern community leadership—plantation plus small-scale business, church, and some political groupings—is being extended to accommodate new corporate leaders. In order for all to accomplish their ends, there is tacit agreement that the South must be integrated into the whole economy of the nation. Thus one finds upon examination that many leaders in southern communities are well known to industrial and business leaders in other regions.[2] There is a definite and obvious connection between national industrial expansion and southern industrial development. Communities are the anchor points of such development.

In the situation one also finds that the movement of large industrial subsidiaries into communities brings shifting patterns of leadership and control, but the shift is often horizontal rather than vertical. That is, there are accommodation and stability factors in

2. The author is now engaged in a pilot study of national leadership and in preliminary examination finds this true.

operation, and no abrupt change in such patterns is as much in evidence as one might be led to believe.

In most communities it would appear that there is a group of men who are considered by their fellow townsmen to be community leaders.[3] They are the wielders of power, if power can be described in terms of moving goods and services toward socially sanctioned goals. The structuring of patterns of power in community affairs encompasses the processes of community organization and fosters or impedes action in relation to community development. Within the leadership group in a given community, certain leaders emerge as "policy makers," or "opinion leaders," as they are sometimes called. That is, certain men are "cleared with," or consulted on most major projects that require a heavy expenditure of time or money in community life. They discuss formally and informally most major moves in relation to industrial, political, and civic development before action is called forth by men below them in prestige and community influence. In the larger communities and cities there may be a loose delegation of responsibility in matters of policy between the top leaders, i.e., one man may be considered an authority on education, another may have his fingertips on information relating to welfare, while still another may be considered an expert on municipal finance, and so on. And while these men may not be fully informed as to minute detail and the intricate technicalities of any one of these fields of endeavor, they do have a hand in their policy determination. Policy making is the key to the flow of activities community-wise. The policy makers in the top group of community leaders most often come from the major industrial and commercial groups in the community.

Owners, operators, and managers of the larger corporate enterprises are men of power within their own businesses, and their status is extended and reflected in matters of power and decision in community affairs. Business organizations contribute sizeable portions of money, through taxes and voluntary gifts, to community support. Consequently, leaders within these groups have consider-

3. These generalizations are taken from studies made by the author in five communities, four of them in the South, varying in size from 7,000 to 500,000. See especially Floyd Hunter, *Community Power Structure* (Chapel Hill: University of North Carolina Press, 1953).

able to say, by assumption, as to how and for what purposes their contributions will be used. Ordinarily their sense of direction in such matters will be influenced by their primary workaday interests, and the rule of thumb measure of any community project up for consideration will take into account the two overriding principles of industrial and agricultural progress.

In southern communities that have experienced a shift from small-scale commercial and industrial operations to those of larger proportions, such patterns of leadership as described here seem to hold true. Local businesses may expand—real estate operations boom, corner grocery stores become supermarkets, garages add facilities, and mercantile establishments add more floor space. Some national chain stores may open branches. The branch managers are invited into the luncheon clubs and commercial organizations along with the managers of new industrial corporate enterprises. In the whole process there is much evidence to indicate that the local, traditional leaders retain a great deal of influence within the total community structure and act as stabilizing factors in the changing situation. They ride the wave of prosperity upward and the whole pattern represents a horizontal expansion of personnel on all levels of social stratification. There is greater prosperity for all, but social patterns remain relatively stable.

In a great many ways southern communities are quite like their counterparts in other sections of the country. The objectives, goals, and functioning of urban centers give them considerable national uniformity, but one also finds different attitudes among the people in matters of religion, race relations, and a host of relatively minor habits of eating, dress, and the like. There is a "flavor" of southern community living just as there is a distinctiveness in New England or mid-western or far western urban life. Waves of foreign immigration have changed New England towns, to be sure, and to the point where the book-model downeasterner may be as hard to find as a julep-drinking southern colonel; but in spite of many changes in these regions, there remain strong institutional patterns of conduct that are stable. The leaders of the South residing in urban centers are not particularly interested in changing institutional arrangements so long as they do not interfere with the work involved in strengthening the economic and political position of the South. "Change for the sake of change" has little meaning.

The changes that are taking place in southern communities—the building of plants, street and sewage systems, development of service industries, and the like—require planning. Within communities one finds new physical planning boards, active chambers of commerce, revitalized school boards, and growing associations for a variety of civic services. Much planning and promotion is going on within and between these associations. In no community, however, can there be said to be a formal, central planning body that coordinates all of the planning that is taking place. Government does not assume the task. Most local governments are restricted by charter and tradition to relatively limited functions. Business institutions cannot alone coordinate all civic planning. Consequently there is much segmented planning. In the process of segmentation, social planning also finds a place of relatively minor importance, but functional to the whole community system. None of the planning agencies is formally tied to state or national authoritative governmental organizations, and yet there is a high degree of order in the whole process. Community systems of organization do hang together in fair balance, and leadership recruited from balancing forces within community power structures is an important drawstring for the whole.

Leadership patterns in southern communities vary in degrees of conservative and progressive action. In a region long noted for its conservative institutions, the ultra-conservative leader finds some support for a certain amount of passive resistance to even the economic changes that find widespread acceptance in other communities. Recently, it came to the writer's attention that one man in a small North Carolina community had successfully blocked the entrance of a large-scale corporate enterprise that wished to locate in the area because he feared that the new corporation would absorb the local labor supply. Contrasted with the aggressive leadership of Houston, Charlotte, and other growing and prosperous cities in the South, the Carolina gentleman in question seems to be a phenomenon out of the past. Most are dedicated to economic progress, and the exceptions noted may prove the rule.

Progressive leaders, while dedicated to expansionist principles, also recognize that there are social needs in communities transcending the requirements of purely economic development. There are many men of goodwill in the South who are overwhelmed, on occasion, with the immensity of problems still facing them.

A quick tour of major southern cities and smaller communities that link them reveals the commonplace signs of social need and community malfunctioning. Deteriorated housing areas from Memphis to Mobile and beyond; recreational desolation; segregated living areas everywhere with inferior street passages, sewage, and lighting facilities; traffic congestion of Atlanta, Charleston, New Orleans, and again, almost everywhere; unregulated, jumbled billboard advertising; rail-line bisections of some communities; tourist court midways; roadside stand and gas station jungles—all these outward signs indicate to the eye that all is not harmony and order.

Deeper analysis into social situations reveals physical and emotional breakdown in families, quiet and sometimes bitter and frustrating struggles for more adequate school facilities, for higher incomes, for better health and welfare facilities, for a lessening of racial discrimination and tensions, and for more control over political destinies.

Traditional arrangements of institutions and often the best intentions on the part of community leaders have not been sufficient to meet the complexity of the problems presented. There has been no manifest conspiracy in the matter, but there has often appeared to be a reluctance on the part of many southern leaders to face up to the reality of the total situation. Those who want rapid change in some of these social situations are admonished that "Rome was not built in a day" and that the South is moving in the proper direction to reclaim its birthright. There is a tendency in some quarters to gloss over the social shortcomings of the region, or to deny in anger that there is any foundation for the charge that all is not well. None of these attitudes, including the attitude that rapid change can be had, is problem-solving. The defensiveness of some leaders dates far back, while for others the more recent social research findings of such organizations as the Southern Regional Council, the Committee for Kentucky, the Georgia Citizens Council, and the Georgia Fact Finding Committee have created an uncomfortable awareness of major social problems.

The social studies made by these organizations, added to such studies as those produced in the university centers of learning, the TVA community studies, and related endeavors, have produced a regional self-awareness that yet needs to be fully translated into specific community action. There is a disposition on the part of many and an intent on the part of others to take such research findings seriously and to continue the whole process. This would appear to be a good start. There is also evidence that adequate support of basic social research in southern community life may be had, but getting the facts is not all that may be required.

The desirability of stressing a strengthened community organization movement in the South has been voiced by many writers. Typical of such statements is that of E. J. Niederfrank, who says,

I believe strongly that community organization and development is fundamentally important, and especially during these times. . . . *It is especially timely here in the South, which is in the early stages of tremendous change and development.* Now is the time to lay a "community" basis for developments, before specialization and diversity produce other patterns that might be less effective in the long run. . . . Processes of community organization and development are especially timely . . . when people will be faced with having to rethink their values. . . . The next ten years will offer a premium on effective community organization.[4] [Italics mine]

The word "effective" used by Mr. Niederfrank leads us to our conclusions.

As was pointed out in the opening paragraphs of this chapter, community organization encompasses two major types of activity: social study and social action. While social study may present some difficult problems, it is at the point of social action that most community organization schemes bog down. In order to remedy the latter defect in some measure, the following factors may be taken into account:

1. If the thesis is true that much current action in southern development springs from the principles of agricultural and industrial improvement, a rider clause needs to be added to the two principles, that is, *"improvement for the social benefit of the whole people."* Most would say that this clause is now *implied,* but there

4. Statement by E. J. Niederfrank in Workshop Proceedings, "Community Development in the South," Section Meeting of the Annual Convention of the Association of Southern Agricultural Workers, Memphis, Tennessee, 1951.

needs to be more than implication in the matter. There needs to be clear and conscious recognition of the reinforced goal.

2. While it may be recognized that social well-being is as important a goal as plant-building and the like, it may also be understood that there is validity in the claim that the general welfare is dependent upon sound economic development and some priority may be given in the allocation of time and materials to undergirding the general welfare base of support.

3. Social structures and organizations must be created that can operate on a policy level of decision in matters of general welfare. Councils of social agencies, as has been pointed out, have proven inadequate to the over-all task of comprehensive community development. They do not involve two important segments of community populations in their present organizational structures. They do not integrate top community leadership in their policy boards, and they do not reach down into the majority citizen groups to solicit their participation. They have become specialized, "welfare agency" organizations. Their financial dependence upon community chest support often makes them obedient to the expediency demands of fund-raising which stifle independent action. Community councils that can coordinate physical, economic, and social planning are needed if institutional problems are to be attacked.

4. Community councils created to make community action goals attainable must have adequate research facilities at their disposal, along with competent personnel and equipment. Freedom to do research on "ticklish" problems and to engage in long-term research within the community would be a partial measure of adequacy. Widespread publicity and discussion of research findings is also a logical sequence of the research process and suggests that solutions to problems come from facing them rather than dodging the facts related to them. More than a "good public relations program" designed to garner financial support for any one organization is required.

5. There needs to be an awareness that communities cannot solve many of their problems alone. Many of the problems facing individual communities are region- and nation-wide, if not worldwide in scope. Studies made by the United Nations would indicate that community boundaries need to be transcended. Certainly, the problems in southern communities are common to other cities of

the nation, and yet there is no adequate social organization through which meaningful information can be shared, community to community. A logical clearing house for information related to community organization would seem to be the newly created federal Department of Health, Education, and Welfare. The existing isolated planning and segmented approaches to various community problems need concerted efforts that only a national clearing house can handle.

6. And finally, there must be the will to do these things. This factor may give us pause because we are in a relatively prosperous period of our history. The demand for social change is to some extent quiescent and is expressed more by the analyzers of social statistics than by overt demands of the population. Minor changes in social relationships within existing organizations are constantly being made, and these changes are reflected in the larger institutional groups, but substantive change on any major scale does not seem to be the order of the day.

Thus, with these things said, the question posed in this chapter may be answered. Community organization, as it now operates, is probably not a lever for institutional change. It does serve a very real need in the adjustive process within the field of social welfare, and as a coordination device it is functional to the larger social system of institutions within which it operates. To meet problems posed within the larger institutions, new social devices must be created that have sanctions potent enough to move the largest of the organizations in society that make the institutions operative. How this may be done is an open and theoretical question.

CHAPTER THIRTEEN

City Planning: Adjusting People and Place

F. STUART CHAPIN, JR.

IN THE SOUTH, as elsewhere in the country, city planning has assumed an increasingly important role as the forces of urbanization have become more and more felt. Compared to the Northeast, Middle West, and parts of the Far West, city planning in the South is a more recent phenomenon. But so also is the industrialization of the South and the accompanying rapid growth of urban areas. The rise of city planning to importance is directly traceable to the many problems created by this rapid growth.

ITS NATURE—CITY PLANNING, AN ADJUSTMENT DEVICE FOR URBAN CHANGE

City planning might be viewed as an adjustment device which urban society develops to acclimate itself to a swiftly changing cultural situation. It is a device which urbanites employ to insure that their physical environment fulfills basic economic, social, and health needs. It is a device which is used in response to pressures of growth and renewal from within the urban setting and from its hinterland. Although these pressures build up during periods of rapid urbanization, they tend to be a continuing phenomenon. Thus while city planning often has its genesis under conditions of stress, when the need for rapid adjustment is greatest, it tends to become an integral part of a complex of devices urban society utilizes in shaping the physical environment to fit the basic needs of living.

As an adjustment mechanism, city planning has become more and more a function of government, the institution which provides many of the physical necessities of urban living. So long as the urban settlement is small, these needs are simple and easily satisfied either by the family or through elemental community institutions. But as the community grows larger, these needs become more complex, and a greater premium is placed on cooperative or community servicing of these needs. Where an urban center is growing at an extremely rapid rate, a lag frequently develops and the once adequate elemental processes by which families adjusted to their setting can no longer suffice. Thus a family can no longer put in its own well and cesspool, but it looks for centrally provided water and sewerage facilities. Instead of walking to town to transact business and satisfy social and economic needs, members of the family now require a network of bus transportation and a system of thoroughfare connections to places of work, central shopping, and amusement. Police and fire protection become increasingly important, and people look for schools, churches, playgrounds, and shopping centers convenient to their home neighborhood. Pressures for a physical environment in which these facilities and services are available, adequate, and properly located have thus given rise to the formalized process of city planning. Just as building and operating many of these facilities have become functions of local government, so it is natural to find that city planning has developed as a continuing official activity of the municipality.

As used in these pages, then, city planning may be considered an over-all process of deriving, organizing, and presenting a broad and continuing program of physical improvements—improvements designed for the social, economic, and physical well-being of the community for both immediate needs and those in the foreseeable future. It examines the economic basis for an urban center existing in the first place; it investigates its cultural, political, physical, and economic characteristics; and it attempts to shape an environment which brings these elements into the soundest and most harmonious combination for the general welfare of the city as a whole.

ITS RAISON D'ÊTRE—FACTORS BRINGING ABOUT THE NEED FOR CITY PLANNING

The complex and diverse nature of the forces of urbanization is brought out in other chapters of this volume. For our purposes here, we shall simply enumerate some of the "problem" manifestations of urbanization which individually or in combination have been factors influential in bringing about the recognition of city planning as an accepted function of municipal government. Listed in random fashion, they include the following:

Traffic congestion and parking problems

Increasing spread between cost of municipal improvements and services and tax revenue being received in various sections of the community

Indiscriminate mixture of land uses

Flight to suburbs

Unsightly and disorderly fringe expansion

Blighted areas and residential, business, and industrial slums

Dislocations in supply and demand of housing

Tax delinquency

Stream pollution

Underlying these and the many other manifestations of urbanization, of course, are more fundamental phenomena—industrialization and decentralization. These are touched on elsewhere in this volume.

To visualize these problems in their proper setting, let us briefly examine an average community reacting to the forces of urbanization. Taking a small southern community as our guinea pig, let us assume that a textile mill selects a site on the outskirts of this rural trading center. Among the factors considered by management in locating in this community, perhaps the potential supply of labor at low wages is more important than the existence of a supply of skilled labor. In any case, the mill moves in. Its presence brings into the community new families—some from distant communities, some from the surrounding rural region. A mushroom development of new residences and stores appears in the vicinity of the mill, and roads and streets are projected out from the town. Problems are numerous but not insurmountable, and adjustments are eventually worked out to meet each situation.

The town makes out for a while improvising in this fashion. Then another mill, attracted by the new supply of trained labor, moves in and locates on the other side of town. New development occurs, new problems arise, and new adjustments are made. Industrial establishments in allied lines are attracted to the community. Some select sites close to the existing mills; some move farther out from the center in leapfrog fashion.

By now the town has grown to a city, and problems of all kinds beset the city fathers. Although in various stages of advancement, nearly every type of problem appearing in the foregoing list is present. Traffic congestion increases in the central sections of the city. The narrow streets which bring shift or shopping traffic into the center from the mill sections and from the new outlying industrial areas become overloaded. These were the roads and streets built only a few years previously—built without any particular thought as to the future. In the center, parking problems develop. The old open lots have disappeared, and curb space must now be divided among many more cars. The old natural order to the community—the business center of the town surrounded by an open-order pattern of residences—has been altered and in many ways destroyed. Inconsistent mixtures of land uses are in evidence: some older sections of the town have given way to commercial places of one kind or another, or the structures have been converted into apartments, rooming houses, or tourist homes.

In the course of growth and expansion, development spills out of the city limits. Along main highway approaches, a ribbon development of roadhouses, gas stations, automobile graveyards, and billboards has sprung up. Along other roads, land subdivided into cheap lots is now occupied by a scattering of small houses, trailer homes, backyard auto-repair shacks, and similar structures. Located beyond the service area of city water and sewerage systems, these areas depend upon wells and privies or septic tanks. As the city continues to expand, it is faced with an increasingly serious health problem in these areas and heavy outlays to install improvements. In still other close-in suburban sections, residential areas have been developed for the more well-to-do. Here, water and sewerage services are extended beyond the city limits, streets are paved, and provision is made for storm drainage. These sections have had these improvements from the beginning when the land was initially subdivided, and the cost was included in the original purchase price of the lots.

Regardless of their character, many of these fringe developments reflect an element of speculation. Few if any developers conduct their business on any calculated analysis of the city's growth and expansion trends. As a result it is not uncommon to find, even in the most exclusive fringe developments, an excessive amount of open country with improvements in place. A general economic recession thus often alters the whole character of these areas. When good times return, other areas frequently catch the public fancy, and the previously developed areas are left to weeds and ruin from lack of use and maintenance.

Meanwhile as families move beyond the city limits, the in-town vacated areas pass through various hands. Neighborhood disorganization which sets in as properties continually change hands, lack of property maintenance, and general deterioration which soon occurs —the implications of these problems are well known. Moreover, as the rate of urbanization slackens, these problems become increasingly acute. Whereas in the early stages of urbanization successive waves of growth operated to replace old uses of land with new ones, particularly in the in-town sections of the city, in the later stages blighted areas and slums no longer become absorbed. In these areas the spread between increasing cost of municipal services and shrinking tax revenues received is a very real problem to the city.

These planning problems are typical of those in most southern cities today. As suggested earlier, they develop out of pressures for growth and renewal—economic and social pressures with origins from within the urban setting and from the surrounding region. Thus the physical form which city planning gives to an urban center must recognize both pressures. Unless development and redevelopment in the city reflect consideration of both pressures, problems will persist and multiply. This then is the *raison d'être* for city planning.

ITS SCOPE—PRESENT CHARACTERISTICS AND EMERGING TRENDS

How does city planning perform its function in the urban setting? At the outset it should be noted that while we have been referring to city planning in the context above as "an adjustment device," in practice it functions as a process in local government, a process which employs highly developed techniques and controls. To be an efficient and productive process in local government (or to be effective as a cultural adjustment device), it requires positive and continuing direction. Such direction is usually provided by a city planning agency consisting of a citizen commission and a professional staff, and the functions and powers of such an agency are usually set down in state enabling legislation and implemented by local ordinances. Thus there is a whole complex of formalized patterns of action which has grown up to give force and effect to city planning as a culturally-oriented adjustment device.

The central interest of the planning agency is focused upon preparation and maintenance of a comprehensive long-range plan for development and redevelopment of the physical environs of the entire urban area, the area over which it has legal jurisdiction and the built-up areas beyond. To illustrate the scope and general sequence of the planning agency's technical activities in pursuit of this objective, a city planning work program of one southern city [1] is reproduced below in abbreviated form:

(1) *Develop a first estimate of existing conditions and significant trends.* This estimate would include the following types of investigations which, though in the beginning would be brief and general, would be developed in progressively greater detail as the program proceeds:

    (a) Mapping the physical, cultural, and economic setting of the city in the region.

    (b) Appraisal of the city's population trends, economy, etc.

    (c) Analysis of the principal services and facilities, noting where adequate and inadequate.

(2) *Determine principal and most pressing problems, briefly evaluate them, and develop an immediate and interim program.* This is necessarily a rough and preliminary formulation of the program developed to provide a starting point. As current problems and needs of the city come more fully into perspective and longer range aspects of the program get underway, this program is progressively refined.

(3) *Formulate a detailed program indicating priorities in planning studies.* These studies would include:

    (a) *Background studies:* Population, economy, culture, topography and physiographic characteristics, land use analysis, etc.

    (b) *Basic plan studies composing comprehensive plan:* Transportation and communications; residential, business, industrial and public land uses; public and semi-public facilities and services (health, welfare, recreation, education, etc.); utilities.

    (c) *Studies in implementation of comprehensive plan:* Zoning, building code, subdivision regulations, sanitation code, public

1. F. Stuart Chapin, Jr., "City Planning in the Southeast," *Journal of the Town Planning Institute,* XXXVI (February 1950).

works improvement program, industrial development programs, urban redevelopment program, etc.

(d) *Specialized studies developing out of basic plan studies:* Redevelopment projects, public housing developments, shopping center design, street intersection design, etc.

(4) *Develop plans on project-by-project basis.* These individual projects would be undertaken in accordance with priorities established above. Each project would include a statement of objectives, an inventory and analysis stage, and finally recommendations and presentation of plan proposals, including methods of financing improvements and steps to be taken in putting plan into effect.

(5) *Integrate various project plans into an over-all plan.* The general framework having been established in stage (2) above, this phase of planning would be essentially one of progressive refinement, coordination of various plan proposals, and elimination of inconsistencies and conflicts.

(6) *Revise plans as conditions alter their applicability.* This would be a continuing activity of observing trends and adjusting plans by restudying each successive stage above.

While it is to some extent an over-simplification of the staging of planning activity, the foregoing summary serves to illustrate that the work of a planning agency follows a circular rather than a straight-line sequence and thus re-enforces an earlier observation of the necessity for city planning to be a continuing activity.

The mere fact that there are plans for growth and renewal in the physical setting of an urban area does not mean that development and redevelopment necessarily will occur according to these plans. As indicated in the illustrative work program above, some means of implementing plans is needed. There are various devices commonly employed for this purpose. Plans for arrangement and rearrangement of land uses are effectuated variously: through zoning and land subdivision control, through stimulants and restraints represented in programs of public improvements, and through slum clearance and redevelopment programs. Similarly plans for major thoroughfares, public utilities, and community facilities of all kinds can be brought into reality through federal, state, and local public works programs.

The planning agency's liaison function with the citizenry of the community also merits comment. While in the early days of city planning there was little direct contact with citizen groups and the public in general, in recent years planning agencies have been developing closer ties with the people of the community. They are interested in broadening public understanding of local problems and the role that planning plays in solving them. Many of these planning agencies are attempting to secure more direct citizen participation in city planning. For example, community councils, citizens' planning organizations, and other civic groups are actively collaborating in planning investigations in many communities today. The educational aspects of these activities have been found so important to the objectives of planning that the work of planning agencies is also being introduced into schools, with public service projects incorporated into civics and other courses.

ITS STATUS—GROWTH OF CITY PLANNING IN THE SOUTH

In the northern regions of the country, where problems of urbanization have been known to cities for a long period of time, urban planning has become firmly established and widely accepted as a necessary function of local government. In the South, where urbanization has been more recent, cities have been slower to experience acute planning problems and have been correspondingly slow in employing the processes of comprehensive planning.

Though slow in getting underway, urban planning in the South is gaining increasing acceptance. Thirty-five years ago, when city planning was first taking hold elsewhere in the country, there were fewer than forty cities in the South in which there was any evidence of interest in city planning problems.[2] Of these, only Norfolk, Tulsa, and Shreveport had official planning agencies. In 1952 there were 39 cities of the over 25,000 population class in the South with resident planning staffs consisting of at least a full-time director (see Table 1); the communities with active official planning agencies number in the hundreds. Of the 33 cities in the South with an urbanized area of 100,000 population or more, nine have no permanent full-time resident city planner. While large metropolitan areas such as Atlanta, Birmingham, Dallas, Houston, Memphis, New Orleans, and Richmond have shown increased activity in planning,

2. For a detailed description of planning activities in this period, see *City Planning Progress* (American Institute of Architects, 1917).

many small cities in the 10, 25, 50 and 75,000 population class, not fully represented in Table 1, are appearing in the picture for the first time.

The areas in which local planning in small cities has made most striking progress are those in which state planning agencies are

TABLE 1. Southern Cities Reported to Have Resident City Planning Staffs With One or More Full-Time Technicians, 1952 *

Urbanized Areas With 1950 Population of 500,000 or More

Houston, Texas	(700,508)	Dallas, Texas	(538,924)
New Orleans, La.	(659,768)	Atlanta, Ga.	(507,887)

Urbanized Areas With 1950 Population of 250,000-500,000

Louisville, Ky.	(472,736)	Norfolk, Va.	(385,111)
Miami, Fla.	(458,647) **	Fort Worth, Texas	(315,578)
San Antonio, Texas	(449,521)	Oklahoma City, Okla.	(275,091)
Birmingham, Ala.	(445,314)	Nashville, Tenn.	(258,887)
Memphis, Tenn.	(406,034)	Richmond, Va.	(257,995)

Urbanized Areas With 1950 Population of 100,000-250,000

Tulsa, Okla.	(206,311)	Baton Rouge, La.	(138,864)
Chattanooga, Tenn.	(167,764)	El Paso, Texas	(136,918)
Little Rock, Ark.	(153,643)	Corpus Christi, Texas	(122,956)
Shreveport, La.	(150,208)	Columbia, S. C.	(120,808)
Knoxville, Tenn.	(148,166)	Montgomery, Ala.	(109,468)

Urbanized Areas and Cities With 1950 Population of 25,000-100,000

Urbanized Areas		Cities	
Winston-Salem, N. C.	(92,477)	Lubbock, Texas	(71,747)
Augusta, Ga.	(87,733)	Alexandria, Va.	(61,787)
Greensboro, N. C.	(83,412)	Greenville, S. C.	(58,161)
Durham, N. C.	(73,368)	Lexington, Ky.	(55,534)
Orlando, Fla.	(73,163)	Lynchburg, Va.	(47,727)
Raleigh, N. C.	(68,743)	High Point, N. C.	(39,973)
		Fayetteville, N. C.	(34,715)
		Paducah, Ky.	(32,828)

Sources: *Municipal Yearbook* (Chicago: International City Managers' Association, 1951), and *ASPO Newsletter* (Chicago: American Society of Planning Officials).

* Does not include communities served by private planning consultants, nor communities in Alabama and Tennessee served by state planning technicians.

** Miami Beach, which has a separate planning agency, included in this population figure.

actively assisting municipalities in organizing and carrying on comprehensive planning programs. Alabama, Kentucky, Tennessee, and Virginia have active programs of this type. The considerable legislative support which state planning agencies in Alabama and

Tennessee enjoy may be attributed in large measure to the success of their programs of local planning assistance—a fact which reflects the growing importance attached to city planning.

The redevelopment legislation of the Housing Act of 1949 has served to increase city planning activity. Under the terms of this act, before cities may take full advantage of loan and grant aids from the federal government in redeveloping blighted areas, they must demonstrate that proposed redevelopment schemes fit into a "general plan" for the over-all development of the community. Of the total of 51 cities in the South which applied for participation in the program by the beginning of 1952, 27 cities do not appear in Table 1. Two-thirds of these are small cities in the under 50,000 population category.

In a review of planning developments in the South, the so-called "model" town should receive mention. These are new towns, built in relatively recent times and developed presumably with benefit of the best available technical aid of their time. The number of these communities which has been developed in the South as compared to other regions of the country is impressive.[3]

Although these communities are too numerous to list in detail, we might single out a few examples in passing. They include towns built by industry, government, real estate firms, philanthropic agencies, and other miscellaneous groups. Kingsport, Tennessee, by virtue of the emphasis placed upon diversification of industry in its early planning, exemplifies the planned community developed by industrial interests. Examples of government-built towns are the World War I shipbuilding villages of tidewater Virginia, TVA's Norris, Tennessee, and the atomic energy city, Oak Ridge, Tennessee. With a war-time population in excess of 75,000 (then fifth largest city in the state), Oak Ridge is one of the most elaborate examples of a planned community built in recent times. In Florida, Coral Gables provides an illustration of a third group of so-called planned communities—those developed as real estate ventures. An example of a fourth group, those developed by philanthropic and miscellaneous agencies, is the relocated community of Columbus, Kentucky.

3. See *Urban Planning and Land Policies*, II (Washington: National Resources Committee, 1939), 18-153.

These and other planned communities which developed in the South have not escaped the influences of urbanization, nor are they modern-day utopias in any planning sense. While they possessed initial advantages over older established communities of the South, few if any provided for continuing planning. For the most part, today they are on equal footing with their neighboring communities in being prepared for the influences of accelerated urbanization.

ITS PROSPECTS—SOME PROBLEMS AND OPPORTUNITIES IN THE SOUTH

While city planning activity is making encouraging progress in the South, cities are facing problems which offer challenging fields of investigation for research resources of the region.

Among the most difficult problems are those which have to do with execution of plans and bringing them to fulfillment. In this category, one problem is developing and sustaining public interest in city planning. As noted earlier in this chapter, southern communities are increasingly becoming aware of this problem. Experience to date indicates that there is close correlation between vigorous public interest in city planning and the extent to which plans are successfully carried out. Without this interest, necessary financing may be voted down and planned improvements never carried out.

Public interest in city planning develops of its own volition only after some critical situation arises and usually when urbanization is in an advanced stage. It has been characteristic of cities which are in the throes of urbanization to be so enamored of bigness and so engrossed in expansion that they have had little inclination to consider the quality of their growth. Unless a concerted effort is made to develop citizen appreciation of the need for planned growth and expansion during the early stages of urbanization, the general public learns about planning after the harm is done.

How can citizen interest be developed and maintained? A fully satisfactory answer to this question is still to be worked out. By trial-and-error experiences, cities have found that customary channels to the general public—newspapers, popular reports, exhibits, radio or television presentations, and the like—are in effect only temporary stimulants to public imagination. Even when incorporated into a carefully worked-out public relations program, citizen interest usually wanes when the campaign period ends. A few cities are now coming to the realization that the missing element in this picture is their failure to effectively bring the people of the community into the planning process. The long-standing practice of creating advisory committees was an early attempt to secure such citizen participation. More recently, citizens' planning associations have been organized in a number of large urban centers and, in some instances, affiliating neighborhood associations have been formed. The Louisville Area Development Association is an example of an active citizens' planning organization. In a few smaller cities, formation of community councils as coordinating committees for the activities of the various civic organizations of the community shows promise of providing means for securing broad participation in the planning process. Modeled after the Committee for Kentucky, which in its most active period aimed to develop interest in sound planning and development of state resources, the Committee for the City and County of Henderson, Kentucky, enjoyed considerable success in securing coordinated citizen participation in planning for the community's development. These are beginnings in the direction of developing broader public interest in urban problems. However, the most desirable relationship between these groups and the official planning agency and the extent to which the general public can effectively take part in the planning process are still matters of conjecture and subjects needing extensive study.

Another problem of some proportions is that of financing local planning—finding funds with which to undertake a comprehensive program in the first place. This is particularly a dilemma for small communities experiencing growing pains of urbanization. It is the time when it is most strategic to plan, yet it is also the time when the community is experiencing the greatest demand upon its tax revenues for needed expansion of municipal facilities and services.

While further intensive study of this problem is clearly needed, the South has brought forth some pioneering solutions. Already mentioned above, the Alabama and Tennessee programs of state aid to communities have had some strikingly successful results in this respect. These state programs received their start from the Tennessee Valley Authority under contractual agreements providing for planning assistance to communities affected by the extensive valley development projects of TVA. The program of the Tennessee State Planning Commission is now past the initial experimental period. Restricting planning assistance services to the small community, largely in the 5,000 to 50,000 population range, the Commission maintains a series of regional offices which in 1952 were actively servicing approximately 50 towns and cities in the state and had provided assistance to about another 30 on various occasions in the past.[4] This is significant when it is considered that less than fifteen years previously only the four large cities of the state had active planning programs.

In Virginia, another approach is receiving a trial. Here the Division of Planning and Economic Development, in line with its interests in regional planning, has attempted to bring together communities in each of several sectors of the state to share the expense of a common planning staff within each region. In order to stimulate this activity, the state extended financial assistance to these regional agencies by offering to match—within limits—funds appropriated by the several cooperating local units of government. The difficulty here is to achieve the necessary inter-city cooperation to get such a joint venture established on a going basis. Such cooperative planning on a regional basis has been attempted in northern Virginia where Arlington, Fairfax, and Prince William counties and the towns of Alexandria, Falls Church, and Manassas have joined to form a Northern Virginia Regional Planning Commission. A newer program in local planning assistance is operating in Kentucky. It is similar to the Tennessee program, but the state development agency is providing assistance through one central office rather than through regional offices.

Still another approach is being tried in Arkansas, North Carolina, Oklahoma, and Texas. In these states limited assistance to small communities is being provided through teaching, research, and service agencies of the state universities. Finally, there are the sources of assistance available through the Leagues of Municipalities, although the extent of planning assistance provided by these agencies varies from one state to another.

One other major problem should be mentioned: the need for

4. See "A Report on the Tennessee State Planning Commission," *The Tennessee Planner*, XIII, No. 2 (1952).

planning and redevelopment techniques especially designed to treat
problems of small cities. This need is particularly pressing in the
South where, of the communities experiencing problems of urbanization, the small cities far outnumber the large urban centers.
Without question there are numerous similarities in the problems
of small and large cities which call for a similarity in approach, yet
because the problems are on a different scale and require different
emphases, distinctly different techniques are needed.

While urbanization is bringing forth these and other problems
in southern cities, it is also providing unusual opportunities for
developing and putting to use new and improved methods of planning—methods which will make it possible for cities of the South
to take the lead in adjusting to changes brought on by modern
science and technology. The trend toward industrial decentralization is introducing numerous new features into urbanization
patterns of cities and is calling for modified planning methods. Likewise, emerging developments in modern aviation clearly indicate
the need for further readjustments in present-day planning concepts. In addition to vast inter-urban freight and transit systems
which are even now developing, there are indications that cities
will soon be occupied with problems of developing local airparks
and concerned with delineation of lanes and regulation of the flow
of local and regional air traffic. With atomic energy being harnessed for peace-time use, we have been alerted for even greater and
more far-reaching changes in the urban environment.

For the most part, the trend of these developments suggests that
in the future the patterns of cities will be more dispersed in form
rather than compact, as was characteristic of other regions in
earlier periods of urbanization. In European nations, notably in
England, some effort is being made in the process of post-war
reconstruction to adjust to these trends. The *Greater London Plan
1944,* implemented by the 1946 British New Towns Act, provides
for a systematic "de-urbanization" of this vast and sprawling
metropolis. It is proposed that more than a million people will be
resettled over a period of time in the process of carrying out a
planned decentralization of London.

It is not the purpose here to discuss the pros and cons of this and
other schemes for reshaping the urban environment, but rather to
suggest that in the South it is possible for cities to bypass the prob-

lems of urban sprawl and haphazard growth and expansion. In the present period of urbanization, southern cities can do much to circumvent physical-social-economic-political problems developing from urbanization and at the same time fall into step with a swiftly changing kind of urban life. This is a great opportunity that cities in the South are facing today.

CHAPTER FOURTEEN

Farewell to "Possum Trot"?

H. C. NIXON

Possum Trot is dead. Long live Possum Trot.

The inhabitants of this rural spot no longer have a local post office, one-room school, grist mill, cotton gin, road foreman, justice of the peace, constable, or baseball team. They no longer gather conspicuously at a country store or railway station for gossip and discussion on rainy days and Saturday afternoons. Their community religious activities have declined, and their political speeches are things of the past. The barns on their largest farms have ceased, in this age of tractors and green pastures, to serve as institutional centers for sharecroppers and other mule-drivers. Possum Trot, in plain terms, has lost its sense, spirit, and status of neighborhood along with the comparative isolation of its horse-and-buggy days. It is no longer an identifying center for persons and families linked by a common and conscious loyalty to that center.

My particular Possum Trot, as well as its Piedmont environs, is not deserted land. It is still an area of homes, farms, and families; but, like Middletown, it is in transition. Acceleration of the transition has stemmed from many factors, including two World Wars, new technology, and the coming of industry to the South, with an increasing urbanization of the territory within a fifty-mile radius of Possum Trot. The pattern of change applies to man and land, to economic and social activities.

Farmers and farm families are less numerous than in earlier days. But they produce more per capita, thanks to mechanization as well as to more and better livestock, especially cattle. They have a higher material standard of living than their predecessors, the rank and file being better fed, clothed, and housed. Many have the benefits of electric service. Much of the income of the inhabitants comes from non-farm sources. One resident is a banker in the nearest town, and a neighbor of the banker has teaching duties in the same town. A city merchant lives on a Possum Trot farm, which he has improved with city earnings. Many cottagers find employment in industrial centers of the county, receiving wages which, even with allowance for dollar inflation, would have seemed rather fabulous in years gone by.

A distinct decline has occurred in the exploitation of human labor and in the depletion of soil resources. Greener fields and pastures have reduced the gashing gulleys. Wider communication with the world and region through mail, press, radio, and modern transportation has reduced the sense of individual frustration and isolation from what it was in former decades. Fewer Possum Trot men seek escape from reality through drunken sprees, as was too frequently the case when I was a boyhood observer. No longer do serious cases of insanity occur to the extent of former years. Fewer go to the county jail or the state penitentiary. In one way or another, individual maladjustments have declined with the passing of isolation. Important credits must be chalked up for Possum Trot of the present day, whatever may be missed from "the good old days."

The inhabitants of Possum Trot today exemplify a diffusion of loyalties, connections, and social contacts, along with their declining concern for the features of a closely knit neighborhood. The diffusion is both geographic and functional, extending to various locales and embracing a wide range of activities or interests. This is indicated clearly by the economic diversity already mentioned. It is illustrated in numerous other ways. There is interest in a consolidated school some miles away and in bus transportation to it. A few families patronize schools and churches in a nearby town. Two cities and two towns regularly attract shoppers and moviegoers from Possum Trot. The county seat means more to these people than formerly, with many matters which were once handled largely by precinct officers now being centralized in offices at the courthouse. These families look forward to daily mail over a rural route from an urban center. A Possum Trot farmer is active in farm committee work, which occasionally takes him to the state capital. Local members of 4-H Clubs look beyond their little valley for recognition. One citizen goes here and there as an earnest worker for the cause of Alcoholics Anonymous. World War II brought a flicker of labor union allegiance to Possum Trot. There are frequent exchanges of visits between Possum Trot families and families of the adjacent urban communities without waiting for Sundays and holidays. And steady followers of radio and television programs are to be found among these rural families.

What is true of Possum Trot is true of thousands of rural villages, hamlets, and neighborhoods throughout the South and America. The pattern of change is not limited to places which, like my native bailiwick, lie in or near urban-industrial districts. With allowance for incidental variations, the new ways are equally observable in numerous small settlements situated in the depths of farm regions, as in the heart of Mississippi or in mountain areas of Tennessee. In important particulars, modern interdependent relations with the outside world are conspicuous in southern farm communities which are distant from industrial centers, for it is most likely the case that such communities are exporters of population, with an accompanying increase in farm income per capita through mechanization and scientific improvement of agriculture. Largely by such a formula have Mississippi and Arkansas reduced sharecropper farming and led all other southern states as well as most of the states of the nation in income gains per capita between 1940 and 1950.

By economic scores, southern rural groups are becoming integral parts of the United States.[1] Widely distributed purchasing power as well as facilities for transportation and communication makes it possible for the small communities of the South, wherever located, to merge their cultural existence intimately with the rest of the country and the world. With more than 14,000 communities of less than a thousand population in the ex-Confederate states, the South has slightly more than a pro rata share of rural people and places and seems destined to retain them, whether of the farm or nonfarm classification. The South and Possum Trot are making a transition together.

---

1. These statements on rural economic improvement are not intended to imply either a dismissal or a solution of the population problems of the South with respect to the prevailing economy. A period of unemployment or depression could shut off the export of rural people and again intensify problems of living for "all these people," as Rupert Vance, T. Lynn Smith, and others would teach us.

Possum Trot, like hundreds of other communities of the southern or American countryside, has been highly susceptible to recent social trends. It has, in fact, manifested a flexibility of economic and social ways from the era of its early settlement in stagecoach days to the present time. It has witnessed the in- and out-migration of population throughout its hundred years of history. It has never had the intimate and enduring characteristics of an old and established neighborhood, such as Walter Terpenning [2] and others have noted for many parts of Europe, or such as one may observe, for example, in a country like Mexico. Neither historically nor currently does Possum Trot provide adequate support for the traditional assumption that God made the country and man made the town or city. It today has little nostalgic longing for a primitive innocence which never existed. It has at no time been classifiable as a Tobacco Road country, but it might have furnished social material for a southern match for Hamlin Garland.

Yet Possum Trot has lost something of significance, although that something may be easily exaggerated and the community's past is subject to serious social discounts. Never a perfect or natural community of active and participating citizens, it is much less so today. There is a sort of unresisting acceptance in the attitude of the inhabitants of Possum Trot toward their community and the world. This attitude is comparable to that of thousands of small stockholders of a giant corporation toward the decisions and policies of the corporation's officials and directors. It is an attitude of complacent, if also hopeful, passivity. The little shareholder knows he can get nowhere voting against corporate destiny as determined by others. The man of Possum Trot knows that he can get nowhere talking back to the radio or arguing with a mail-order catalogue. The inhabitants of Possum Trot had no direct voice in the widening and relocation of their principal highway some years ago, if that paved portion of a national system can be called "their" highway. Not by their determination did R. F. D. mail service, telephone lines, and electricity become available to them. It is not easy or natural to show loyalty to such facilities as mail routes, bus lines, or endless highways, however much these modernizing instrumentalities may remove older civic roots and minimize the "enamored localism" of Possum Trot.

The decline of "enamored localism" is pointedly exemplified by the passing, without replacement, of institutionalized personalities. Possum Trot no longer has persons who are locally important and who have achieved their importance locally. If a gentleman farmer went from this community to the state legislature some years ago, his election resulted largely from the fact that he was a retired banker and former resident of the county seat. He did not have Possum Trot in his bones. His career was not primarily associated with that rural locality. The locality has no successor to Jason Scott, who served a period as a justice of the peace and who for years upon years was a Sunday school superintendent as well as an officer of his church. There is no successor to Butler Green, who was the community's leading hog-raiser for forty years and who went to town barely more than once a month during his life, sometimes bringing back a whiskey supply for his occasional "dram." There is no successor to Bill Nixon, forty-five years a country storekeeper and the community's only postmaster prior to the coming of R. F. D. There is no successor to Robert McCain, the largest land-holder in his day, who lived beyond ninety, was married three times, systematically smoked a clay pipe, entertained preachers, and was an easy mark for the occasional book agent or peddler. There is no successor to Martin McCain, ex-slave of Robert Mc-Cain, tenant farmer, and Methodist minister with a voice which could send gospel words in natural tones for a distance of half a mile. There is no successor to Julia Carpenter, ex-slave, who was midwife to two races, a practical philosopher in her own right, and a folk historian with learning not gleaned from books. There is no successor to Bud Medders, whose rural wit and humor would have filled a book but would have been barred from the mails.

Possum Trot, in fact, has lost much of its local idiom and its local history, although its inhabitants have increased their knowledge of written history. For example, they know more in a general way than did their immediate forebears about the facts and significance of the Civil War, but less about the incidents of "the Yankees coming" through Possum Trot.

It is incorrect to say that Possum Trot is a land of hastening ills or a land where men decay. But it is correct to say that more than in former times this community exemplifies a lack of local roots for those who share its homes and soil. If it is true, as Simone Weil observes in *The Need for Roots*, that community rootage is perhaps the most important need of the human soul, Possum Trot and its kind in rural America stand in need of prayer for a genuine renaissance. In some way civic vitamins must be utilized to provide a re-enrichment for something which has gone out of the collective life. How can that vitalizing process be accomplished?

Local leadership would be one essential for restoring or developing local associational life in neighborhoods like Possum Trot. There are examples in the South of small communities looking ahead under the power and influence of dynamic leaders in the spheres of education, religion, recreation, civic activity, and economic cooperation.[3] The importance of good leadership can hardly be overestimated, and Possum Trot would profit by it if, by some special dispensation, such a feature could be provided. But a leader coming into that community would not find an institutional base of operation, either in the physical or organizational sense. It would be necessary to find both a place and a cause for bringing the citizens together, not to mention the serious matter of overcoming their habit of not coming together as a representative local group. It has become easy and natural for the individuals and the families of Possum Trot not to participate cooperatively in community activities but to concern themselves with private affairs or with affairs that transcend the bounds of Possum Trot. Home and farm life in this neighborhood has become more satisfying and less monotonous than formerly for the average person, with less cause for emotional escape, whether through intoxication, "muscular" religion,[4] or acts of reformation. This improved life, moreover, merges or blends conveniently with the culture of larger geographical units of society, and there is little awareness of problems to be faced on the strictly local level, little feeling of need for any

3. See Wayland J. Hayes, *The Small Community Looks Ahead* (New York: Harcourt, Brace and Company, 1947).

4. There is a Holiness church at Possum Trot, with members and worshippers from areas beyond the immediate vicinity. It is ignored and neglected by the sophisticated classes of the community. The shouting type of worship has declined among the Negro members of the community. They too have increased their reading and radio habits, becoming more outer-worldly and less other-worldly.

leadership or movement in the interest of the civic salvation of Possum Trot.

Leadership alone will not resolve the Possum Trot dichotomy of energetic activity with respect to most economic or material interests and a rather acquiescent passivity with respect to the broader field of social relations or civic affairs. The problem of civic non-participation must be met on a systematic basis for all rural hamlets and neighborhoods, not for any one alone. It calls for a new decentralization to balance the new centralization of the machine age. The new decentralization has, in fact, already arrived, but it has not yet adequately recognized the existence of Possum Trot.

The modern scheme of things might be set forth by noting the elements of centralization and the consequent impact upon our public life. It is tritely emphasized in texts and studies in political and social science that the twentieth century has witnessed a great shifting of authority to the center, with the national government taking over many responsibilities formerly entrusted entirely to the states, which in turn have assumed many tasks and powers formerly belonging to counties and other local units of government. But it should be equally emphasized that in this process of change the functional role of states and counties as well as cities has enormously expanded. The states carry out many undertakings and perform many services under the stimulus of federal authority and funds. Counties and cities carry out many operations under the sponsorship and standards provided at the state and national capitals, generally becoming the last basic unit or subdivision in the administration of a new functional federal system. This system has largely replaced what Alexis de Tocqueville described for us in observing that America in his day had a centralized government with local administration. Seeing the new system at its best in the TVA country, David Lilienthal explained it as centralized authority with decentralized administration.[5]

Possum Trot and the county should look to each other in the process of adjusting to the grand strategy of centralizing and decentralizing American civic life. The county is the most universal unit of local government inside the United States, and it has always

5. He develops this thesis in his *TVA: Democracy on the March* (New York: Harper and Brothers, 1944).

served important purposes in the rural South. It is the primary tactical unit in the new order of systematic or bureaucratic administration. The delegation of functions, sponsorship of projects or services, and assumption of supervision downward from higher to lower levels of government customarily stop with the county, which sometimes has to yield or share this basic position with city or town.

The county is basic in two related respects. It is normally the last in the hierarchy of decentralization of functions and powers, bringing national, state, and local government to citizens in its borders in a variety of matters, such as welfare, elections, taxation, law enforcement, highways, and schools. It is likewise normally the first in the scale of centralization of actual government, performing a wide range of old and new services in or for Possum Trot instead of leaving them for Possum Trot to administer or neglect. This systematic order ensures a measure of uniformity within and among the counties of a state, with a few fundamental similarities for all counties of the nation. Gone is much of the variety in local administration which de Tocqueville discovered in this country a century and two decades ago, or which James Bryce discovered half a century later in observing that local government reflected the most conspicious failure in the American Commonwealth. The progress toward better county government has brought gains to Possum Trot, but ways and means are yet to be developed for encouraging the inhabitants of such a community to participate actively, intimately, and consciously in this progress.

It is important for civic and human reasons that villagers and rural dwellers have a feeling of belonging to the county as formerly did rural people have a feeling of belonging to places like Possum Trot. It should be the order of the day to arrest an unhealthy and unfortunate trend toward a sort of exclusive and super-loyalty to state or nation and an accompanying sense of nonentity on the part of citizens, whether living in a rural district or a giant city. The southern cultivators of the soil have a heritage of county identity as old as the founding of Virginia, and that heritage is worth preserving even at the cost of administrative imperfections. It might be remarked in passing that any theory or system of administration in democratic government should make allowance for popular processes of participation and decision-making, if only for the purpose of political pedagogy.

The best leadership for Possum Trot is good county leadership, and the best government for Possum Trot is good county government. The people of this neighborhood like to go to the county seat, which is the largest urban center in the county. They go there for business, for pleasure, for attending to matters at the courthouse. City and county officers measure up to satisfactory levels of competence and efficiency, and a farmers' market serves to link city and country. A daily newspaper serves both the urban and rural population, but not to the exclusion of papers from Birmingham and Atlanta. The county paper carries "local" news items from points like Possum Trot. Relations between the urban center and the rural constituencies are healthy, although the patterns of harmony are largely set at the center. The ties might be closer and more mutual at times when election campaigns are not under way.

It is not enough to say that the county seat, especially in rural regions, should bestir itself to cultivate good relations with its Possum Trots through the serving of educational, recreational, welfare, agricultural, and other civic interests for all. It is important that, in the increase and improvement of these services, democratic processes as well as goals be kept in mind. It is important that "politics" not be completely removed from county government, that "courthouse rings" not disappear in the drive for efficiency and economy under bureaucratic dominance from higher and higher levels of government. Within limits and established standards, the movement for decentralization must apply to policy or politics as well as to administration. Otherwise, county officialdom will become merely a retail dispensary for the blessings and burdens of big government as handed down from the state and national capitals, and Possum Trot will look upon the dispensary as a branch of a chain-store system providing or permitting self-service but not self-determination. A few large agencies of government have recognized the democratic importance of policy-making at the bottom levels of government, notably the Department of Agriculture in several programs. But much of this discretion at the bottom has been largely on a plebiscite type of take-it-or-leave-it instead of the actual formulation of opinion on alternatives to be followed from top to bottom. The TVA has made headway with developing policy-making at the local or group level, although grass-roots democracy has not been the goal of all local or regional organizations participating mutually in the process.[6]

This discussion is intended in no way to offer a theory of county sovereignty, either in the manner of the little states of ancient Greece or in the sense of wide autonomy in local affairs as exercised by southern counties in the agrarian era of another century. There must be centralized power at the top, including power to prevent abuse of power down the line. But upper centralization can allow and provide leeway for participation and responsibility at the grass roots, on democratic principles, to the end that Possum Trot and its county may not find it natural merely to echo and re-echo the voice from the big capital city with no additional sense of civic duty. Application of this precaution will save not so much the identity but the life of Possum Trot. And it is the life that counts.

Possum Trot is dead. Long live Possum Trot.

6. This point is discussed by Philip Selznick, *TVA and the Grass Roots* (Berkeley: University of California Press, 1949). For broader and more various aspects of the subject, see Harold Stein (ed.), *Public Administration and Policy Development* (New York: Harcourt, Brace and Company, 1952).

Contributors

HENRY ALLEN BULLOCK, Professor of Sociology and Chairman of Graduate Research at Texas Southern University, is a native of North Carolina. He attended Virginia Union University (A.B.) and the University of Michigan (M.A. and Ph.D.). He is the author of a number of articles on southern urban life, with particular reference to its bi-racial aspects.

F. STUART CHAPIN, JR., Associate Professor of City Planning at the University of North Carolina, is a native of Minnesota. Mr. Chapin received his A.B. degree from the University of Minnesota and the B.Arch.C.P. and M.C.P degrees at the Massachusetts Institute of Technology. Before coming to the University, he was director of city planning in Greensboro, N. C., and a community planner with the Tennessee Valley Authority. He has written a number of monographs and articles in the field of city planning.

NICHOLAS J. DEMERATH is Professor of Sociology, University of North Carolina. Born in Illinois, he was educated at De Pauw (A.B.) and Harvard (A.M. and Ph.D.). He has served as an adviser on housing and urban rehabilitation for the United States and Philippine governments, and is the author of various articles and textbooks on urban problems and administrative organization.

ROBERT M. DINKEL is Professor of Sociology at Guilford College. He was educated at Notre Dame (A.B.), the University of Minnesota (M.A.), and the University of North Carolina (Ph.D.), and has written a number of journal articles on various phases of sociology. Dr. Dinkel is president of the Quality Block Company of Greensboro, N. C., and of the Cape Fear Block Company of Fayetteville, N. C.

CORTEZ A. M. EWING is Professor of Government at the University of Oklahoma. Born in Indiana, he was educated at Earlham College (A.B.) and the University of Wisconsin (Ph.M. and Ph.D.). He has held membership and offices in a number of professional organizations and is the author of several books on politics, among them *Federation, Congressional Elections 1896-1944,* and *Primary Elections in the South.*

ELIZABETH M. FINK is Executive and Editorial Assistant in the Institute for Research in Social Science, University of North Carolina. A native of Tennessee, Miss Fink received the B.S. degree from East Tennessee State College and the M.A. degree from the University of North Carolina.

HARLAN W. GILMORE, Associate Professor of Sociology at Tulane University, was born in Arkansas. He received the B.A. degree from Hendrix College and the Ph.D. degree from Vanderbilt University. His publications in the field of urbanism include *Social Disorganization in a Southern City, New Orleans Population Handbook 1950,* and *Transportation and the Growth of Cities,* as well as numerous journal articles.

RUDOLF HEBERLE is Professor of Sociology at Louisiana State University. He was born and educated in Germany, receiving the Doctor of Political Science degree from the University of Kiel. Before coming to LSU in 1938, he held university posts in Germany and was a Fellow of the Rockefeller Foundation, studying in England and the United States. Dr. Heberle is the author of *Social Movements* and books and articles dealing with urbanism and regionalism both in this country and Germany.

HOMER L. HITT, head of the Department of Sociology at Louisiana State University, is a native of Texas. He was graduated from Louisiana State University and from Harvard (M.A. and Ph.D.). A frequent contributor to professional journals, Dr. Hitt is the author of a number of monographs dealing with Louisiana and in 1952 collaborated with T. Lynn Smith on the book, *The People of Louisiana.*

FLOYD HUNTER is Associate Professor in the School of Social Work, University of North Carolina. Educated at the University of Chicago (A.B. and M.A.) and the University of North Carolina (Ph.D.), he was for several years a practitioner in the field of community organization. He is the author of *Community Power Structure,* a study of decision-makers in a southern metropolis.

HAROLD F. KAUFMAN is Thomas L. Bailey Professor of Sociology and Head of the Division of Sociology and Rural Life, Mississippi State College. A native of Ohio, he was educated at the University of Missouri (A.B. and A.M.) and Cornell (Ph.D.). His major publications have been in the fields of social organization, social stratification, and community life.

H. C. NIXON is Professor of Political Science at Vanderbilt University. Born in Alabama, he was educated at Alabama Polytechnic Institute (B.S. and M.S.) and the University of Chicago (Ph.D.). In addition to articles in the rural and regional field, he has written *Forty Acres and Steel Mules, Possum Trot,* and *Lower Piedmont Country.*

AUSTIN L. PORTERFIELD is Professor of Sociology at Texas Christian University. He was born in Arkansas and educated at Oklahoma City University (A.B.), Drake University (A.M.), and Duke University (Ph.D.). Dr. Porterfield's chief area of research interest is criminality, and he is the author of a number of books and journal articles in this and other fields.

SARA SMITH is an instructor in the Department of Sociology, Woman's College of the University of North Carolina. A native of Pennsylvania, Miss Smith took her undergraduate work at Wilson College and Indiana (Pa.) State Teachers College and received the M.A. degree from the University of North Carolina, where she is now a doctoral candidate.

T. LYNN SMITH is Professor of Sociology at the University of Florida. He was born in Colorado and was educated at Brigham Young University and the University of Minnesota (M.A. and Ph.D.). Dr. Smith has served as chairman of the Sociology Departments of Louisiana State University and Vanderbilt University and has done extensive traveling and research in Latin America. He is the author of two books on Brazil, texts in rural sociology, urban sociology, and population, and of numerous articles in professional journals.

ROBERT H. TALBERT is Professor of Sociology, Texas Christian University. A native of Missouri, he was educated at Southeast Missouri State College (A.B.), University of Missouri (A.M.), and Duke University (Ph.D.). He has written and collaborated on a number of books and articles in the fields of urbanism, minority relations, and crime and delinquency.

LORIN A. THOMPSON has been director of the Bureau of Population and Economic Research, University of Virginia, since 1944. A native of Colorado, he attended Ohio State University (B.A., M.A., and Ph.D.). He is the author of numerous articles in professional journals of sociology, economics, and psychology, and is editor of monographs published by the Virginia Population Study.

JAMES E. TITUS is a native of Nebraska. He received the B.A. and M.A. degrees from the University of Oklahoma and is a Ph.D. candidate at the University of Wisconsin. He is currently making a study of American liberalism during the 1930's. A former Instructor in Government at the University of Texas, he is now in the Dallas Regional Office of the Wage Stabilization Board.

RUPERT B. VANCE is Kenan Research Professor of Sociology, University of North Carolina. He was born in Arkansas and was educated in Arkansas (A.B., Henderson-Brown), Tennessee (M.A., Vanderbilt), and North Carolina (Ph.D., University of North Carolina). Population, regionalism, and ecology are his special areas of interest, and his books in these fields include *Human Geography of the South* and *All These People*.

Subject Index